CHINA'S MONETARY CHALLENGES

Despite the People's Republic of China's remarkable growth over the post-1978 reform period, questions have arisen about the sustainability of its exchange rate policy and the soundness of its financial system. This book focuses on the key monetary challenges to China's continued advancement and addresses such topical issues as the buildup of foreign exchange reserves, monetary control, credit allocation difficulties, and the expanding role of China's asset markets and stock exchanges. Current and past monetary policy strategies are examined in detail, as are the banking sector reforms leading up to fuller foreign competition after December 2006. The analysis also assesses the People's Republic's role within Greater China (including Hong Kong and Taiwan) and the potential for future renminbi monetary hegemony within Asia. The treatment of these issues is intended to be accessible to non-economists and does not assume prior immersion in the underlying formal models.

Richard C. K. Burdekin is Jonathan B. Lovelace Professor of Economics at Claremont McKenna College and is an Editorial Board Member of *The Open Economics Journal*. He was a Visiting Senior Fellow at Hawaii's East-West Center in August 2005 and was previously a Visiting Scholar at the Federal Reserve Bank of Dallas and Assistant Professor at the University of Miami. Richard Burdekin first visited China in 1998. His main research interests include Chinese economic reforms, inflation and deflation, and central bank policymaking. Richard Burdekin has published in journals such as the *American Economic Review*, *Economica*, *Economic Inquiry*, the *Journal of Financial Economics*, the *Journal of International Money and Finance*, and the *Journal of Money, Credit, and Banking*. His book *Deflation: Current and Historical Perspectives* (co-edited with Pierre L. Siklos) was published in 2004 by Cambridge University Press. Prior books include *Distributional Conflict and Inflation* (with Paul Burkett, 1996); *Establishing Monetary Stability in Emerging Market Economies* (with Thomas D. Willett, Richard J. Sweeney, and Clas Wihlborg, 1995); *Confidence, Credibility, and Macroeconomic Policy* (with Farrokh K. Langdana, 1995); and *Budget Deficits and Economic Performance* (with Farrokh K. Langdana, 1992).

China's Monetary Challenges

Past Experiences and Future Prospects

RICHARD C. K. BURDEKIN

Claremont McKenna College

CAMBRIDGE
UNIVERSITY PRESS

CAMBRIDGE UNIVERSITY PRESS
Cambridge, New York, Melbourne, Madrid, Cape Town, Singapore, São Paulo, Delhi

Cambridge University Press
32 Avenue of the Americas, New York, NY 10013-2473, USA

www.cambridge.org
Information on this title: www.cambridge.org/9780521880169

First published 2008

Printed in the United States of America

A catalog record for this publication is available from the British Library.

Library of Congress Cataloging in Publication Data
Burdekin, Richard C. K. (Richard Charles Keighley), 1958–
China's monetary challenges : past experiences and future prospects / Richard C. K. Burdekin.
    p.   cm.
Includes bibliographical references and index.
ISBN 978-0-521-88016-9 (hbk.)
1. Monetary policy – China.   2. Money – China.   I. Title.
    HG1285.B87   2008
    339.5′30951 – dc22   2007052907

ISBN   978-0-521-88016-9 hardback

TO YANJIE, EILEEN, EMMA, & JOSEPHINE

Quand la Chine s'eveillera, le monde tremblera...
[When China rises, the world will tremble...]

Napoleon Bonaparte[1]

If we isolate ourselves and close our doors again, it will be absolutely impossible for us to approach the level of the developed countries in 50 years.

Deng Xiaoping, 1984[2]

---

[1] Quote attributed by Alain Peyrefitte, *The Chinese: Portrait of a People*, translated from the French by Graham Webb (Indianapolis/New York: Bobbs-Merrill, 1977).

[2] October 1984 "Speech at the Third Plenary Session of the Central Advisory Commission of the Communist Party of China" – as quoted by Jinglian Wu, *Understanding and Interpreting Chinese Economic Reform* (Mason, OH: Thomson, 2005), p. 294.

Contents

Preface

Work on this book was funded by a 2005–2006 Scholar Grant from the Chiang Ching-kuo Foundation, and I am immeasurably grateful for this support. Some of the initial research was conducted while I was a Visiting Senior Fellow at Hawaii's East-West Center, which provided a very hospitable and helpful environment for my work. My home institution, Claremont McKenna College, also helped with support for databases and other research needs.

I have been fortunate to work with many excellent co-authors over the years, and I am grateful to a number of them for kindly consenting to have some of their joint work presented in this volume. In particular, I wish to thank William Brown and Pierre Siklos, as well as my former students Gregory Arquette, Emily Kochanowicz, and Hsin-hui I. H. Whited, for their contributions to several of the chapters in this volume. Gregory Arquette also played a major role in keeping the analysis of China's securities markets as up-to-date as possible, allowing the book manuscript to incorporate the most recent numbers available at the time.

Chapters 3 and 6 include material previously published by the *Cato Journal* and the *China Economic Review.* I thank Jim Dorn, editor of the *Cato Journal,* and Elsevier, publisher of the *China Economic Review,* for their respective permission to reprint.

This book greatly benefited from three excellent sets of reviewer comments, including those kindly provided by Jim Dorn and Elliott Parker. I am most appreciative too of Scott Parris's support for the book at Cambridge University Press. Kishen Rajan and Tom Willett contributed much valuable time in offering a host of helpful comments on earlier versions of many of the book chapters. Marc Weidenmier also gave helpful feedback. Meanwhile, Nancy Tao provided outstanding research support, both in terms of data work and Chinese language support and by cheerfully putting up with my incessant demands as this book neared completion. Yeqin Zeng also supplied valuable translation help.

My family made perhaps the most essential contribution of all, putting up with the many hours spent tying together the wide-ranging strands of research contained in this volume. My wife, Yanjie Feng Burdekin, also did her best to save me from the most egregious errors in my understanding of China and its people – although any remaining failings in this regard should be firmly attributed to the author. My oldest daughter, Eileen Burdekin, valiantly waded through drafts of all the chapters, finding numerous errors that I and others had missed. Meanwhile, my middle daughter, Emma Burdekin, also assisted with the book and helped ensure that the youngest member of the family, Josephine Burdekin, did not get the chance to destroy the work in progress.

I would also like to offer a special thank-you to my father-in-law, Feng Delong, whose personal reminiscences of the 1949–1950 inflationary spiral helped spark my interest in China's monetary and inflation history.

Let me add a brief word on the Chinese language references, names, and places. In most cases, the modern *pinyin* system has been used for converting Chinese characters into Roman letters. All Chinese references not expressed in English use the *pinyin* form, except for an old 1958 reference, which has been kept in the Wade-Giles form in which it was originally catalogued. Some proper names, such as Mao Tse-tung and Chiang Kai-shek, have also been kept in the old form that is likely to be more familiar to most readers. Finally, among the place names, the old province of Manchuria enters the discussion of the 1930s experience. Referring to the modern-day "North-East Provinces" in that context seemed a recipe for confusion.

With regard to China's currency, the post-1949 money issues are known as *renminbi* (meaning "people's currency"). Although the unit of account is technically the *yuan renminbi*, I have simply stuck with the designation renminbi – or RMB for short. (Rather confusingly, different writers variously use both *renminbi* and *yuan* in this context, and it seemed best to be consistent.) Earlier Chinese money issues mentioned in this book include the pre–November 1935 silver coin standard, the *fapi* paper currency of 1935 to 1948, and the *gold yuan* issued by the Nationalists in 1948–1949 – before their defeat in the Chinese Civil War ushered in the new People's Republic under Chairman Mao.

I hope that readers will find this volume helpful and not confusing. The exciting events in China and their historical antecedents certainly demand the West's attention, and it has been a pleasure to assess some of the remarkable strides China has made in recent years.

China Today and Lessons from the Past

Shanghai, the Paris of the East!
Shanghai, the New York of the West!
Shanghai, the most cosmopolitan city in the world...
(*All About Shanghai and Environs* – a 1934 guidebook)[1]

For decades China's economic progress was stifled and hidden from the rest of the world behind Chairman Mao's "bamboo curtain." However, the remarkable growth over the post-1978 reform period has launched the country into a major player in the world economy. By 2007, the Shanghai Stock Exchange had reached center stage with coming initial public offerings that looked likely to rival, or even exceed, those of New York. Many tough challenges remain nonetheless, including the sustainability of China's exchange rate policy and the soundness of a financial system that is still dominated by four big state-owned banks. This book addresses some of the key monetary challenges to China's continued advancement, such as potential inflationary pressures under the continued buildup of foreign exchange reserves, the need for additional liberalization of interest rates and financial market development, and external pressure for faster exchange rate adjustment.

Such issues as the causes and consequences of exchange rate pressures are interpreted in terms of standard economic principles and past experiences – taking into account some illustrative lessons deriving from events in China's own history prior to the days of the bamboo curtain. Besides considering how past lessons help put current pressures in perspective, this book looks forward to the ongoing challenges posed by China's accession to the World Trade Organization and the potential for Chinese monetary

---

[1] As quoted by Wasserstrom (2003, p. 51).

The author thanks Tom Willett and Yanjie Feng Burdekin for their helpful comments.

1

hegemony within the Asian sphere. The goal throughout is to present the reader with relevant empirical analysis and an explanation of the theoretical underpinnings but to do so in an accessible fashion that does not assume prior immersion in the underlying formal economic models.

The pegged exchange rate between China's currency, the renminbi, and the US dollar that was maintained until July 2005 ensured that, as the US dollar weakened against most other world currencies in the early twenty-first century, the renminbi automatically followed. This had the effect of making the renminbi cheaper and cheaper in world terms. The apparent exchange rate misalignment tended to boost Chinese exports because these exports were now being priced on the basis of this cheaper currency. China's export growth continued unabated even after the modest 2.1% revaluation of the renminbi against the dollar on July 21, 2005, and the subsequent gradual movement upwards. Meanwhile, accelerating inflows of foreign exchange reserves required increasingly large-scale interventions by the People's Bank of China in order to offset upward pressure on the exchange rate and domestic money supply growth and, hence, inflation. This pressure has been augmented, at times, by "hot money" flowing into China as holders bet on new appreciation of the renminbi against the dollar that would yield capital gains to those exchanging dollars for renminbi at the original, lower rate.

In addition to exploring the current situation in detail, Chapter 1 seeks to put it in perspective by assessing the evolution of the People's Republic's exchange rate policy over the years and the gradual movement toward more market-based rates. One key episode was during the 1997–1998 Asian financial crisis when, even as most Asian currencies depreciated dramatically against the US dollar, China stuck with its commitment to a constant, pegged exchange rate with the US dollar. While "taking one for the team" and resisting pressures for devaluation, China was hit by deflation in 1998. The pressures for devaluation of the renminbi in the late 1990s were abruptly replaced by pressures for revaluation, however, in the face of the reversal in the upward trend of the US dollar against other world currencies after 2001. The renminbi was no longer being propped up, but rather being held down, by major People's Bank of China intervention in the foreign exchange market. Chapter 1 addresses the charges of alleged renminbi undervaluation that have, if anything, become more strident since China's 2005 break from the old dollar exchange rate peg. Although there seems to be no doubt that the renminbi became more undervalued (or less overvalued) over time, different approaches to measuring the degree of undervaluation produce quite different answers. This leaves the overall degree of undervaluation far from clear-cut.

Chapter 2 assesses the recent pressures on the renminbi in the light of global economic imbalances. Worsening US current account deficits have been accompanied by a widespread trend toward growing trade surpluses among emerging economies, which is certainly not just a "China phenomenon." Recent strains appear to largely reflect downward pressure on the dollar in the face of rising US trade deficits with the world as a whole – accompanied meanwhile by high savings rates in the surplus countries and low savings rates in the United States. China has itself been running a relatively balanced trade position with countries other than the United States, while incurring deficits with other Asian nations like Japan. Especially given the cautionary lessons from the Japanese and Taiwanese experiences with rapidly rising currency values in the 1970s and 1980s – which are reviewed in Chapter 2 – there certainly seems to be no good reason for China to accede to US pressure for sudden exchange rate appreciation. The chapter also reviews the move toward the creation of new state investment agencies (known as "sovereign wealth funds") by China and other large holders of dollar reserves. These agencies seek to achieve higher returns on their dollar assets by moving beyond the US Treasuries that have served as the typical mainstay of China's holdings in the past.

Chapter 3 turns to the inflationary and deflationary cycles experienced in the People's Republic of China, beginning with the inflationary spiral that was already in full sway when Chairman Mao originally proclaimed the People's Republic on October 1, 1949. Parallels are drawn between the methods of inflation control adopted at that time, such as the indexing of bank deposits, and the anti-inflationary policies adopted during the post-reform era in the face of the inflation spikes of 1988–1989 and 1993–1994. The question of repressed inflation is also addressed along with evidence that this phenomenon remained important even after the economic reforms that began in 1978. Chapter 3's review of the deflation experience of 1988–2002 includes comparisons with the similar deflationary pressures experienced by Hong Kong.

The closing discussion of post-2002 inflationary pressures in Chapter 3 feeds into the focus on the recent policy of the People's Bank of China in Chapter 4. The growing liquidity of the interbank market is assessed along with the People's Bank's increasing reliance on more market-based methods of monetary control such as open market operations. A major policy tool in "sterilizing" the inflationary effects of China's large reserve inflows has been the sale of "central bank bills," the rapidly growing issuance of which is documented in the chapter. Chapter 4 also provides some new empirical evidence on People's Bank monetary policy responses to reserve flows and exchange rate changes. The results are consistent with the effects of reserve inflows on the Chinese money supply being largely offset over our 1994–2006 sample period.

Part II of the volume offers three case studies of episodes that illustrate the past and present importance of international factors to China. The 1930's experience reviewed in Chapter 5 shows that it is certainly nothing new for the Chinese economy to be pressured by a weakening US dollar. In this regard, Federal Reserve Chairman Ben Bernanke (2002) once credited the 40% devaluation of the dollar against gold in 1933–1934 as a "key policy shift that permitted sufficient monetary expansion to reverse US deflation during the Great Depression." The expansion in Federal Reserve notes was generated, in part, via Franklin D. Roosevelt's silver purchase program, which actually had severe deflationary effects on China in the mid-1930s because its currency was linked to silver. As the value of China's currency rose with the world price of silver, its exports became more and more expensive abroad. Chapter 5 discusses the difficulties faced by China at that time and documents the damage exerted by the massive silver outflow that eventually forced both China and Hong Kong to exit the silver standard by 1935. The damage to Chinese and Hong Kong business interests is also reflected in the response of share prices, such as that of the Hong Kong and Shanghai Banking Corporation (HSBC), which was then, as it is today, a major financial player in East Asia.

Whereas China suffered from the sudden currency appreciation that was artificially generated by the 1934 US silver purchase program, the opposite dangers arising from keeping the exchange rate at an artificially low level have seldom been more vividly illustrated than by China's own past experience in the late 1940s, which is analyzed in Chapter 6. The Nationalist government forced Taiwan to maintain a fixed, artificially low exchange rate against mainland China's gold yuan currency – itself the successor to the heavily depreciated *fapi* that was adopted after China abandoned silver in 1935. Indeed, in August 1948 the combination of the fixed exchange rate for the gold yuan and Nationalist control over both the Central Bank of China and the Bank of Taiwan created an almost ideal vehicle for massive capital flight from mainland China to Taiwan. The rate of exchange between the gold yuan and the Taiwanese currency was held fixed through the fall of 1948 in spite of rapidly accelerating money growth on the mainland and a collapsing military situation. Holders of gold yuan naturally took advantage of the fixed exchange rate that forced the Bank of Taiwan to accept the depreciating Nationalist currency and exchange it for the separate Taiwanese currency at an overvalued rate. The net capital inflow between August and October 1948 accounted for almost all of Taiwan's rapid money growth during September–October 1948. This episode shows, in sharp relief, how inflationary pressures can indeed be fueled by an artificially cheap, fixed exchange rate.

The exchange rate question is, of course, just one aspect of the challenges to monetary control in mainland China today. The credit allocation issue and China's banking sector problems are discussed in Chapter 7 in the context of both the changing macroeconomic landscape and the transition to full foreign bank competition mandated in December 2006 under China's World Trade Organization commitments. In preparation for this development, the government began the process of transforming its major policy banks into publicly traded companies. Although three out of the big four state-owned banks enjoyed successful initial public offerings in 2005–2006, their apparent newfound balance sheet strength was achieved only through successive government-funded capital injections. Concerns about remaining "hidden" bad loans continued to stoke fears that further large bailouts may be needed in the future. Government funds could also be required to bail out the group of asset management companies established to take many of the bad loans off the banks' balance sheets, in the process paying prices way above subsequent realized market values. Another concern is the continued concentration on lending to the nation's state-owned enterprises and correspondingly low levels of lending to China's growing private sector. The private sector's reliance on informal finance is also discussed in Chapter 7. Meanwhile, the fresh acceleration of loan growth as foreign capital flooded into China during 2006–2007 raised fears that new nonperforming loans are being generated, illustrating how exchange rate pressures and banking sector pressures may well remain linked.

Finally, Part III of the book considers the People's Republic of China in the context of the Greater China region (including Hong Kong and Taiwan) – with a focus on ongoing financial linkages as well as more general economic integration associated with trade ties and flows of foreign direct investment. Chapter 8 includes an assessment of the development of China's bond, equity, and real estate markets. Whereas in the early 1980s China had no secondary market for government debt and no stock exchanges, the establishment of both these key institutional features in the late 1980s and early 1990s began the progress toward meaningful financial market development in China. Although many missteps have occurred along the way, including disruptions associated with sudden government policy reversals, China's financial markets have advanced greatly in recent years with considerably higher liquidity and an enhanced array of financial instruments. This includes, for the first time, genuine prospects for a corporate bond market that might chip away at China's long-standing and near-complete dependence on bank credit.

The growth in China's stock exchanges accelerated in 2006–2007, leading to record highs in the major market indices. The question of valuations on the Shanghai Stock Exchange is assessed by comparing stock prices there to prices of the same companies' stock traded on the neighboring Hong Kong stock market. The data suggest that, relative to the more established market in Hong Kong, any overvaluation of Shanghai shares was, for the most part, greater *before* the rally period that began in late 2005. Although prices in Shanghai did accelerate faster than Hong Kong prices after April 2006, as of June 2007 the differential remained quite low relative to its own past history – thereby rather casting doubt on the timing of any allegations of "irrational exuberance."

Chapter 9 moves the comparative focus from Hong Kong to Taiwan and offers a detailed examination of the macroeconomic linkages between mainland China and Taiwan. The growing trade links and flows of foreign direct investment from Taiwan to mainland China, in spite of ongoing political animosity, are indicative of China's increasing integration with other East Asian economies. Moreover, the importance of external influences on Chinese monetary policy, as emphasized in Part I of this volume, receives further support from the mutual sensitivity of money growth in mainland China and Taiwan to developments on the other side of the Taiwan Strait. The chapter's empirical work shows that trade and investment ties have been reflected in significant co-movement not only between mainland China and Taiwan money supply growth rates but also inflation rates, output growth, and stock market performance over the post-1994 period. The overall sensitivity to mainland China effects appears to be highest for Taiwanese output and money growth. This is combined with evidence of weaker, but still significant, responses of mainland China variables to developments in Taiwan.

Chapter 10 concludes and also looks forward to consider whether the People's Republic of China could plausibly serve as the future monetary leader in Asia. The renminbi has become increasingly important as a "vehicle" currency in recent years, especially in Hong Kong, where almost all banks now offer renminbi services to their customers. A potentially major step toward greater renminbi penetration in Hong Kong was the June 2007 launch of China Development Bank's 5-billion renminbi bond issue in

Hong Kong. This represented the first renminbi-based issue outside the mainland. More and more transactions are being settled in renminbi, not only in Hong Kong (and Macau) but also as part of the border trade conducted with other neighboring Asian economies like Taiwan, Malaysia, and Thailand. Although the renminbi is certainly not yet ready to take on the dollar, or even the euro, as a major world reserve currency, continued slow but steady capital account liberalization should help pave the way for the much greater role it seems destined to achieve going forward.

PART I

CHINA'S EXCHANGE RATE REGIME AND MONETARY POLICY

ONE

The Renminbi–US Dollar Exchange
Rate Controversy

Renminbi's further appreciation is megatrend...
  (Wu Xiaoling, Vice Governor of the People's Bank of China, 2005)[1]

Introduction

Mainland China's surging exports in the early twenty-first century, and growing importance in world trade, have been accompanied by unprecedented scrutiny of its exchange rate policy not only by academics but also by politicians and policymakers, especially those in the United States. The controversy initially focused on China's maintenance of a constant pegged exchange rate with the US dollar. Although US policymakers had repeatedly urged China to maintain this pegged rate during the 1997–1998 Asian financial crisis, the exchange rate parity of 8.28 RMB/$US was subsequently seen as too cheap, making China's exports cheaper in US dollar terms and accounting for China's growing trade surpluses with the United States. Since China's movement away from a pegged exchange rate in July 2005, the debate has shifted to the question of whether the currency's rate of appreciation against the US dollar is sufficiently rapid. This chapter discusses the evolution of China's exchange rate policy and offers some historical perspective on the valuation of China's currency, the renminbi (which

[1] As quoted in *People's Daily Online*, October 26, 2005c.

Part of this chapter includes material previously published in Burdekin (2006), and the author thanks the East-West Center in Honolulu, Hawaii, for their hospitality while researching the exchange rate question. The author also thanks Kishen Rajan and Tom Willett for their helpful comments, is most grateful to Nancy Tao for her valuable research assistance, and greatly appreciates Jim Barth's willingness to provide historical data on the Milken Institute's "Renminbi Pressure Indicator."

means "people's currency," in Chinese). Recent renminbi valuations do not seem to have been too out of line with levels recorded in the 1990s, nor has ongoing empirical analysis of the currency's purchasing power yielded any consistent support for US charges of drastic renminbi under-valuation.

However, Chinese authorities are right to be concerned about growing flows of funds into the country, and the renminbi. Even if the currency is not artificially cheap, the accumulation of foreign funds remains an inevitable result of the nation's trade surpluses – an inflow that, in China's case, has been heavily augmented by its attraction as a destination for foreign direct investment (FDI). Moreover, speculation regarding renminbi appreciation has been a factor encouraging "hot flows" of money into the currency by individuals and businesses seeking to profit from this appreciation. As described in Chapter 6, there is certainly historical precedent for worrying about the potential inflationary effects of such large-scale capital inflows. In the late 1940s, as the Nationalist regime faced defeat in the Chinese Civil War, capital flight from the mainland to Taiwan precipitated a massive monetary expansion and hyperinflationary spiral on the island. The situation was greatly exacerbated by the Nationalist government's decision to peg Taiwan's currency at an artificially low value against mainland China's currency, however. Fears that such a mechanism could reemerge in today's People's Republic of China are mitigated by the fact that, in real terms, China's currency, the renminbi, remained in-line with its own historical levels of the 1990s. Nevertheless, China's own history certainly provides a vivid warning as to the potential consequences stemming from an excessively undervalued fixed exchange rate.

The Evolution of the People's Republic's Exchange Rate Policy

The renminbi was introduced by Mao Tse-tung's Communist forces as they gained territory from the Nationalist government under Chiang Kai-shek during the Chinese Civil War. Chairman Mao proclaimed the formation of the People's Republic of China on October 1, 1949. Continued rapid renminbi issuance was accompanied by high rates of inflation during 1949–1950 until stabilization was achieved in March 1950 (see Chapter 3). During the last inflationary surge in early 1950, wholesale price rose by 56% in Shanghai, and by 77% in Tianjin, between January and March 1950 (Burdekin and Wang, 1999). The renminbi depreciated by 100% against the US dollar, by 106% against the pound sterling, and by 115% against

Table 1.1. *Early Renminbi Exchange Rate Fluctuations, 1950–1951*

	Exchange Value of the Renminbi*		
	Pound Sterling	US Dollar	Hong Kong Dollar
January 1, 1950	48,000	21,000	3,000
January 6, 1950	64,400	23,000	3,498
January 21, 1950	70,000	25,000	3,816
February 1, 1950	77,000	27,500	4,167
February 8, 1950	81,200	29,000	4,538
February 23, 1950	82,150	31,000	4,733
February 24, 1950	89,500	34,500	5,267
March 2, 1950	97,500	39,000	5,990
March 11, 1950	98,708	42,000	6,460
April 2, 1950	98,400	41,000	6,400
April 10, 1950	96,000	40,000	6,244
April 19, 1950	97,194	39,000	6,310
April 24, 1950	93,000	37,500	6,000
May 26, 1950	98,900	37,500	6,120
July 3, 1950	94,280	35,500	5,870
July 8, 1950	93,200	35,000	5,800
July 26, 1950	91,440	35,000	5,690
August 7, 1950	81,220	32,200	4,950
September 5, 1950	78,210	31,000	4,750
December 25, 1950	73,570	27,360	4,500
January 4, 1951	68,370	24,900	4,200
January 20, 1951	63,350	22,890	3,880
May 22, 1951	62,350	22,270	3,880

* These figures are for "old" renminbi convertible into today's renminbi on a 1:10,000 basis (see text).

Source: Cheng (1954, pp. 120–122).

the Hong Kong dollar over this same three-month period (Table 1.1).[2] The renminbi's official foreign exchange value gradually recovered after March 1950 before the People's Republic's effective exclusion from trade with the

[2] Although these figures denote official exchange rates set by the government, they appear to have initially been reasonably representative of actual market rates. According to Cheng (1954, p. 120): "Chinese foreign exchange policy then was aimed at boosting exports, absorbing foreign exchange and getting as much overseas remittances as possible. Hence, fluctuations in foreign exchange rates followed the principle of conforming to black-market rates." Zhang (2003, p. 54) adds that a weighted index of the cost of eighty key export goods served as the main reference for exchange rate adjustments over the 1949–1952 period.

West following its November 1951 entry into the Korean War. The share of China's trade with non-communist countries plunged from 74% in 1950 to 28% in 1952 (Durdin, 1953, p. 14) and complete monopoly control of the foreign exchange system followed in 1956. China's share in world trade stood at only 1.5% in 1953 and declined even further to just 0.6% in 1977 on the eve of the economic reforms launched under Deng Xiaoping (Wu, 2005, p. 292).

After 1951, the exchange rate with the US dollar was adjusted in December 1952, January 1953, and January 1955 (Zhang, 2003, p. 55), but otherwise remained constant until a succession of appreciations against the dollar were employed during the 1970s (see Table 1.2). The Table 1.2 exchange rate values reflect the currency reform of February 1955, under which all past renminbi issues were called in and replaced with "new" renminbi at the rate of 1:10,000 (Jao, 1967–1968, p. 111). The 1952 and 1972 exchange rates of 2.26 and 2.25 RMB/$US are, in reality, almost unchanged from the last May 22, 1951, data point given in Table 1.1 – with 22,270 RMB/$US in the old currency being equivalent to 2.23 RMB/$US in new currency. International trade remained under monopoly control by the government from 1956 until 1978. Under the planned economy regime, the exchange rate was fixed at an artificially overvalued level to support the state's emphasis on import substitution, and stringent foreign exchange controls were maintained (Lardy, 1992, chapter 2; Zhang, 2003, pp. 46–48). Zhang (2001) estimates that, except for a brief period between 1971 and 1973, the renminbi essentially remained overvalued throughout the 1957–1977 period.

Gradual liberalization took place after 1978, accompanied by a series of devaluations in the official exchange rate that progressively moved the rate from 1.56 RMB/$US in 1979 to 5.76 RMB/$US in 1993.[3] Although the official exchange rate remained overvalued in the early post-1978 period, an internal settlement rate that applied only to trade transactions was established in January 1981 at a rate of 2.80 RMB/$US as compared to an official rate of just 1.53 RMB/$US at that time. The resultant dual exchange rate system ended on January 1, 1985, however, as the official exchange rate was itself devalued to 2.80 RMB/$US – leaving this more competitive rate to apply to all currency transactions (Lin and Schramm, 2004, pp. 82–84). Foreign trade authority had itself been decentralized as early as 1979 and more than 5,000 trading companies were in place by the end of the 1980s (Lardy, 1992, p. 39). A limited secondary market for foreign exchange was

---

[3] See also Lin and Schramm (2004, p. 80) for a compact summary of the main exchange rate system reforms over the 1979–2004 period.

Table 1.2. *Renminbi/US Dollar exchange rate,*
1952–2007

Year	RMB/$US	Year	RMB/$US
1952	2.26	1980	1.50
1953	2.62	1981	1.70
1954	2.62	1982	1.89
1955	2.47	1983	1.98
1956	2.46	1984	2.32
1957	2.46	1985	2.94
1958	2.46	1986	3.45
1959	2.46	1987	3.72
1960	2.46	1988	3.72
1961	2.46	1989	3.77
1962	2.46	1990	4.78
1963	2.46	1991	5.32
1964	2.46	1992	5.51
1965	2.46	1993	5.76
1966	2.46	1994	8.62
1967	2.46	1995	8.35
1968	2.46	1996	8.31
1969	2.46	1997	8.29
1970	2.46	1998	8.28
1971	2.46	1999	8.28
1972	2.25	2000	8.28
1973	1.99	2001	8.28
1974	1.96	2002	8.28
1975	1.86	2003	8.28
1976	1.94	2004	8.28
1977	1.86	2005	8.19
1978	1.68	2006	7.97
1979	1.56	2007	7.61

Note: Data are average values over the course of each year.
Sources: 1952–1956 data are from Lardy (1992, p. 148) and sub-sequent data are from the International Monetary Fund's *International Financial Statistics* database.

permitted in some localities in 1980, with more regularized foreign currency "swap" markets developing by 1985–1986. This practice was spearheaded by foreign-funded enterprises that, as part of the Chinese government's drive to attract more foreign investment, were allowed to swap foreign exchange among themselves in the coastal cities and the newly established Special Economic Zones like Shenzhen. Access to the swap market remained limited for domestic firms until April 1988, when quota controls on foreign exchange retention rights were abolished and domestic enterprises began to enjoy an essentially level playing field with foreign-funded enterprises (Lardy, 1992, p. 60; Lu and Zhang, 2000, p. 125).

Trading volumes in the swap market increased markedly after the 1988 abolition of quota controls and accelerated further with the December 1991 removal of all restrictions on domestic enterprises and residents' ability to sell foreign exchange into the swap market (World Bank, 1994, pp. 31–32; Lin and Schramm, 2004, pp. 84–87). Transaction volumes in the swap market rose from $US 4.2 billion in 1987 to $US 8.6 billion in 1989 and $US 25 billion in 1992 (World Bank, 1994, p. 32). By September 1988 the Shanghai swap market price was seen as reflecting actual supply and demand for the currency. A "marginal pricing auction" mechanism was employed, under which the price was adjusted in response to any excess demand or supply at the starting price – with a switch to a standard "Dutch auction" ensuing in August 1990 (Lu and Zhang, 2000, p. 125). Although swap market rates still varied significantly from city to city, considerable convergence with the black market rate appears to have been achieved by the end of the 1980s (see Lardy, 1992, pp. 57–66). Moreover, Lu and Zhang (2000) point to a causal relationship between the swap rate and the official exchange rate over the 1988–1992 period, implying that the swap market helped facilitate the adjustment of the official exchange rate in a direction consistent with market forces. A national swap center was established in Beijing in 1988 and by the end of 1993 there were as many as 119 swap centers nationwide, with every province possessing at least one (Zhang, 2006, p. 12).

The continued gap between the official exchange rate and the more-market-determined swap rate was closed on January 1, 1994, as part of a comprehensive reform of the official exchange rate system. At that time, the official exchange rate and the swap market rate were unified at a rate of 8.70 RMB/$US, which represented the prevailing secondary market rate at the end of 1993.[4] The change from the 1993 official exchange rate of 5.76 implied a devaluation of nearly 50%. However, Lardy (2005a, p. 43n) demonstrates that this greatly exaggerates the actual impact of the exchange rate revision. If 80% of all current account transactions were already based on the swap rate, the weighted average effect of the exchange rate change would amount to only 10% ((0% × 80%) + (50% × 20%)).[5] The 1994

---

[4] There was still no unified swap market rate even in 1993, however, and the World Bank (1994, p. 42) noted a range from 8.0 RMB/$US to 8.5 RMB/$US in March 1993.

[5] This assumed weighting of 80% for the swap market rate and 20% for the official exchange rate reflects the fact that, under the pre-1994 regulations, exporters were required to provide 20% of their foreign exchange to the state at the official rate (World Bank, 1994,

reform also replaced the foreign exchange swap market with an interbank foreign exchange market that, for the first time, offered a single, unified secondary market for the renminbi. This interbank market was implemented under the Shanghai-based China Foreign Exchange Trading System, which began operations on April 4, 1994.[6] Access was initially provided only to domestic enterprises, however, and foreign-funded enterprises still had to use the swap centers until July 1996; only then were they finally permitted to purchase foreign currency on demand on the interbank market (Zhang, 1999, pp. 10–11). In December 1996 the renminbi became fully convertible on the current account (Zhang, 2006, p. 14).

As the new arrangements eliminated any remaining scope for the authorities maintaining balance through foreign exchange controls on current account transactions, exchange rate pressure emerged as a potentially important source of monetary and price fluctuations. The effect of 1994's $US 30.5 billion balance of payments surplus on the renminbi/US dollar exchange rate, for example, was contained only via People's Bank of China dollar purchases that tripled China's reserve holdings to $US 77.9 billion (Lin and Schramm, 2004, p. 89). Although the absolute level of reserve holdings reached in 1994 pales in comparison with the $US 1,202 billion that had been amassed by the end of the first quarter of 2007 (see Chapter 2), there certainly seems to be a parallel in terms of the monetary consequences. Recent reserve inflows pushed Chinese money growth up near 20%; while the 1994 intervention added to inflationary pressures whereby the growth rate of consumer prices reached 24.2% in 1994, up from 14.6% the previous year (Chapter 3). A key difference, though, is that post-2002 expansionary pressures were seemingly being manifested more in sharp run ups in asset prices rather than goods price inflation (see Chapters 2 and 8 on this issue).

Pressures for Depreciation and Appreciation Since 1994

Even after the dollar began weakening against other world currencies in 2002 (see Figure 1.1), China kept the exchange rate between the renminbi and the dollar in the close range maintained since the major devaluation of January 1, 1994. After the initial adjustment to 8.62 RMB/$US in 1994, the

---

p. 43). Going beyond current account transactions, though, the official rate assumed more importance given that "the coverage of transactions at the official exchange rate [was] considerably wider, and include[d] debt service payments and all the central government imports that [were] financed from foreign loan proceeds, the draw down of reserves, or foreign exchange earnings from the exports of invisibles" (World Bank, 1994, p. 42).

[6] See Lin and Schramm (2004, pp. 87–89) for further details of the operation of the new interbank market.

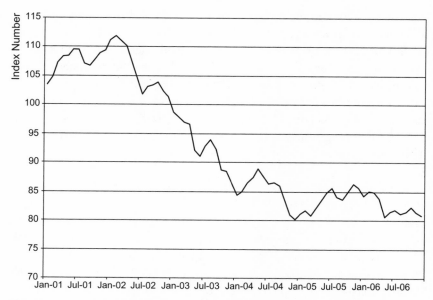

Figure 1.1. US Dollar Trade Weighted Exchange Index: Major Currencies (Index March 1973 = 100). *Sources:* Board of Governors of the Federal Reserve System, Federal Reserve Bank of St. Louis.

exchange rate was allowed to gradually strengthen to 8.28RMB/$US by 1998 but then remained fixed at this same 8.28 level for seven years. Although the exchange rate policy adopted in 1994 always allowed for daily fluctuations of up to 0.3%, the permitted range of fluctuation was, in practice, quite limited and the effective bands were tightened over time as the People's Bank intervened more and more in order to minimize volatility. By late 2004, the permitted range of fluctuation approached zero and "Chinese practice was virtually indistinguishable from a full outright fixed exchange rate" (Anderson, 2006b, p. 5). On an annual basis, the renminbi/$US dollar exchange rate had remained near constant since 1995, varying only from 8.35 RMB/$US to 8.28 RMB/$US and consistent with the maintenance of a very rigid dollar peg over this whole period preceding the July 21, 2005 revaluation.

Pressure for adjusting a pegged exchange rate with the US dollar emerges if China's goods' prices do not keep pace with US prices. If, for example, China's price level doubled while the US price level remained constant, China's exports would become twice as expensive in the United States. In reducing China's sales abroad this would also reduce the demand for the renminbi needed to purchase such goods, and in turn put pressure on

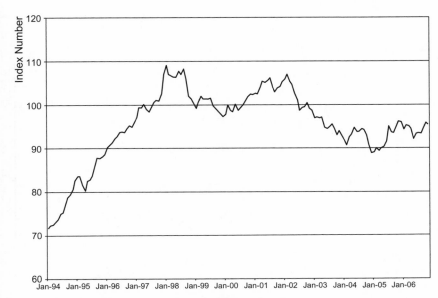

Figure 1.2. China's Real Effective Exchange Rate Index (2000 = 100). *Source:* International Monetary Fund.

the (now unwanted) renminbi to fall in value against the US dollar. If the People's Bank of China sought to maintain a fixed exchange rate under this scenario, the central bank would have to buy back its own currency to support its value, thereby reducing the rate of domestic monetary expansion. This situation would represent a constant *nominal* exchange rate but a rising *real* exchange rate that reflects the rising world price of Chinese goods. Moreover, a rising real exchange rate implies increasing pressure for currency depreciation that the central bank must try to forestall by buying back its own currency if the fixed nominal exchange rate is to be maintained.

Given that China trades with many countries besides the United States, a representative real exchange rate measure should take into account price movements relative to all of China's major trading partners. The International Monetary Fund calculates such an index, known as the *real effective exchange rate*, that weights each foreign country by its share of trade with China. This real exchange rate measure, shown in Figure 1.2, enjoyed a steady rise from 1994–1998. Over this period, China's price level rose more rapidly than most of its trading partners, making Chinese goods more expensive abroad. Although the renminbi was fixed against the US dollar, and the dollar remained strong against most other major currencies, China's real exchange rate appreciated both relative to the dollar and relative to the full set of countries considered in the effective exchange rate

Figure 1.3. China's Inflation Rate (Consumer Price Index). *Source:* Great China Database.

measure. The pressures for devaluation peaked at the time of the 1997–1998 Asian financial crisis, when almost all Asian countries outside China and Hong Kong abandoned their own pegged exchange rates with the US dollar. As these other currencies fell against the dollar (in some cases to a dramatic degree such as the near 90% depreciation of the Indonesian rupiah), they fell against the renminbi as well. Thus China faced a sudden additional loss of competitiveness against its Asian rivals and renminbi devaluation seemed almost inevitable at the time. Indeed, the writer can attest from personal experience that the unofficial exchange rates offered for US dollars in Beijing in the summer of 1998 were significantly more generous than the official rate of 8.28.

The pressure for renminbi depreciation during the Asian Financial Crisis was forestalled by tight monetary policy, and tight credit, as the People's Bank of China intervened and bought back its own currency to support its value. The maintenance of the pegged rate was also aided by the fact that capital controls limited foreign access to the renminbi. It was not possible for speculators to sell short (sell borrowed renminbi) against the US dollar, for example, and so the renminbi was spared the kind of speculative attack that was orchestrated against the Hong Kong dollar in 1997–1998. Nevertheless, the tight monetary policy helped push China into deflation in late 1998 as shown in Figure 1.3, which depicts China's inflation rates over the post-1990 period. As China's price level fell from 1998 through the beginning of 2001, China's exports tended to become cheaper in world terms, pressures for depreciation were alleviated, and the rise in the real exchange rate started to reverse. Economic growth slowed, however, and there was marked acceleration of savings relative to consumption in the face of economic uncertainty and tight credit markets. China certainly paid a price for warding off currency depreciation and received kudos from the US administration at the time that were apparently quickly forgotten when the pressures on the currency later reversed after 2002.[7]

The fall in the real exchange rate was temporarily interrupted in 2000–2001 as the strength of the US dollar against other most major world currencies, including the euro, carried the renminbi upward against these same currencies. The renewed upward pressure on the real exchange rate at this time can be seen in Figure 1.2. However, after the dollar's decline began in early 2002, China's real exchange rate fell as well and China's goods started to become cheaper and cheaper in non-US dollar countries. Demand for renminbi to purchase Chinese exports soared, and there was a natural pressure for renminbi appreciation in the face of all this extra demand. Offsetting this pressure required the People's Bank to reverse its intervention of the late 1990s. The goal now was to hold the renminbi down by buying the relatively weak US dollar and issuing in exchange larger and larger quantities of renminbi. This helped make renminbi more abundant and the dollar scarcer, thereby offsetting the underlying impetus for the renminbi to rise above its pegged exchange rate with the US dollar.

Matching the post-2002 dollar depreciation not only had the effect of making the renminbi artificially cheaper in world terms, therefore, but has also induced more rapid expansion in the supply of renminbi that threatens inflation to the extent that too much money ends up chasing too few goods. Broad money supply growth accelerated to nearly 20% in 2003 before dropping back to 15% in 2004. Money supply growth then rose again to 17.6% in 2005 and remained at 16.9% in 2006 – standing at an annualized 17.3% through the first quarter of 2007 (People's Bank of China, 2007). The People's Bank of China has attempted to dampen the rate of credit expansion through sales of government bonds that withdraw money from circulation and by taking steps to discourage credit creation by the banking system (Chapter 4). Inflationary pressures were further augmented by "hot

---

[7] As discussed in Chapter 3, Hong Kong like mainland China entered deflation in 1998 and suffered considerable economic weakness in holding on to its own fixed link to the US dollar.

money" flowing into China after 2002 as speculators bet on revaluation of the renminbi against the dollar that would yield capital gains to those exchanging dollars for renminbi at the original, cheaper pegged rate of 8.28 renminbi to the dollar. Following the limited revaluation implemented in July 2005, a renewed surge of capital inflows beginning in late 2005 led to accelerating reserve accumulation that made it increasingly difficult for the People's Bank to contain money growth and credit creation.

Exchange Rate Expectations, Capital Flows, and Pressure for Appreciation

The market for forward contracts in a currency, with prices agreed upon now for delivery at a set future date, can provide useful insights into exchange rate expectations. Expectations of currency depreciation typically lead forward contracts for that currency to trade at values below today's spot market price, that is, producing a forward exchange discount, while expectations of currency appreciation should be associated with a forward exchange premium. Mainland China's own foreign exchange market has offered little beyond spot market transactions, however. The interbank foreign exchange market established in 1994 did not provide for forward and swap transactions until August 2005, following the new exchange rate regime adopted in the preceding month. Meanwhile, daily turnover in China's foreign exchange market reached only $US 0.83 billion in 2004, compared to $US 102 billion in Hong Kong, $US 125 billion in Singapore, and $US 199 billion in Japan (Zhang and Liang, 2006, p. 71). Individuals and businesses seeking to hedge their exposure to renminbi have typically had to rely upon offshore markets, therefore, where an alternative "nondeliverable" forward market emerged in the late 1990s, with quite active trading in Hong Kong and Singapore and, increasingly, the United States.

The nondeliverable forward market for the renminbi is a cash-settled futures contract, whose value reflects the expected exchange rate of the renminbi in terms of the US dollar. Expectations of renminbi appreciation are first evident in the RMB/$US forward data from November 13, 2002, when the renminbi moved from a forward discount to a forward premium (Figure 1.4). The new forward premium for the renminbi implied that market participants expected the US dollar to exchange for fewer renminbi in the future (i.e., at less than the old 8.28 pegged rate) and was followed by an increase in the daily contract volume to over $US 600 million (Fung, Leung, and Zhu, 2004). The implied expected appreciation peaked around 6% in the first half of 2005 before falling back somewhat in the face of the

Figure 1.4. Expected Change in the RMB/$US Exchange Rate (One Year Nondeliverable Forward Contract). *Source:* Bloomberg.

actual 2.1% appreciation imposed by the Chinese authorities on July 21, 2005. An earlier spike in revaluation pressure occurred in September–December 2003 in the midst of rising US emphasis on renminbi revaluation reflected in congressional initiatives and a series of strong statements by administration officials – as well as an October 7, 2003 rumor from Japan that renminbi revaluation was imminent (see Zhang, 2004, p. 246).[8]

The expected appreciation implied by the nondeliverable forward market persistently exceeded actual appreciation over the 2002–2006 period. As pointed out by Higgins and Humpage (2005), this likely reflects the effects of the so-called "peso problem," whereby market participants seek protection against a possible sudden, large adjustment. In the case of the renminbi, attaching even a small probability to major revaluation would be sufficient to push the appreciation implied by the nondeliverable forward market persistently above the actual exchange rate moves. Although the

---

[8] Movements in the expected exchange rate also appear to have exerted significant effects on Chinese stocks listed in Hong Kong and New York – with increases in the renminbi forward premium boosting the price abroad as investors expected exchange rate gains that would translate underlying renminbi values into larger US or Hong Kong dollar amounts (see Chapter 8, this volume; Arquette, Brown, and Burdekin, 2008).

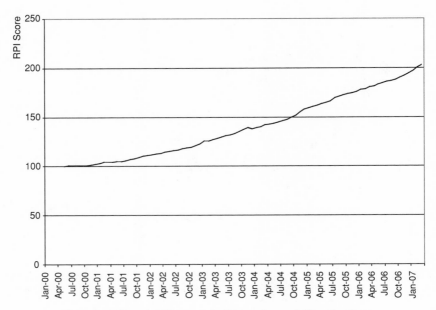

Figure 1.5. Renminbi Pressure Indicator. *Source:* Milken Institute.

emergence of this effect in 2002 preceded the actual policy move by three years, there was certainly tangible evidence of rising pressure for renminbi appreciation at the time. The falling real exchange rate discussed earlier was accompanied by rising levels of capital inflows and growing foreign exchange reserves.[9] According to the "Renminbi Pressure Indicator" developed jointly by Xinhua Finance and the Milken Institute, the pressure for appreciation rose by over 25% between 2000 and 2002 before further intensifying to a level of 202.7 in March 2007 relative to its base of 100.0 in 2000 (see Figure 1.5).[10] Although this rise in the indicated pressure level takes into account exchange rate changes and domestic interest rate changes, the largest contributor became the soaring level of foreign exchange reserves, which reached $US 1.33 trillion in June 2007 for a 41.6% year-on-year increase. A key policy question is whether this reserve buildup reflects a fundamental imbalance that justifies more substantial renminbi appreciation or that it has, instead, been made up of more speculative capital inflows

---

[9] The enormous growth in reserves, together with China's exports and imports, over the post-1990 can be seen in Table 1.3.

[10] Details on the "Renminbi Pressure Indicator" and data updates can be found at the Milken Institute's website (http://MilkenInstitute.org).

hoping to benefit either from self-fulfilling expectations of a further shift in exchange rate policy or from participation in mainland China's recently explosive asset markets.

Just as expectations of renminbi revaluation first emerged in 2002, so too did errors and omissions in China's balance of payments turn positive in that year after many years of deficit. This latter development suggested that prior capital flight out of the renminbi had reversed and is likely indicative of unrecorded capital inflows into China. Although the renminbi was made fully convertible for current account transactions in 1996, mainland China's official capital account has remained officially closed other than to FDI and a small range of other transactions.[11] The ongoing restrictions have kept China's capital account ranked as the most closed in the Asian region (Anderson, 2006b, pp. 18–19). To the extent that flows of funds into and out of China take place outside the formally authorized range of activities, they will be captured only in the errors and omissions section of the official balance of payments statistics. Anderson (2006b, p. 24) describes how some of these unauthorized flows have been engineered:

[D]uring the 1990s trading companies routinely overstated the value of import shipments in order to take money out of the country, and banks and firms shuttled a great deal of unrecorded cash across borders as well. In the first half of this decade, banks took strong advantage of regulatory loopholes to borrow offshore and repatriate the funds to invest in China.

The deficit in the errors and omissions category peaked at $US −22.1 billion in 1997 during the Asian financial crisis (see Table 1.3). The subsequent movement into positive territory during 2001–2004 reached $US 26.8 billion in 2004, with waning demand for dollar deposits by Chinese residents offering further evidence of expected future renminbi strength (Hu, 2005, p. 364). The errors and omission category returned to deficit in the year of the July 21, 2005 exchange rate reform, however, accompanied by a decline in China's capital account surplus that set in just as the current account surplus was accelerating. After standing at over $US 100 billion in 2004, the capital account surplus was just $US 10 billion in 2006, with strong portfolio outflows nearly offsetting FDI of $US 63 billion (see Cohen, 2007). These developments have occurred on the heels of an apparent rise

---

[11] See Zhang (2006) for a detailed account of the recent policy moves that have largely eliminated restrictions on long-term capital transactions while still attempting to check short-term movements.

Table 1.3. *Mainland China Balance of Payments and Reserves Position, 1990–2006*

	Exports	Imports	Foreign Exchange Reserves	Net Errors and Omissions
1990	62,091	53,345	29586.2	−3205.17
1991	71,910	63,791	43674.3	−6766.93
1992	84,940	80,585	20620.4	−8211.15
1993	91,744	103,959	22386.9	−10096.40
1994	121,006	115,614	52914.1	−9100.25
1995	148,780	132,084	75376.7	−17823.20
1996	151,048	138,833	107039.0	−15504.00
1997	182,792	142,370	142762.0	−22121.80
1998	183,712	140,237	149188.0	−18901.80
1999	194,931	165,699	157728.0	−17640.50
2000	249,203	225,094	168278.0	−11747.90
2001	266,098	243,553	215605.0	−4732.46
2002	325,596	295,170	291128.0	7503.53
2003	438,228	412,760	408151.0	17985.40
2004	593,326	561,229	614500.0	26834.20
2005	761,953	659,953	821514.0	−16440.60
2006	969,380	791,605	1068490.0	n.a.

Source: All data are as reported in the International Monetary Fund's *International Financial Statistics* database and are in millions of US dollars.

in the effective degree of capital mobility evident from the latter part of 2004.[12]

Meanwhile, Prasad and Wei (2007) show that the reserve buildup during 2001–2003 had been accompanied by a shift in the nature of capital inflows and a movement away from the dominant role previously played by FDI in favor of more volatile "hot money" flows reflected in growing levels of portfolio inflows as well as the aforementioned rise in errors and omissions. By late February 2004, Guo Shuqing, head of the State Administration of Foreign Exchange, was voicing the government's concern that the billions of investment dollars flowing into China could generate an asset bubble and inflation (see Goodman, 2004). Initial empirical support for this assertion seemed lacking, given that property prices actually began declining in 2004, the stock market remained in a downtrend, and consumer price inflation

[12] Ouyang, Rajan, and Willett (2007) find that an increasing fraction of domestic monetary base movements started to be offset by international capital flows during 2004, with the estimated "offset" coefficient rising from approximately 0.1 to 0.2 in 2003 to as much as 0.71 in the third quarter of 2005.

stayed relatively low.[13] An asset bubble in the stock market did seem to be a real danger later on, however, even though available data suggest that the "hot flows" dissipated after the July 21, 2005 policy move. The main Shanghai index rose by 130% in 2006 in a strong advance that continued into 2007, as discussed further in Chapter 8.

Doubts as to the Question of Renminbi Undervaluation

In the period leading up to the July 2005 announced change in exchange rate policy, debate over the extent to which economic conditions justified exchange rate adjustment in China reached crescendo pitch. The needed degree of revaluation, depending upon the source and the particular estimation method employed, was seen as ranging anywhere from zero to 50% or more. Much analysis focused on purchasing power parity, the premise that, after converting domestic currency into foreign currency at the going exchange rate, internationally traded goods should be purchasable for essentially the same price abroad as at home. Empirical application of this premise is complicated, however, both by the need to capture prices on a broad range of goods and by the need to abstract from the contribution of "nontradables," that is, such factors as land and labor inputs that, even if they differ substantially in price across countries, cannot be readily or legally shipped from place to place. Although the narrow focus on a single item under *The Economist's* popular "Big Mac Index" hardly addresses these requirements, its transparency and popularity have given considerable prominence to its implication that the renminbi was dramatically undervalued in the period preceding the July 2005 policy adjustment.

The Big Mac Index compares the price at McDonald's restaurants abroad to the US price, and assesses whether dollars converted into local currency at the current exchange rate would have more or less purchasing power than in the United States. The Big Mac has tended to be considerably cheaper in dollar terms in mainland China, implying that, by 2003, revaluation of over 50% would have been needed to equalize prices across the two countries. As pointed out by Yang (2004), however, most of the Big Mac's price is accounted for by nontradable local services like labor, rent, and electricity, which are substantially cheaper in China than in the United States. Allowing

---

[13] Although the authorities actually seemed to remain successful in sterilizing most of the inflationary effects of the inflows (Chapter 4), the subsequent lending surge that began near the end of 2005 led to new concerns with potential inflationary pressures in 2006 and after.

for these cheaper nontradable components could quite easily account for the apparent price discrepancy, even assuming full equality in the portion of the price reflecting tradable components like the meat, the bun, and the paper. Meanwhile, *The Economist*'s own alternative "Tall Latte Index" showed the dollar-equivalent Tall Latte price at Starbucks to be, over essentially the same time period, nearly identical across the two countries – costing $2.80 in the United States and requiring $2.77 to make the same purchase in China (Max, 2004). The greater equality in price for the Tall Latte may well reflect a more important role for tradable components like (relatively more expensive) coffee beans but, more importantly, it suggests that considerable caution needs to be applied in inferring renminbi under- or overvaluation from product-specific price comparisons.

The "Apple Index" compiled by Laurenceson and Tang (2006), based on the price of Apple Inc.'s globally available electronic products like iMac and iPod, not only focuses on products with a high value share for tradable components (principally flash memory) but also attempts to control for tariffs and taxes and for the value of the residual nontradable inputs. This "Apple Index" consistently suggests closer approximations to purchasing power parity than the Big Mac Index across a broad range of countries both in Asia and elsewhere. And there is no support for renminbi undervaluation. Moreover, Laurenceson and Tang (2006) show that the Apple Index does not share the Big Mac Index's tendency toward higher degrees of exchange rate undervaluation at lower national per capita income levels. To the extent that nontradable goods are cheaper in lower income countries, the prices of goods with substantial nontradable value components will be biased downwards in such cases and produce erroneous estimates of exchange rate undervaluation – estimates that should be based only on tradable goods.[14] Some, if not all, of the extreme renminbi undervaluation suggested by the Big Mac Index simply reflects the operation of this bias.

Among broader price indices, the World Bank's International Comparison Program is generally considered the best source of data for purchasing power parity comparisons. However, even this series features a strong inverse correlation between the degree of implied exchange rate undervaluation and per capita income levels similar to that seen for the Big Mac Index (Funke and

---

[14] Lower nontradable ingredient costs follow naturally from the lower hourly wages that are typical of lower-income countries – with average hourly wages in the United States still standing at approximately twenty times the average Chinese level at the time of Yang's (2004) Big Mac comparison.

Rahn, 2005, pp. 467–468). A considerable number of studies have recently sought to extend the purchasing power parity approach by incorporating the effects of nontradables via a relative productivity measure. This is based on the premise that cheaper nontradable goods in countries like China reflect the relatively lower wages that would tend to follow from lower productivity levels. As relative productivity rises, therefore, wages and nontradable goods prices should tend to catch up with more advanced economies, implying a higher real exchange rate. Recent time series analysis, incorporating alternative sets of additional macroeconomic control variables, suggests estimated degrees of undervaluation ranging from minimal (Shi and Yu, 2005; Goh and Kim, 2006) to a moderate 11–12% (Funke and Rahn, 2005) through the end of 2002.[15] Shi and Yu (2005, p. 43) do point to a recent rising trend, however, with the estimated degree of undervaluation increasing from an average of just 4.24% from the third quarter of 1999 through the first quarter of 2002 to 10% over the period from the second quarter of 2002 to the third quarter of 2004.

Still another approach is to incorporate the effects of relative productivity levels by employing cross-sectional analysis to assess the "average" relationship between relative productivity levels, or relative per capita income levels, and real exchange rates across countries. Frankel (2006) suggests that, based on the extent to which China's real exchange rate failed to keep up with the "average" reaction to income growth, the renminbi was undervalued by around 35% in 2000. Using a similar technique, Coudert and Couharde (2007, p. 574) suggest undervaluation in at least the 44–46% range for 2000–2004.[16] Controlling for other factors, including sampling uncertainty, and considering trends over time as well as across countries, Cheung, Chinn, and Fujii (2007b) conclude, however, that such strong findings of renminbi undervaluation are not robust. Meanwhile, Dunaway, Leigh, and Li (2006) show that relatively small changes to the sample period, specific set of variables included, or particular set of countries included, tend to have disproportionately large effects on the findings, producing variations of up to 50 percentage points in the implied deviations of the exchange

---

[15] For additional references, and discussion of the different methodologies employed, see Siregar and Rajan (2006) and Cheung, Chinn, and Fujii (2008).

[16] Coudert and Couharde (2007) find that the indicated degree of undervaluation is lower when panel data over multiple years are employed but also offer calculations based on flow equilibria and implied current account imbalances that suggest even higher potential degrees of undervaluation – ranging overall from 16% to 54% across their different sets of results.

rate from its equilibrium value. Extended purchasing power analysis, of the type described earlier, is also seen to be highly sensitive to relatively small changes in the setup of the empirical test.

Dunaway, Leigh, and Li's (2006, p. 9) conclusion that "estimates of a country's equilibrium real exchange rate need to be treated with a great deal of caution" is certainly worth bearing in mind when confronted with overly-strong statements implying that a specific degree of renminbi under-valuation is a proven fact (cf. Bergsten, 2007). Although it is true that the available empirical studies do consistently point to a movement in the *direction* of renminbi undervaluation in recent years, this must be placed in the context of likely significant *overvaluation* in the aftermath of the 1997–1998 Asian financial crisis. Examination of the historical record seems to offer further reason for being wary of the case for very large renminbi revaluation. As Figure 1.2 shows, China's effective real exchange rate in 2006, far from being unprecedented, represented nothing more than a return to the levels seen during 1996. Indeed, the effective real exchange rate actually trended slightly upward during 2005–2006. This occurred in the midst of gradual appreciation of the nominal renminbi exchange rate against the US dollar, strengthening from 8.28 RMB/$US on July 20, 2005 to 7.62 RMB/$US by June 30, 2007. Rising reserve inflows and Chinese trade surpluses may well justify continued appreciation. However, neither historical comparisons nor recent empirical evidence seems to offer any real, consistent support that more drastic moves are justified by *Chinese* economic fundamentals – rather, recent political pressure seems to be driven more by concerns about US and global imbalances, as discussed in Chapter 2.

Post-2005 Developments and Future Prospects

In undertaking a limited 2.1% revaluation of the renminbi against the dollar (to 8.11 RMB/$US) on July 21, 2005, the People's Bank of China also referred to the adoption of a more "flexible" policy and of tying the renminbi to a "basket" of foreign currencies that would include the euro, the Japanese yen, and the Korean won in addition to the dollar. The renminbi remained in a tight range following the initial adjustment, however, and appreciated by only an additional 0.49% through the end of 2005. Ogawa and Sakane (2006) find that estimation using daily data over a six-month period before and after the July 21 reform suggests only a slight decline in the response to the US dollar, with the estimated coefficient on the dollar declining from unity to 0.91. Meanwhile, the weights attached to the euro, Japanese yen, and Korean won appear to have increased only slightly and

Table 1.4. *Correlations of the Renminbi with the US Dollar, Japanese Yen, Korean Won, and the Euro Before and After the July 2005 Regime Change*

	RMB	US Dollar	Japanese Yen	Korean Won	Euro
Sample Period: January 2004 to June 2005					
RMB	1.000000	0.999963	0.808829	0.856309	0.206646
US dollar	0.999963	1.000000	0.808020	0.855107	0.203347
Japanese yen	0.808829	0.808020	1.000000	0.664864	0.516583
Korean won	0.856309	0.855107	0.664864	1.000000	0.173425
Euro	0.206646	0.203347	0.516583	0.173425	1.000000
Sample Period: July 2005 to December 2006					
RMB	1.000000	0.967076	0.819270	0.929362	−0.710814
US dollar	0.967076	1.000000	0.674787	0.874554	−0.570388
Japanese yen	0.819270	0.674787	1.000000	0.825229	−0.788857
Korean won	0.929362	0.874554	0.825229	1.000000	−0.752094
Euro	−0.710814	−0.570388	−0.788857	−0.752094	1.000000

Note: Each currency is defined relative to the Swiss franc, which serves as the numeraire for the comparisons.
Sources: Swiss National Bank (http://www.snb.ch) and the *International Financial Statistics* database.

the coefficients attached to these other currencies are generally insignificant. Table 1.4 reports correlation coefficients between these currencies calculated over an extended period of approximately 18 months before and after the reform.[17] The correlation between the renminbi and the US dollar is seen to drop only marginally from unity to 0.97. There are only slight changes in the correlations with the Japanese yen and the Korean won – whereas a negative correlation with the euro over the post-July 2005 period appears to belie any focus on stabilizing that particular cross rate.

Although the apparent continued dominant role for the US dollar seems to support Goldstein and Lardy's (2006, p. 422) conclusion that "the July 2005 reforms have had little visible effect," the pace of appreciation actually increased to 3% during 2006 – with the RMB/$US rate appreciating from 8.08 in December 2005 to 7.82 in December 2006. The cumulative appreciation through the first quarter of 2007 reached 7.01% against the US dollar, 11.47% against the Japanese yen, and 2.84% against the euro (People's Bank of China, 2007, p. 14). The People's Bank of China subsequently announced an increase in the daily fluctuation band with the US

---

[17] Following Frankel and Wei (1994) and Ogawa and Sakane (2006), these correlations are calculated with each currency expressed in terms of the Swiss franc, which serves as the necessary numéraire.

dollar from 0.3% to 0.5% that took effect on May 21, 2007. The rate of currency appreciation had, of course, been lagging well behind the rapid rate of reserve buildup and expansion of China's trade surplus. Although these latter factors are often cited as justification for much more drastic renminbi appreciation, past reserve inflows, to some extent, reflected "hot money" speculative flows. Allowing the currency to appreciate in face of such flows would validate revaluation expectations that may well have motivated the inflows in the first place, but would not necessarily be justified on any more fundamental basis. The size of China's rapidly growing trade surplus, which reached 9.1% of China's gross domestic product (GDP) in 2006, is certainly a concern and would seem to imply substantial renminbi undervaluation (cf. Goldstein, 2006; Roubini, 2007). Essentially the whole of this surplus has been derived from trade with the United States, however, and China ran close to a balanced trade position with the rest of the world in 2006 (and a substantial deficit in 2005). It is important, therefore, to look not just at possible imbalances on the Chinese side but also on the US side. As discussed in Chapter 2, while continued renminbi appreciation may indeed be warranted, extreme currency adjustment seems justified only if one takes the view that China is somehow responsible for correcting US and world imbalances single-handedly!

TWO

China's Reserve Buildup and Global Imbalances

[The International Monetary] Fund should focus its surveillance on the systemati-
cally important countries issuing major reserve currencies. The frequent outbreak
of crises since the collapse of the Bretton Woods system indicates that the fundamental weakness of the international monetary system lies in its undue reliance on
a single currency.[1]

(Zhou Xiaochuan, Governor of the People's Bank of China, 2006b, p. 4)

Introduction

The upward pressure on the renminbi in the early twenty-first century arose
in the midst of generalized dollar weakness. Sharp interest rate reductions by
the US Federal Reserve after September 11, 2001, coupled with mushrooming US current account deficits, were met by a decline in the value of the
US dollar against most major world currencies from 2002 onwards. Subsequent Federal Reserve rate hikes were insufficient to more than temporarily
suspend the dollar downturn in 2005, and dollar depreciation quickly reaccelerated in the face of continued record US trade deficits and new Federal
Reserve rate cutting initiated in the second half of 2007. Whereas a past
major devaluation of the dollar in 1933–1934 has itself been seen as a key
policy shift that permitted sufficient monetary expansion to reverse deflation pressures in the 1930s (Bernanke, 2002), its impact is remembered
more negatively in China – where it put great pressure on the economy
and induced a monetary regime change that facilitated an ultimately disas-
trous inflationary spiral (see Chapter 5). Dollar depreciation is certainly not

[1] The Bretton Woods fixed exchange rate system, with the US dollar as the central reserve
currency, broke down after 1971 in the midst of rising US budget deficits and current
account deficits.

an official goal today. However, so long as mounting trade deficits require the purchase of more and more foreign currency in exchange for US dollars, the Federal Reserve could only seek to offset the resulting downward pressure on the dollar by raising interest rates sufficiently to attract more demand for a high-yielding US currency. Such a high-interest rate strategy would threaten severe deflationary consequences, however, and doubts as to the Federal Reserve's willingness to undertake such a step only underpin continued dollar weakness.

This chapter discusses the recent pressure on the renminbi in light of US and global imbalances. The United States' bilateral trade deficit is put in perspective with overall US and Chinese current account positions as well as the worldwide trend toward rising current account surpluses among emerging market economies. Should surplus countries like China retreat from the large-scale dollar purchases that have helped finance the burgeoning US current account deficits, there would likely be not only an acceleration of the pace of dollar depreciation but also significant upward pressure on US interest and inflation rates. China's 2007 creation of a sovereign wealth fund may well be the beginning of a move away from the prior practice of allocating most new reserve accumulation to US Treasuries. Meanwhile, as discussed later in this chapter, it does not seem likely that renminbi appreciation offers any viable hope of reining in US current account deficits. Even double-digit renminbi appreciation would almost certainly leave intact the worsening trend in the US current account position. However, drastic renminbi appreciation would pose considerable risks for China. Although assessment of post-Bretton Woods episodes of rapid currency appreciation in Japan and Taiwan does not yield an unambiguously negative perspective, these experiences raise concerns not only regarding the effects on investment and export performance but also the likelihood that, once begun, the appreciation process would end up overshooting any reasonable equilibrium exchange rate value. Given the very real questions surrounding current renminbi undervaluation, as discussed in Chapter 1, continued limits on the rate of currency adjustment may well be justifiable on economic grounds.

The United States vs. China

China's rise to prominence both in terms of global trade and bilateral trade with the United States has been quite extraordinary. China became the world's third largest exporter in 2005, and in 2006 overtook Japan to become the United States' second largest trading partner (after Canada). As has been widely noted, the pegged exchange rate of 8.28 renminbi per dollar maintained by China until July 21, 2005, meant that dollar depreciation could not make US goods cheaper in China in the way that US goods prices were falling in terms of euros, pounds, or yen. Concern that the renminbi remained too cheap in dollar terms in spite of the post-July 2005 appreciation ensured that "China bashing" remained very much in vogue in 2007–2008, threatening, in fact, to surmount the heavy level of "Japan bashing" that emerged in the 1980s. As further confirmation of the changing world situation, the United States' former role as Japan's largest trading partner was, for the first time, surmounted by mainland China over the fiscal year ending in March 2007. In contrast to the mushrooming US bilateral trade deficits with China, Japan actually enjoyed a bilateral surplus even as its imports from China reached an all-time high, rising by 13% over the year (Nakamoto, 2007, p. 5). Other East Asian economies have also generally run bilateral trade surpluses with China. To some extent this reflects Asian neighbors like Korea and Taiwan, as well as Japan, using China as the final assembly point for their own US-bound exports – leading Jin and Li (2007 – emphasis added) to argue that "China's trade surplus with the U.S. actually represents the trade surplus of the [East Asian] *region*."[2]

As discussed further later, there is a whole array of reasons why the actual size of the United States' own bilateral trade deficit with China may be substantially overstated in official US statistics, which show the overall bilateral trade deficit reaching $232.5 billion in 2006. The rapid growth in bilateral trade is undeniable, however, and, as shown in Figure 2.1, the monthly level of Chinese imports nearly tripled over the 2001–2006 period, reaching approximately $24.2 billion in December 2006 (for a cumulative total of $287.8 billion over the preceding twelve months). US exports to China have actually been growing nearly as quickly as Chinese imports, with US exports growing by an average of 23% a year over the 2001–2006 period.[3] The problem is that the disparity in the starting levels means that US exports would have to grow nearly six times faster than imports to close the bilateral trade deficit in dollar terms. In comparison, the highest

[2] Such "displacement" effects of China's surplus are, of course, not so easily pinpointed in the data. Although US trade deficits with the Asian region as a whole have certainly risen strongly, the question is whether bilateral US deficits with other individual countries would have been higher still in the absence of China's assembly-point role.

[3] Growth in US exports to China has, in fact, dwarfed export growth elsewhere. Bergsten et al. (2006, p. 84) note that between 2000 and 2005, cumulative growth in US exports to China reached 160% whereas exports by US firms to the rest of the world increased by just 10%.

Figure 2.1. US Imports from China, Mainland, Customs Basis (in millions of dollars). *Source:* US Department of Commerce: Bureau of Economic Analysis, US Department of Commerce: Census Bureau; Federal Reserve Bank of St. Louis.

import-export ratio faced against Japan in the mid-1980s was only three-to-one (Hufbauer, Wong, and Sheth, 2006, p. 8).

It should be emphasized, however, that mainland China's economic open-ness to both imports and foreign direct investment (FDI) is, in quantitative terms, substantially higher than Japan's. Indeed, while the share of imports in China's economy soared from just 5% in 1978 to 30% in 2005, the import ratio has remained closer to 15% for the United States and 10% for Japan (Bergsten et al., 2006, p. 84). Meanwhile, as noted by Siebert (2007, p. 905), net FDI inflow into China has steadily risen from an average of just $US 1.4 billion per year during the 1980s, to $US 26 billion in the 1990s, and $US 48.3 billion over the 2000–2005 period. The annual growth rate of FDI inflows accelerated after China joined the World Trade Organization in 2001 (see Whalley and Xin, 2006) and stood at $US 63 billion in 2006. Accordingly, whereas Japan's large bilateral trade surpluses of the 1980s largely reflected sales by domestic corporations, more recent Chinese surpluses incorporate substantial exports by US, European, and other non-Chinese multinational corporations. Whalley and Xin (2006) illustrate the rapid growth in exports by foreign-invested enterprises, which accounted for 57% of China's total exports in 2004 – as opposed to less than 2% in 1985. As discussed next, reexporting by US multinationals, in particular, implies that a significant portion of China's bilateral surplus with the United States reflects the activity of US, rather than Chinese, firms.

In 2004 the Bush administration and the Kerry campaign found agreement in asserting that the US trade deficit was primarily a Chinese problem, deriving from the Chinese currency, the renminbi, being too cheap relative to the US dollar and thereby making Chinese goods overly cheap as well. Former Treasury Secretary John Snow's September 2003 call for Chinese exchange rate adjustment was followed by increasingly vehement rhetoric during the 2004 election year and a series of individual congressional initiatives culminating in the June 2005 proposal by Senators Charles Schumer and Lindsey Graham that threatened a 27.5% tariff on Chinese imports. A new flurry of bills threatening punitive action against China for its currency policy followed in 2007.[4] As argued later, even assuming that such actions proved to be effective in improving the US bilateral trade balance with China, it is simply not plausible that any such moves could reverse the recent trends toward widening *overall* US trade deficits. The merchandise trade deficit reached $765 billion during 2006 (representing approximately 5.6% of the total US economy) and the deteriorating trend is readily apparent in Figure 2.2. US attempts to dictate the renminbi's value against the US dollar seem singularly inappropriate given the uncertainty that surrounds the whole question of renminbi undervaluation, as discussed in Chapter 1.[5] Indeed, McCary and Batson (2007, p. A4) point out that "[m]ost of the anti-China bills introduced so far would impose penalties until the currency was no longer deemed 'misaligned,' but don't specify what that level is."

Considering that the United States has recently been accounting for more than 70% of the *world's* current account deficits, it seems rather doubtful that all the imbalances could be on the Chinese side.[6] Indeed, in only five advanced economies (Greece, Iceland, New Zealand, Portugal, and

---

[4] Hufbauer, Wong, and Sheth (2006) offer a detailed account of the evolution of the recent trade tensions and congressional initiatives while excerpts from a number of recent Congressional Research Service reports on this issue are collected in Morrison, Labonte, and Sanford (2006). Concerns about the apparent protectionist sentiment in Congress were expressed in an August 2007 petition signed by 1,028 economists opposing retaliatory trade measures against China. This petition, sponsored by the Club for Growth (www.ClubForGrowth.org) and published in the *Wall Street Journal*, drew attention in China as well (see, for example, *China Daily*, August 2, 2007).

[5] As Dorn (2006, p. 433) validly points out, the popular "negotiated approach to resolving trade imbalances presumes that 'experts' know the relevant market-clearing exchange rates and that governments can enforce them – neither of which has proved to be true."

[6] And, as the Bank for International Settlements (2005, p. 145) put it: "[P]olicymakers who blame the policies of others for causing external imbalances, while denying their own culpability, risk destabilizing financial markets in the meantime and exacerbating the problems that policymakers should be seeking to resolve."

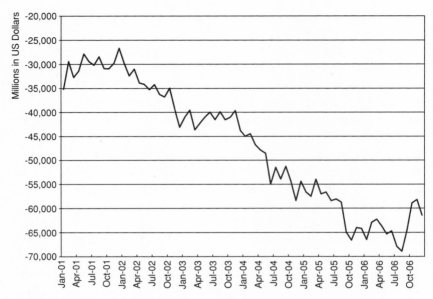

Figure 2.2. US Trade Balance: Goods and Services, Balance of Payments Basis (in millions of dollars). *Source:* US Department of Commerce: Bureau of Economic Analysis, US Department of Commerce: Census Bureau; Federal Reserve Bank of St. Louis.

Spain) was the 2006 current account deficit a bigger percentage of the economy than the US case. And, in absolute terms, the $856.7 billion 2006 US current account deficit was nearly eight times that of the runner-up, Spain, with $108.0 billion (International Monetary Fund, 2007, pp. 248–249). China's trade surplus, although large, is by no means such an outlier as the United States' deficit. As discussed in the previous chapter, the US trade deficit has also continued to rise unabated even while the dollar depreciated considerably after 2001. By the time of China's July 2005 exchange rate policy change, the dollar had lost nearly a quarter of its value on average against other major world currencies in little over three years, even after including the short-lived "bounce" in the first half of 2005. With China still only accounting for 11.9% of total US trade in 2006, one has to wonder whether *any* plausible adjustment of the Chinese currency could, on its own, yield any sustained reversal of this trend.

Would Renminbi Appreciation Really Help the US Trade Balance?

The deficits that mainland China has consistently run with its Asian partners reflect China's role as "final assembler" of many products made elsewhere in the region. Hufbauer, Yong, and Sheth (2006) point out that approximately 55% of China's total exports, and as much as 65% of China's exports to the United States, have represented goods assembled from imported parts and components. Owing to China's position in Asian production networks, "the US bilateral trade balance with China rises as its trade imbalance falls with other Asian countries, especially Hong Kong, Taiwan, Korea, and Japan" (Hufbauer, Yong, and Sheth, 2006, p. 6). This would naturally tend to make unilateral renminbi appreciation an unlikely solution for overall US trade imbalances. The more probable outcome would be to "shift Asian countries' assembly plants to other low-cost Asian countries, not back to America" (Jin and Li, 2007). Past growth of the US bilateral trade deficit with China itself includes substantial gains at the expense of other developing economies. A case in point is the way in which a rise in Chinese textile sales to the United States was largely offset by reduced imports from other countries after import quotas ended in December 2004 (Stiglitz, 2005).

The nature of China's exports to the United States is another factor working against the scope for renminbi appreciation reining in the US trade deficit. With US imports from China being concentrated among basic necessities and low-tech products, the elasticity of substitution is likely considerably lower than for high-tech and high value-added products imported from elsewhere.[7] Zhang, Fung, and Kummer (2006) suggest that volumes of Chinese imports may not decline sufficiently to prevent the dollar value of Chinese imports from actually rising in the face of a renminbi revaluation that drives up the US price of Chinese goods. Their computational general equilibrium model actually implies continued deterioration in the US bilateral trade deficit when allowing for renminbi revaluation of up to 12%. Meanwhile, Barrell, Holland, and Hurst's (2007, p. 10) recent examination of the effects of a simulated 10% appreciation in the renminbi within their world model suggests only a very short-lived reduction in China's overall trade surplus – leading the authors to conclude that "the policy driven structural factors that have given China a current account surplus are largely independent of the exchange rate regime."[8] Lardy (2005b, p. 136), in

[7] Rodrik (2006) concludes that China's exports are nevertheless significantly more sophisticated than would normally be expected for a country of its income level – pointing to success in China's industrial policies based not just in terms of export quantity but also rising export quality.

[8] Intellectual property right piracy is a factor that could help produce a sizeable trade surplus largely independent of the valuation of the currency (Laurenceson and Tang, 2006). Limited central government initiatives aimed at reducing intellectual property right infringement have so far tended to be frustrated at the provincial and municipal level (Hufbauer, Wong, and Sheth, 2006, chapter 4). Greater US pressure on China to eliminate such piracy would

considering a more drastic 15% to 25% revaluation of the renminbi against the US dollar, suggests that even a move of this magnitude would do no more than slow the rate of increase of the bilateral US–China trade deficit.[9]

According to US statistics, China's overall current account surplus reached $US 238.5 billion in 2006, rising from $US 160.8 billion in 2005 and representing approximately 9.1% of its total economy, up from 7.2% in 2005, but still not the largest in the region in relative terms. Elsewhere within Asia, Singapore's current account surplus was 27.5% of its economy in 2006, for example, whereas Malaysia's was 15.8%, and the Hong Kong SAR weighed in at 10.2% (International Monetary Fund, 2007). The tremendous growth in China's imports has, in fact, generally not lagged far behind the more-widely-noted surge in export performance since the 1990s – although the gap did widen over the 2004–2006 period (see Figure 2.3). China's overall trade surplus in 2006 actually combined an increased $US 232.5 billion surplus with the United States with a mere $6 billion surplus with the rest of the world. If all the imbalances were on the Chinese side, it would be hard to explain why the United States has continued to run large deficits with the rest of the world as well as China, whereas China's "excess" surplus essentially disappears once US imports from China are removed from the equation.

US statistics on China's bilateral trade surplus with the United States are themselves almost certainly overstated because of transshipment of goods via Hong Kong. Discrepancies arise if goods reexported from Hong Kong are mistakenly classified as if Hong Kong were their final destination. For example, US goods exported to China via Hong Kong may be erroneously reported in US customs statistics as an export to Hong Kong while also erroneously recorded in Chinese customs statistics as an import from Hong Kong. Schindler and Beckett (2005) find that most of the discrepancy between US and Chinese trade statistics is removed by correcting for such

certainly seem more justifiable than the repeated attempts to dictate the value of China's currency.

[9] The effects would admittedly be magnified if such a Chinese policy move triggered a more general upward adjustment of other Asian currencies. It is unclear whether any such widespread reaction would emerge in practice, however – with the July 21, 2005, Chinese revaluation seen by Ogawa and Kudo (2007) as having only limited and quite mixed effects on other neighboring currencies. What if Hong Kong, Korea, Malaysia, Singapore, Taiwan, and Thailand did, in fact, all follow a hypothetical freeing of the renminbi exchange rate against the dollar? Laurenceson and Qin (2006, p. 202) emphasize that even a 25% collective appreciation in their currencies could only reduce the overall effective dollar exchange rate by approximately 5%, given that their share of total US trade remains little more than 20%.

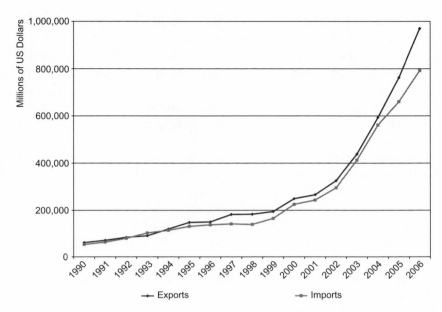

Figure 2.3. China's Exports and Imports Since 1990 (in million of US dollars). *Source:* International Monetary Fund.

distorting effects arising from Hong Kong's transshipping role. Based on Schindler and Beckett's analysis, the Chinese numbers are understated just as the US numbers are overstated. After making further adjustments for factors such as reexport markups and trade in services, Fung, Lau, and Xiong (2006) estimate that the United States' bilateral deficit with China was $US 170.7 billion in 2005, representing approximately 85% of the official US figure of $US 201.6 billion and 149% of the official Chinese figure of $US 114.2 billion. Broadly similar ratios are implied by Schindler and Becket's (2005) findings for 2003 data.

The actual overstatement in the US figures could be still higher, however, after considering reselling to US-based parent companies by multinational corporations operating in China. Chinese Ministry of Commerce calculations suggested the degree of overstatement could have been 30% or more in 2004, with sales by US-funded enterprises operating in China reaching US $75 billion in that year (*People's Daily Online*, August 12, 2005b). This reflects mainland China's importance as a destination for foreign direct investment. Such activities may distort the reported trade position, not only by counting US affiliate reexports to the United States as Chinese exports, but also by treating US affiliate sales in China as purely domestic output rather than as US exports. Both US affiliate reexports and US affiliate sales in China have been growing strongly in recent years (see Li, 2006, p. 64).

Although these qualifications suggest that official US figures significantly overstate the extent of the underlying trade imbalance, this would still leave a substantial US–China bilateral deficit. No matter how much China's impact may have grown, it has, however, been far from the only driver behind the burgeoning US current account deficit and the United States' transition to a debtor nation. The United States' $4 trillion net debt to foreigners was accumulated over many years and did not suddenly spring from any alleged recent exchange rate imbalance with the renminbi. Moreover, China's relatively balanced trade with the rest of the world, contrasted with the United States' massive trade deficit with the rest of the world, begs the question of whether it is really the renminbi that is too weak or the US dollar that is too strong. From the perspective of Fan Gang, a member of the People's Bank of China's monetary policy committee: "[T]he real problem the world faced was an overvalued dollar, not only against the renminbi but against all the leading currencies."[10]

Reserve Accumulation and the International Role of the Dollar

Limiting the renminbi's appreciation against the increasingly weak US dollar has required large-scale central bank purchases of dollars that induce more rapid expansion in the domestic supply unless these purchases can be "sterilized" through offsetting withdrawals of currency from circulation (see Chapter 4). Expansionary pressures were further augmented by "hot money" flowing into China with a renewed surge of capital inflows following the new exchange rate policy announced in July 2005 that was widely seen as setting the stage for further renminbi revaluation over time. The rate of increase in consumer prices in China initially remained relatively benign, with the inflation rate only briefly exceeding 5% in the third quarter of 2004 before dropping back below 2% in 2005–2006.[11] Nevertheless, the rate of accumulation of foreign reserves continued at an ever-accelerating rate over the post-2000 period (see Figure 2.4). In addition to speculative capital flows, other factors in the recent surge in China's foreign exchange reserves include ongoing steps toward capital account liberalization and the dollar

---

[10] As quoted in Garnham, Giles, and Brown-Humes (2006, p. 11).
[11] While apparently reflecting the success of the authorities' efforts to sterilize the inflationary effects of the inflows (see also Chapter 4), renewed inflation concerns emerged in 2007 as the annualized rate of increase in consumer prices reached 6.5% in August 2007.

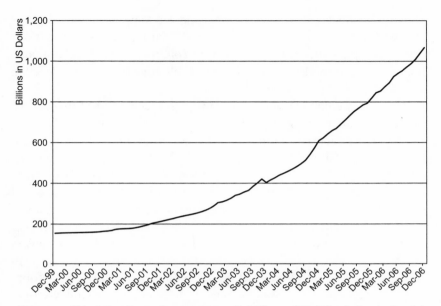

Figure 2.4. China's Foreign Exchange Reserves (in billions of US dollars). *Source:* People's Bank of China.

purchases required to maintain the managed exchange rate bands (see also Zheng and Yi, 2007). As discussed in Chapter 8, almost certainly some of the liquidity influx was being channeled into the stock market and housing market.[12]

The reserve accumulation and accompanying growth in the US current account deficit with China is itself part of a worldwide trend toward larger current account surpluses among emerging economies. In 2006, for example, China's balance of payments surplus of US $238.5 billion was almost matched by a $212.4 billion surplus in the Middle East (International Monetary Fund, 2007, p. 251). Elsewhere, Russia enjoyed a $95.6 billion surplus and there has also been an increasing move to current account surpluses in Latin America, reaching an aggregate $48.7 billion in 2006. The trend toward US current account surpluses being matched primarily by emerging market current account surpluses has been emphasized by Bernanke (2005, 2007), who points to reserve accumulation in East Asian and Latin American countries since the financial crises of the late 1990s as well as the effects of rising oil prices in boosting surpluses in the Middle East, Russia, and

---

[12] Wu (2003) suggests that absorption of excess currency in these assets markets became empirically significant even before 2001.

other oil-producing nations such as Nigeria and Venezuela. Between 1999 and 2006, a $534.8 billion increase in the US current account deficit was countered by a $501.8 billion swing in the collective current account position of emerging market economies from a collective $21.2 billion deficit in 1999 to a $544.2 billion surplus in 2006.[13]

John Lipsky (2007), First Deputy Managing Director of the International Monetary Fund, recently acknowledged the Fund's worry that "rather than shrinking as anticipated [with the post-2002 recovery in global growth], global payments imbalances reached a record high, leading to growing concerns about the threat of impending economic and financial instability."[14] The Fund's Multilateral Consultation on Global Imbalances was launched in 2006 to address these developments, with participation from China and other major surplus countries such as Saudi Arabia and Japan in addition to representation of the euro area and the United States. Based on Bernanke's (2005, 2007) view, the imbalances primarily reflected high savings growth abroad combined with the attraction of US financial markets as a destination for this saving. Bernanke (2005) points to foreign capital inflows being drawn, first by rising US equity prices in the 1990s and then by a booming US housing market after the 2000 market crash – as well as the ensuing post-2003 stock market recovery. With the sophisticated US financial system essentially intermediating savings originating in China and elsewhere, Dooley, Folkerts-Landau, and Garber (2004) see the United States serving as the *de facto* center country in a "Revived Bretton Woods System." If their "portfolio balance" view of global imbalances is correct, such capital flows are the result of portfolio optimization and not indicative of any need for drastic exchange rate adjustment (cf. Xafa, 2007).

The dollar's role as the major international reserve currency has certainly played a major part in drawing foreign funds into US assets. The total inflow from foreign central banks reached $498 billion in 2004, financing as much

---

[13] There was also a $29.9 billion increase in the current account surpluses of the "newly industrialized Asian economies," including Hong Kong, Korea, Singapore, and Taiwan, over this same period (International Monetary Fund, 2007, p. 247).

[14] Were the US current account deficit to remain around 6% of GDP then, coupled with nominal GDP growth that has recently also been around 6%, Mussa (2005) concludes that this would eventually push up US net foreign liabilities to an unprecedented 100% of GDP – compared with just over 20% of GDP in 2006. Eichengreen (2007, chapter 4) suggests that raising nominal GDP growth via allowing more rapid inflation is the most likely path to containing the net debt ratio if the current account deficit cannot be brought down. The downward trend of the dollar would, of course, itself be a factor facilitating such an inflationary "solution" – but also, quite possibly, a major financial crisis.

as 75% of the 2004 trade deficit. The willingness of other central banks to, thus far, continue accumulating dollar assets goes a long way toward explaining why, even in the face of such large trade deficits, the dollar did not fall further over the 2002–2007 period. Mainland China, in fact, became the second largest foreign holder of US Treasuries after Japan in 2006, with its holdings of US Treasuries more than doubling since June 30, 2004 (when China's holdings stood at $341 billion). As of June 30, 2006, US Treasury figures assessed mainland China's reserve accumulation of US Treasuries at $699 billion, up from $527 billion on June 30, 2005 (US Department of the Treasury et al., 2007).

Observers such as Eichengreen (2007) have questioned whether the dollar will remain such a dominant reserve currency of choice in the future, however, suggesting that this role will be increasingly shared with other currencies like the euro. There is also the question of the dollar's role in pricing, and settling trades in, most internationally-traded commodities such as oil. Were oil invoicing to switch from the dollar to the euro, for example, the "petrodollar" recycling of the surpluses enjoyed by the oil-producing nations could well be transformed into "petroeuros" instead (Rajan and Kiran, 2006). Some signs of a limited move away from the dollar emerged in 2006 as a number of central banks, ranging from Italy, Russia, and Switzerland to the United Arab Emirates, announced plans to reduce the proportion of dollar holdings in their reserves (see Garnham, Giles, and Brown-Humes, 2006, p. 11). In addition, in May 2007, Kuwait elected to delink its currency from the dollar as the combination of a weakening dollar and a strong domestic economy produced increasing inflationary pressures. This not only shows that China is far from the only economy facing difficulties in dealing with the downward trend in the dollar, but also could potentially be an early sign of more widespread retreat from foreign central bank dollar purchases.

Kerr (2007, p. 13) points out:

If Kuwait's oil-rich neighbours also dropped their dollar pegs, the impact would be felt way beyond the Gulf. Countries in the region could buy fewer dollars and put less of their booming foreign exchange reserves into US assets such as Treasury bonds.

Possible effects of flight from the dollar likely include higher yields on Treasury securities if foreign central bank purchases declined, but there is little consensus as to how important this effect would be. Recent estimates as to the impact of central bank reserve accumulation on US Treasury yields have

Table 2.1. *China's New Foreign Investment Agency and Other Sovereign Wealth Funds*

Country	Sovereign Wealth Fund	Estimated Size*	Year Begun
United Arab Emirates	Abu Dhabi Investment Authority	$625.0 billion	1976
Norway	Government Pension Fund	$322.0 billion	1990
Singapore	Government Investment Corporation	$215.0 billion	1981
Kuwait	Kuwait Investment Authority	$213.0 billion	1953
China	China Investment Corporation (CIC)	$200.0 billion	2007
Russia	Stabilisation Fund	$127.5 billion	2004
Singapore	Temasek Holdings	$108.0 billion	1974
Qatar	Qatar Investment Authority	$60.0 billion	2005
US State of Alaska	Permanent Reserve Fund	$40.2 billion	1976
Brunei	Brunei Investment Authority	$30.0 billion	1983

* As of October 2007.
Source: Larsen (2008, p. 2).

ranged from zero to 200 basis points (see European Central Bank, 2006, pp. 23–25). Warnock and Warnock (2006) subsequently suggested that, after controlling for other factors, foreign official purchases of US securities exerted an approximate 90 basis point effect on 10-year Treasury yields over the 1984–2005 period. However, future surpluses may not translate so automatically into reserve holdings of US Treasuries. A growing array of *sovereign wealth funds* has been created by a number of surplus countries, including the United Arab Emirates (whose Abu Dhabi Investment Authority is considered the largest such fund, weighing in at perhaps US $625 billion), as well as Norway, Singapore, Kuwait, and China (see Table 2.1).[15] Sovereign wealth funds appear to be on track to surpass total official reserve holdings as early as 2011, with Stephen Jen of Morgan Stanley predicting growth from a total estimated size of $2,510 billion in early 2007 to perhaps $6,500 billion by 2011 and $12,000 billion by 2015 (Jen, 2007).

China's own sovereign wealth fund, China Investment Corporation (CIC), was formally inaugurated on September 29, 2007, with initial registered capital of $200 billion. It actually commenced operations earlier in the year, with a relatively aggressive investment stance suggested by the May 2007 move to invest $3 billion in the initial public offering (IPO) of the Blackstone Group, a major US private equity firm. This is likely to form part

[15] Estimates vary considerably owing to the limited reporting by many of these funds, and the 2007 size of the Abu Dhabi Investment Authority, in particular, has actually been placed as high as $875 billion.

of a potentially major move away from surplus countries' emphasis on US Treasuries, although, as the Blackstone purchase implies, not necessarily a move away from US assets altogether.[16] In fact, China's Premier Wen Jiabao stated that the establishment of CIC would "not have any adverse impact on U.S.-dollar denominated assets."[17] However, it is still possible that new funds accumulated via China's ongoing current account surpluses with the United States could be invested on a more diversified basis than has been the case in the past. Should funds be reallocated to the euro, as the most viable alternative major currency, the higher demand may well boost the euro's value – but also have the rather less welcome effect of furthering the loss of competitiveness vis-à-vis the United States already experienced by the euro-zone countries in the post-2001 period. Blanchard, Giavazzi, and Sa (2005, p. 39) characterized the old status quo as follows:

> The trade deficits of the United States with Japan and the euro area imply an appreciation of both the yen and the euro against the dollar. For the time being, this effect is partly offset by the Chinese policies of pegging and keeping most of its reserves in dollars. If China were to give up its peg or to diversify its reserves, the euro and the yen would appreciate further against the dollar.

Cautionary Lessons from Japan and Taiwan

Clearly China is not the only nation to be concerned about the scope for further, and perhaps stronger, appreciation against the US dollar. Despite mounting US pressure, however, renminbi appreciation was kept to a measured, quite gradual pace over the first two years following the July 2005 currency reform. This begs the question of what consequences might be expected if China, like Japan, were to accede to US demands for more dramatic currency appreciation. In this respect, parallels can also be drawn with the experience of Taiwan, which entered the US congressional spotlight in the midst of its own rising trade surpluses in the 1980s. The Taiwanese authorities, in fact, allowed the New Taiwan dollar to appreciate by over one-third against the US dollar between 1986 and 1988 in the face of US pressure. The United States threatened trade retaliation unless Taiwan's markets were

---

[16] The relatively low return on China's existing vast US Treasury bill and bond holdings implies a sizable opportunity cost if the returns earned on such securities are compared to the approximate 15% returns accruing to inward foreign investment in China (Zheng and Yi, 2007, pp. 21–22). The 2007 launch of China's sovereign wealth fund naturally offers a chance for more profitable use of the growing reserve holdings.

[17] See *People's Daily Online*, March 16, 2007a.

Table 2.2. *Comparison of Japanese and Chinese Export and Current Account Performance*

	Japan			China		
	Export Growth	Share of US Imports	Current Account ($US billion)	Export Growth	Share of US Imports	Current Account ($US billion)
1950s	12.4%	3.9%	$0.1		0.2%	
1960s	16.6%	10.8%	$0.3		0.0%	
1970s	14.6%	13.3%	$3.1	13.5%	0.2%	
1980s	5.3%	18.5%	$42.0	25.0%	1.4%	−$1.8
1990s	2.3%	15.6%	$99.4	23.4%	6.4%	$12.5
2000s	3.5%	10.7%	$114.0	22.4%	10.4%	$24.4

Notes: Export growth is based on home-country currency values; share of US imports is based on US dollar values; share of US imports in the 2000s uses data from 2000–2003; China's current account figures are based on 1982–1989 data for the 1980s and 2000–2002 data for the 2000s; Japan's current account figures for the 2000s are based on data from 2000–2004.
Source: Eichengreen (2007, p. 77).

opened to US goods in conjunction with an immediate and substantial rise in the New Taiwan dollar (Hon, 2004). The effects of Taiwan's experience with sharp currency appreciation are considered along with the lessons from Japan's experience. Japan, after having initially negotiated currency appreciation quite successfully following the breakdown of the Bretton Woods system in 1971 (Eichengreen, 2007, chapter 3), subsequently appeared to suffer considerably from acceding to incessant US pressure for additional currency appreciation in the 1980s. McKinnon (2005, p. 77) actually sees "the appreciating yen up to the mid-1990s as the main source of Japan's deflation and low-interest-rate liquidity trap."[18]

Overall, the Japanese and Taiwanese experiences suggest that currency appreciation carries substantial risk but does not necessarily have the calamitous consequences suggested by McKinnon (2005).[19] Indeed, Japan continued to enjoy export growth of 14.6% in the 1970s, down only slightly from the 1960s, and a rising share of US imports, even as the yen appreciated by approximately 41% from its old Bretton Woods parity of 360 yen/$US to an average of 211 yen/$US in 1978 (see Table 2.2). The yen initially

[18] Such a "liquidity trap" scenario implies that interest rates have fallen so far that they can go no lower, leaving no room for the central bank to boost the economy through engineering rate cuts.

[19] Obstfeld (2007) also draws parallels with Germany's relatively favorable experience after being forced off its former dollar peg in 1971 in the face of an influx of speculative capital inflows and expanding US liquidity – a scenario certainly not so unlike the pressures recently experienced by China.

appreciated by 17% in 1971 alone (see McKinnon, 2005, p. 88). The continued rise in Japan's share of US imports, reaching 18.5% in the 1980s, triggered further US pressure on Japan but, at the same time, suggests considerable resilience to the already substantial currency appreciation since 1971. Eichengreen (2007, chapter 3) concludes that although the appreciation did negatively affect Japanese exports and investment, the contractionary effects were offset by rapid growth in the world economy – with world income enjoying a cumulative 12% gain during 1972–1973. Eichengreen (2007) also points to beneficial effects of continued Japanese exchange rate intervention to lessen volatility, coupled with expansionary monetary and fiscal policy. This favorable perspective is disputed by Ito (2006), however, who argues that Japan should have more quickly moved to a free float and thereby avoided the reserve inflows and inflationary pressures during 1971–1973 that accompanied the authorities' attempts to resist further currency appreciation. The rise in Japan's inflation, reaching 10% in the summer of 1973 following the March 1973 adoption of the free float, is seen by Ito as indicating that the Japanese authorities waited too long to free the exchange rate – and that Chinese authorities should move more quickly in that direction today.

The Japanese real economy clearly fared less well in the face of renewed US pressure that, following the Plaza Agreement of September 1985, saw the yen appreciate from an average of 239 yen/$US in 1985 to a high value of 128 yen/$US in 1988 – representing a fresh overall appreciation against the dollar of approximately 46%. Renewed strengthening of the yen in the early 1990s took the exchange rate all the way to 80 yen/$US in April 1995. Although Japan's current account surplus continued to rise, export growth declined from 14.6% in the 1970s to 5.3% in the 1980s and only 2.3% in the 1990s (Table 2.2). There was also a noticeable shift of manufacturing FDI from Japan to South-East Asia after the Plaza Agreement. Japan actually moved into deflation in the 1990s following the collapse of its hitherto rapidly rising equity and housing markets. The collapse of land values proved particularly damaging given its role as collateral for loans, with severe balance sheet effects for individual and commercial landholders as well as Japan's banking system (on this linkage, see, for example, Kuttner and Posen, 2001, and Burdekin and Siklos, 2004). The asset price collapse came not only at the end of an extended period of currency appreciation but also at the time of an abrupt tightening of monetary policy by the Bank of Japan.

Although many factors undoubtedly explain Japan's failure to weather the second period of sharp appreciation, Japan's current account surpluses, like its foreign exchange reserves, continued to rise – making it unclear that US pressure ever secured the trade benefits thought to accrue from a stronger yen. As McKinnon and Schnabl (2006, p. 282) point out:

When Japan was forced into appreciating the yen several times from the mid-1980s into the mid-1990s, it was thrown into a decade-long deflationary slump with no obvious decline in its large trade surplus, which has persisted up to the present.

However, the earlier 1970s experience seems to refute the premise that deflationary effects of currency appreciation are inevitable.[20] Taiwan's experience in the late 1980s also suggests that substantial appreciation, while naturally weakening export performance, need not have such drastic consequences.

As shown in Table 2.3, Taiwan's export growth slowed from 29.41% in 1986 to 1.67% in 1990 in the face of a 30.2% currency appreciation between 1986 and 1989. Taiwan's current account surplus declined from a peak of $US 18,003 million in 1987 (representing nearly 20% of Taiwan's economy) to $US 10,923 million in 1990, thereafter generally remaining around 1984–1985 levels before trending upward again after the Asian financial crisis. The rate of foreign reserve accumulation slowed in the face of the currency appreciation but continued to trend upward. Adjustment to the rapid currency appreciation may have been aided by central bank intervention that limited the rate of appreciation to no more than one cent a day, thereby preventing any sudden, discrete jumps in the exchange rate (Hon, 2004). Another factor was that negative effects of the appreciation on Taiwan's exports to the United States were partially offset by gains in Europe and elsewhere, with the New Taiwan dollar actually depreciating against such currencies as Germany's Deutsche mark and the Japanese yen during the same late 1980s time period. Even as Taiwan's US market share fell back from 48% in 1985 to 32% in 1990, Taiwan's European market share rose from just 10% in 1980 to 18% by 1990 (Gee, 1994, pp. 93–94).

Xu (2008) concludes that the New Taiwan dollar appreciation exceeded what was justified on a purchasing power parity basis and was likely driven upward more by short-term capital inflows than a nonsustainable current account balance. Similar arguments that recent pressure on the renminbi also manifested such short-term flows, themselves reflecting expectations

---

[20] Although McKinnon and Schnabl (2006) stress the negative effects of expected currency appreciation on domestic wages and interest rates (an argument repeated in, for example, McKinnon, 2005, and McKinnon, 2007), the question is whether any such mechanism can be assumed to dominate other factors influencing wage and interest rate determination.

Table 2.3. *Taiwan's External Position, 1982–2000*

	NTD/$US Exchange Rate	Rate of Export Growth	Current Account Surplus (in millions of US dollars)	Foreign Exchange Reserves (in millions of US dollars)
1982	39.11	−2.46%	2,251	8,532
1983	40.06	15.04%	4,416	11,859
1984	39.60	20.54%	6,980	15,664
1985	39.85	0.81%	9,206	22,556
1986	37.82	29.41%	16,287	46,310
1987	31.77	34.43%	18,003	76,748
1988	28.59	13.23%	10,200	73,897
1989	26.40	9.35%	11,416	73,224
1990	26.89	1.67%	10,923	72,441
1991	26.81	13.55%	12,468	82,405
1992	25.16	7.25%	8,550	82,306
1993	26.38	4.68%	7,042	83,574
1994	26.46	9.71%	6,498	92,455
1995	26.48	20.18%	5,474	90,310
1996	27.46	3.79%	10,923	88,038
1997	28.66	5.69%	7,050	83,502
1998	33.44	−9.32%	3,436	90,341
1999	32.27	9.77%	7,993	106,200
2000	31.23	22.73%	8,899	106,742

Note: NTD/$US refers to the number of New Taiwan dollars per US dollar.
Source: Central Bank of the Republic of China (Taiwan) (http://www.cbc.gov.tw).

of pending currency appreciation, would seem to justify caution in the permitted range of exchange rate adjustment. In the late 1980s, Taiwan's central bank maintained a relatively easy money stance, reducing interest rates to cushion the effects of the currency appreciation, and the rate of real GDP growth remained relatively robust, dipping only from 7.8% in 1987 to 5.4% in 1990 (Xu, 2008). While producer prices actually declined during 1987–1991 in spite of accelerating rates of credit expansion, asset prices surged – with the Taiwan Stock Index rising from 1,100 at the end of 1986 to 12,000 in early 1990 while average housing prices in the area around the island's capital, Taipei, more than quadrupled (Chen, 2001).

As with Japan at the end of the 1980s, Taiwan's asset price boom ended with a major collapse, and the island's stock market lost approximately 75% of its value in six months during 1990. Also in common with Japan was the central bank's adoption of an easy money policy to compensate for the negative effects of the currency appreciation. Even though China's own currency appreciation has so far been quite tightly contained, the parallels with inflationary pressures being channeled into asset markets rather than goods markets are all too obvious in light of China's stock market gains in 2006–2007 – as addressed more thoroughly in Chapter 8 of this volume. It also does not seem that permitting rapid currency appreciation to occur did anything to alleviate overall credit expansion rates in Japan and Taiwan in the 1980s.

Taiwan's appreciation may admittedly have conferred longer-run benefits in encouraging an advance into more advanced, technologically-intensive export activities that are Taiwan's hallmark today. For example, Chen, Schive, and Chu (1994) note a sharp increase in the ratio of products with higher degrees of capital intensity, and a decline in the ratio of products with high degrees of labor intensity, among Taiwan's exports over the 1986–1991 period. Xu (2008) also emphasizes expansion in the service sector aided by the effects of the currency appreciation in raising domestic real income levels as tradable goods became relatively more affordable.[21] It is doubtful that China could readily handle even the modest slowdown experienced by Taiwan, however, and there must also be concern that allowing freer appreciation of the renminbi would run the risk of allowing speculative capital flows to push the currency too far too fast.[22] The less severe consequences experienced by Taiwan, as well by Japan in the 1970s, must also be set against the calamitous developments in Japan following its own "second round" of major currency appreciation in the 1980s. Perhaps the most vivid cautionary lesson of all is China's own experience in the 1930s, however, to which we will return in Chapter 5 of this volume. There is certainly good precedent for Chinese authorities to be concerned about the risks of more rapid currency appreciation – whereas past experience suggests that such appreciation has had surprisingly little effect on the trade surpluses enjoyed by the countries concerned, leaving little hope that a move by China today

[21] The 77.6% increase in Taiwan's unit labor costs between 1985 and 1990 was influenced by labor law changes as well as by currency appreciation (Chen, Schive, and Chu, 1994) – nevertheless, it does seem to contradict the view that currency appreciation necessarily prevents domestic wages from catching up with more advanced country levels (cf. McKinnon and Schnabl, 2006).

[22] Indeed, Shi (2006) finds that even the limited real currency appreciations experienced by China over the 1991–2005 period exerted significant negative effects on China's GDP. China's manufacturing sector seems particularly vulnerable – with Hua (2007) identifying statistically significant negative effects of real currency appreciation on manufacturing employment over the 1993–2002 period.

could be expected to have much, if any, lasting effect on the United States' own yawning trade deficits.

Where We Stand Today

Whatever the weakness or strength of the case for further immediate additional renminbi appreciation, a sudden move in this direction could very well hurt, not help, the United States – insofar as this led the Chinese to significantly cut back on their purchases of US dollar assets. Indeed, the US government should almost certainly be hoping that China does not make any major move to pull its funding of the US trade deficit – and instead invest either in other foreign currencies or, indeed, in its own economy. Notwithstanding recent US pressure for immediate freeing of the renminbi exchange rate, and threats of punitive tariffs on Chinese imports, the United States, as the deficit country dependent on Chinese inflows, is arguably the one that is more vulnerable. China, in contrast, appears to be holding the strong hand. Joseph Stiglitz (2005), for example, has argued that

China could easily make up for the loss of exports to America – and the well-being of its citizens could even be improved – if some of the money it lends to the US was diverted to its own development.

China abandoning exchange rate control entirely and allowing the renminbi to strengthen freely against the US dollar remains unlikely in the short term because it could jeopardize the high rates of economic growth demanded by the Chinese leadership. Pronounced renminbi revaluation would make China's exports more expensive and likely slow the economy. There are serious political concerns about the unemployment that might be generated by any slowdown. Following the bold initiatives laid out by Jiang Zemin at the 1997 15th Party Congress, the Chinese government has acknowledged the need for ongoing closures of at least some of the country's loss-making state-owned enterprises. However, in order to ensure that the workers cast out of these state-owned enterprises are able to find new employment, the government finds it hard to accept even a modest reduction in the country's high rates of overall economic growth.[23] Moreover, bad loans to loss-making state-owned enterprises have contributed to

---

[23] Nobel laureate Robert Mundell was quoted as saying that large exchange rate revaluation could even cut China's recent rapid growth rates in half (*People's Daily Online*, February 14, 2006b).

significant financial sector weakness in the past (see Chapter 7). Continued concerns about China's banking sector add to the risks associated with restrictive policies and help explain the limited nature of the exchange rate adjustments undertaken in 2005 (Eichengreen, 2005).[24]

---

[24] Besides the obvious risk to the export sector, another concern is that rapid appreciation might well worsen inequalities between regions, and between skilled and unskilled workers. This would follow from lower real income levels in China's countryside if the domestic currency price of agricultural products falls, suggesting that any such currency move would be appropriate only as part of a more balanced package of reforms (Blanchard and Giavazzi, 2006).

THREE

Combatting Inflation and Deflation

Beijing is preparing to step on the brakes – Chinese style. The 10 per cent annualized growth in first quarter domestic product came on the back of surging liquidity. Banks lent $137bn in the first quarter, about half the amount targeted for the whole year. Monetary tightening is overdue... China has opted for administrative measures and is likely to do so again. Possible actions include stricter bank reserve and lending rules and limiting land supply...

(*Financial Times*, April 26, 2006a, p. 16)

Introduction

For much of its existence, the People's Republic of China was essentially free of open inflation. Rigid controls kept official prices of many goods virtually unchanged for decades before economic reforms began in 1978. Limited inflationary pressures emerged after 2002 in the face of rising capital inflows and growing pressure for renminbi appreciation, as discussed in Chapter 1. However, Chinese authorities previously had to confront much more severe upward spikes in inflation in both 1988–1989 and 1993–1995. Inflation peaked at over 24% in 1994 before falling back to single digits in 1996 and less than zero in 1998. By 1998, the government's concern clearly shifted to the slowing growth rate of the economy and the weaknesses in the nation's banking system. The increased government expenditures aimed at boosting growth and recapitalizing the banks helped end China's deflation episode but also set the stage for new inflation worries in the early twenty-first century.

This chapter includes some material previously published in Burdekin (2000) and the author is most grateful to Jim Dorn, editor of the *Cato Journal*, for permission to reprint. The author thanks Xiaojin Hu, Yanjie Feng Burdekin, Tom Willett, Pierre Siklos, Mack Ott, Charles Hu, Bill Brown, and Marc Weidenmier for their helpful comments on the original piece and extends gratitude to Ida Whited, Ling Cao, and Ran Tao for their research assistance.

Table 3.1. *Early Renminbi Note Issue and Prices, 1948–1950*

	Cumulative Note Issue (in billions of renminbi)	Wholesale Prices (index for 13 major cities)
December 31, 1948	19	100
January 31, 1949	–	153
April 30, 1949	–	287
July 31, 1949	280	1,059
September 30, 1949	810	–
October 31, 1949	1,100	–
November 30, 1949	2,000	5,376
December 31, 1949	2,670	–
February 28, 1950	4,100	–

Source: Burdekin and Wang (1999, p. 213).

This chapter offers an overview of the main inflationary and deflationary challenges faced by the People's Republic since 1949. Parallels are drawn between some of the early methods of inflation control and more recent anti-inflationary policy in the 1990s and 2000s. Over the post-1978 period, the authorities have increasingly moved toward more market-based policies, with reduced reliance on administrative methods, aided by progress in such areas as price liberalization and the institutional separation of monetary and fiscal policy. Further financial and interest rate liberalization is still called for, however, and external factors have also posed especially strong challenges for Chinese policymakers in recent years. The deflationary pressures that emerged with the 1997–1998 Asian financial crisis were quickly replaced by new worries about increasing current account surpluses and reserve inflows. A brief overview of the latest People's Bank policy measures aimed at combatting these expansionary pressures leads into the more detailed policy analysis that follows in Chapter 4.

Early Methods of Inflation Control

The People's Republic was initially confronted by a rampant inflationary spiral that had begun under the earlier Nationalist regime. As noted in Chapter 1, when Mao Tse-tung proclaimed the People's Republic of China on October 1, 1949, prices were skyrocketing. There was a fourteenfold increase in the renminbi money supply, and more than tenfold increase in wholesale prices, between December 1948 and July 1949 – followed by a sevenfold increase in the money supply and a more than fivefold increase in prices over the July 1949–November 1949 period (Table 3.1). By March 1950, wholesale prices were more than two hundred times above the levels reached in June 1949, just after Shanghai fell to the Communists in the final stages of the Chinese Civil War. With little initial formal tax apparatus and no bond issuance until 1950, the surging money growth represented the only ready way by which the new regime could fund its expenditure needs. Although there was no national budget at this time, Chen Yun, who was in charge of the People's Republic's Committee on Financial and Economic Affairs, estimated that two-thirds of total expenditures were funded by deficit finance in 1949 (Chen, 1984, p. 77).

The Communist authorities responded to inflationary pressures by direct intervention in commodity markets. Such an approach had been attempted, less successfully, by the preceding Nationalist regime (Burdekin, 2007). The basic premise behind this intervention, however, goes all the way back to practices adopted during China's Imperial era and endorsed by Confucius as early as the sixth century B.C.E. Stabilization of grain prices became an important part of Imperial policy, and Chen (1911, p. 572) observes that in 54 B.C.E. it was formally

proposed that all the provinces along the boundary of the empire should establish granaries. When the price of grain was low, they should buy it at the normal price, higher than the market price... When the price was high, they should sell it at the normal price, lower than the market price...

The People's Republic itself quickly established a battery of state trading units, which obtained their supplies through levying a tax-in-kind, from the output of state enterprises, and by purchase of private sector output. During the 1949–1950 inflationary spiral, these state trading companies sought to mobilize supplies of key commodities like grain and cotton cloth, and release them onto the market in the cities to combat shortages and offset the successive price jumps that arose there (Burdekin and Wang, 1999). Their operations became a key element in the Communist policy of conducting "economic warfare" against speculators (Hsia, 1953) and containing inflation in the cities. The supplies collected and put onto the market by the state trading companies represented important support for the early renminbi issues – and, according to Eckstein (1977, p. 170), the state trading companies

performed an initial distribution function, buying up surpluses and channeling them into cities and regions experiencing acute scarcities, into areas where prices of consumer goods were rising and where demand pressures were acute. In this way, they could contain speculative price rises and assure reasonable price stability.

The first nationwide intervention by the state trading companies took place in November 1949. In an attempt to bring down prices and withdraw currency from circulation, the state trading companies unloaded commodity stocks in the big cities. Sales by the state trading companies withdrew as much as 30 billion renminbi from circulation in Shanghai alone between October 10 and November 10, 1949 (Chung-kuo k'o-hsüeh yüan, 1958, p. 362). Effective March 10, 1950, the state trading companies were reorganized into a full nationwide system, boosting their ability to equilibrate relative prices of commodities over the different regions and offset any local spikes in price. Stabilization was essentially achieved by the end of March 1950, with the actions of the state trading companies aided by vigorous promotion of bond sales that appear to have funded more than one-half of the budget deficit in the first half of 1950.[1] The bond purchases by the private sector were apparently not entirely voluntary, however, and, after being "asked to subscribe to their full financial capacity... Cheap sale or sale below cost was the last resort for most businessmen to raise funds... " (Hsin, 1954, p. 15). Fiscal consolidation measures were implemented also, although significant deficit reduction was not achieved until the second half of the year (see Burdekin and Wang, 1999).

In high inflation cases like China's 1949–1950 experience, the rate of price increase typically exceeds the rate of money supply growth as individuals unload the depreciating currency faster and faster, causing the velocity of circulation to accelerate. This velocity represents the average number of times the currency changes hands over the year. Each time the currency changes hands and is spent, still more upward pressure is added to prices and so rising velocity only exacerbates the extent to which too much money is chasing too few goods. Beginning in 1949, China's new government sought to reduce the turnover of the currency by offering bank deposit accounts that were indexed for inflation. Under the "parity deposit system" introduced by the People's Bank of China on April 20, 1949, the value of deposits was set in terms of a commodity unit that conformed to the consumption pattern of the local population. This essentially indexed deposits to commodity prices and appears to have motivated substantial growth in bank deposits despite continued rapid inflation. In Tianjin, for example, the volume of bank deposits in June 1949 quickly rose to 20.8 times the March level (Burdekin and Wang, 1999, p. 216). In addition, after the "parity deposit system" was adopted by the Shanghai authorities on June 14, 1949, a United Nations study confirmed that bank deposits grew substantially faster

---

[1] As discussed in Burdekin and Wang (1999, p. 223), this is based upon taking the ratio of Chen's (1984, p. 117) estimate of private sector bond sales in the first half of 1950 to Chen's (1984, p. 40) estimate of the budget deficit over that same period.

Table 3.2. *Money, Prices, Output, and Velocity in China, 1950–1957*

Year	Wholesale Prices	Retail Prices	Renminbi Money Stock	Net National Product	Real Money Balances	Velocity of Circulation
1950	100.0	100.0	100.0	100.0	100.0	100.0
1951	117.8	111.8	191.6	131.7	162.6	69.1
1952	118.0	112.7	313.8	166.4	265.9	53.1
1953	116.5	117.4	418.6	182.3	359.3	43.8
1954	117.0	117.5	449.8	192.6	384.4	42.6
1955	117.7	119.2	500.2	202.6	424.9	40.7
1956	117.0	119.2	601.6	227.4	514.1	37.6
1957	117.1	122.0	595.5	240.6	508.5	40.1

Note: Real money balances are calculated by taking the ratio of the money stock to the wholesale price level (where 1950 = 100).
Source: Jao (1967–1968, p. 105).

than commodity prices over the July–October 1949 period (Hsia, 1953, p. 61).

Repressed Inflation in the Pre-Reform Period and After

After the movement toward a planned economy got substantially underway in 1952, measured inflation generally remained negligible until after the opening up process that began under Deng Xiaoping in 1978. However, there appear to have been periods of substantial excess money growth and inflationary pressure during the pre-reform period. Although price controls ensured that these inflationary pressures were largely "repressed" and hidden from official inflation data, the extent of this repressed inflation is suggested, for example, in the rapid accumulation of money balances over the 1950–1957 period (Table 3.2). Real balances, that is, the renminbi money stock divided by the price level, rose by more than fivefold between 1950 and 1957 while the velocity of circulation declined by approximately 60%. Over this period, the money supply rose from RMB 2,632 million to RMB 15,675 million, far outstripping the increase in output from RMB 42,842 million to RMB 103,072 million (Jao, 1967–1968, p. 104). If velocity had remained at its original 1950 level of 16.2, prices should have risen 146.4% during 1950–1957, as compared to the measured cumulative wholesale price advance of 17.1% and retail price increase of 22.0% shown in Table 3.2. It is difficult to see why individuals should have voluntarily accumulated so much more money over this period, and the "great divergence between the increase in the quantity of money and the increase in price level indicates that monetary excess demand was being severely repressed" (Jao, 1967–1968, pp. 105–106). In practice, this repressed inflation "manifested itself predominantly in the form of chronic shortages, long queues, and extensive rationing... " (Jao, 1991, p. 2).

Feltenstein and Farhadian (1987) point to the latent inflationary pressures associated with rising real money balances in the 1950s being repeated in the late 1970s in a trend that continued into the early post-reform period. Feltenstein and Farhadian estimate that, over the 1954–1983 period as a whole, the underlying rate of inflation implied by excess demand pressures was two and a half times the inflation rate suggested by official price data. Inflationary pressures were likely especially high in 1953, 1956, and 1961 (Hsiao, 1971; Peebles, 1991). Consistent with Feltenstein and Farhadian's (1987, p. 148) finding of a strongly significant positive effect of the government's budget deficit on the rate of broad money growth in China during 1954–1983, these three episodes of severe repressed inflation all coincided with signs of deterioration in the government's fiscal position. Although the 1953 and 1956 episodes were, in part, a manifestation of the state's investment and socialization policies, Hsiao (1971, pp. 236–251) points to a significant role played by fiscal factors in each case. Hsiao (1971, p. 236) suggests that the annual inflation rate in 1953 and 1956 would have been 10% to 15% in each case if estimated repressed inflation were added to open inflation.

A still more serious upsurge in inflation occurred in 1961, when a 16.2% retail price increase may have been accompanied by as much as a 260% increase in free market prices (see Peebles, 1991, p. 24). Whereas basic necessities continued to be rationed, this surge in free market prices apparently reflected a deliberate strategy of selling high-price goods in order to withdraw money from the market (Peebles, 1991, pp. 28–29). Underlying inflationary pressures in 1961 reflected not only the collapse of industrial and agricultural output in the aftermath of the failed "Great Leap Forward" but also a large expansion in the size of the state's budget during 1958–1960.[2] Moreover, as in the post-reform period, standard budget deficit figures were understated and failed to take into account the use of the People's Bank as a provider of the state enterprises' working capital needs. Loans from the People's Bank provided 100% of quota working capital from 1959 through

---

[2] Imai's (1994) estimates of repressed inflation over the 1954–1992 period confirm heightened inflationary pressures in 1956 and 1958–1961 – although estimated total inflationary pressure is limited to 2.1% in 1956 and 30.2% in 1961. Imai (1994, p. 149) also points to one further inflationary spell in the pre-reform era that appears to have been linked to the Cultural Revolution (with total inflationary pressure peaking at 9.6% in 1968).

July 1961, which "relieved the budget of its share of the burden and thus ensured the appearance of a budgetary surplus by means of credit inflation during a period of high fiscal investment" (Hsiao, 1971, p. 78).

Although the inflationary pressures of the 1950s and early 1960s occurred while the Chinese economy remained more or less entirely "socialized," repressed inflation certainly did not disappear overnight when economic reforms began in 1978. "Planned prices" set by the government remained in force for key commodities and for housing, forming part of a two-tier pricing system that combined market-based prices with administrative prices until the 1990s. Indeed, consumer fears about the inflationary consequences of the removal of the remaining price controls helped fuel the inflation spike in 1988–1989 that is discussed in more detail later in this chapter. Interest rates also remained tightly regulated and, despite considerable gradual liberalization since 1978, were still subject to limited administrative controls in the early twenty-first century.[3] Meanwhile, as discussed in Chapter 1, the exchange rate remained tightly controlled at first, and the renminbi did not become fully convertible even for current account purposes until 1996. Consequently, it is not surprising that Feltenstein and Ha (1991) find evidence of repressed inflation continuing into the 1979–1988 post-reform period.[4]

Inflationary Pressures in the 1980s and 1990s

High inflation is almost always associated with rapid rates of money growth and large budget deficits, both of which were abundantly present in the People's Republic's early inflation experience. Although deficits that are not financed through money issue need not be as inflationary, the pressures to at least partially monetize such deficits are often strong – especially in countries where private financial markets are not fully developed. Table 3.3 provides some data on inflation, broad money (M2), budget deficits, and real output growth over the 1979–2006 reform period. Although M2 has grown at a double-digit rate in every year since 1979, the inflationary consequences

---

[3] The ongoing progress in this area is discussed in Chapters 4 and 7. Until at least 1985, administrative controls were reflected in an "inversion" of interest rates, whereby the rate charged for fixed investment loans was actually held *below* the rate paid on savings deposits (Jao, 1991, p. 18).

[4] Feltenstein and Ha's calculations suggest that underlying inflationary pressure was approximately 12% above the movement in the official price index during 1979–1988. Ma (1993) offers some confirmation of ongoing repressed inflation through the 1980s but finds that this occurred in conjunction with some increased voluntary savings owing to greater monetization of the economy – as well as strong evidence of structural shifts around 1959–1961 and after 1978.

Table 3.3. *Inflation, Money, Budget Deficits, and Output in the Post-Reform Era,*
1979–2006

	Rate of Growth of the Consumer Price Index	Rate of Growth of Broad Money (M2)	Broad Money as Share of Output	Budget Deficit as Share of Output	Rate of Growth of Real Output
1979	2.0%	49.2%	32.9%	3.4%	7.7%
1980	6.0	25.9	37.0	1.5	7.8
1981	2.4	18.3	40.7	−0.8	4.5
1982	1.9	14.6	42.8	0.3	8.3
1983	1.5	19.7	45.7	0.7	10.4
1984	2.8	32.6	50.2	0.8	14.6
1985	10.7	35.5	54.4	0.0	16.2
1986	5.7	30.2	62.2	0.8	8.9
1987	7.2	25.3	66.5	0.5	11.6
1988	18.7	20.7	64.3	0.9	11.3
1989	18.8	18.7	67.4	0.9	4.1
1990	3.2	28.9	79.2	0.8	3.8
1991	3.6	26.7	86.0	1.1	9.2
1992	6.3	30.8	91.3	1.0	14.2
1993	14.6	42.8	100.5	0.8	13.5
1994	24.2	34.5	100.4	1.2	12.6
1995	16.9	29.5	103.9	1.0	10.5
1996	8.3	25.3	112.1	0.8	9.6
1997	2.8	17.3	122.2	0.8	8.8
1998	−0.8	15.3	133.4	1.2	7.8
1999	−1.4	14.7	146.1	2.1	7.1
2000	0.4	12.3	150.5	2.8	8.0
2001	0.9	14.4	162.7	2.6	7.4
2002	−0.6	16.8	175.9	3.0	9.6
2003	1.2	19.6	188.5	2.5	9.3
2004	3.9	14.4	184.8	1.5	9.5
2005	1.8	17.6	163.2	1.2	9.9
2006	1.8	16.9	–	–	10.7

Sources: The consumer price data are the Great China Database (http://www.finasia.biz/tejonline/
tejonline.htm) and the 1998 *China Statistical Yearbook* (Table 9.1) – with pre-1985 data based on
the "overall retail price index"; the money supply data are from the Great China Database and the
International Monetary Fund's *International Financial Statistics* database (sum of series 34 and 35);
the ratio of broad money to output is obtained by dividing the money supply data by gross domestic
product in current prices from the Great China Database; the budget deficit figures and real output
growth (based on constant price gross domestic product) are from the Great China Database.

have been damped. Rapid real output growth averaging 9.5% over the 1979–2006 period offers a natural impetus for increased money demand, consistent with the standard premise that the transactions demand for money rises at higher levels of real income. However, falling income velocity of circulation is also a major part of the rising share of M2 in gross domestic product (GDP).

The fivefold increase in the M2/output ratio between 1979 and 2005 enabled the government to obtain substantial seigniorage revenue from expansion in the real money supply. This is usually interpreted as evidence of rising desired money holdings as the Chinese economy became increasingly monetized. The early gains in the M2/output ratio could also represent a continuation of the repressed inflation phenomenon discussed earlier, however, with Feltenstein and Ha (1991), for example, suggesting that no significant trend toward higher real money balances during 1979–1988 remains if account is taken of the effects of repressed inflation. Yet the repressed inflation hypothesis becomes less plausible with the ending of the two-tier pricing system and a move toward a more market-based system of prices by the 1990s. The continued advance in the M2/output ratio after the 1980s almost certainly reflects a voluntary increase in money holdings, and such rising real money demand is consistent with a more than proportionate response of money holdings to rises in real income, as well as to price increases, over the post-1990 period (Burdekin and Siklos, 2008).[5] Revenue from real currency expansion reached an estimated 3.8% of gross domestic product in 1992 (World Bank, 1995, p. 125) and the level of the M2/output ratio has remained above 100% since 1993. Although the rate of increase in the M2/output ratio slowed relative to the prior 1979–1993 pace, the M2/output ratio still recorded an 88.5% advance from 1994–2003. The M2/output ratio subsequently declined slightly in 2004–2005, falling from 188.5% in 2003 to 163.2% in 2005. It is as yet too early to say if this reflects a trend, frequently observed in other economies going through a rapid monetization phase (cf. Siklos, 1993), whereby an initial trend toward rising real money balances (and falling velocity), is followed by a growing financial sophistication phase manifested in declining real money balances (and rising velocity).[6]

---

[5] Gerlach and Kong (2005) suggest an even higher income elasticity of 1.65 (as compared to 1.35 in Burdekin and Siklos, 2008) based on estimation over an extended 1980–2004 period that includes the tail end of the two-tier pricing system.

[6] In the 1990s, China's M2/output ratio actually rose above levels seen in other East Asian economies like Japan and Singapore. Qin (2003), in emphasizing the close relation between China's M2/output ratio and bank deposits over the 1983–1999 period, attributes China's

Even in the face of such seemingly strong appetite for real money balances in the early 1990s, the rise in M2 growth to 42.8% in 1993, followed by 34.5% in 1994, was accompanied by a surge of inflation above the 20% level.[7] Although the officially recorded budget deficit remained low, representing only an approximate 1% share of output, lending by the People's Bank of China for policy purposes (chiefly loans to loss-making state enterprises) added significantly to the government's actual financing needs.[8] Taking account of such lending, World Bank (1995, p. 28) estimates tied the jumps in inflation in 1988 and 1993 to a near doubling of the consolidated deficit to 6.4% of output in 1988 and another sharp jump to 8.9% in 1993. At the same time, sharp increases in the People's Bank's lending to the financial system were seen in both 1988 and 1992 (World Bank, 1995, pp. 53–54), consistent with the funding needs represented by off-budget loans – encompassed by the consolidated budget deficit but not the official, unadjusted figures. Wong, Heady, and Woo (1995, p. 28) offer even higher numbers on the Chinese government's consolidated deficit, suggesting that it amounted to 7.6% of output in 1988 and rose above 10% by 1990–1991. The World Bank (1995, p. 39) argues that the People's Bank's "obligation to finance a persistent CGD [consolidated government deficit] ... caused the repeated buildup of inflationary pressure in China" and accounted for more than two-thirds of the annual growth in reserve money over the 1987–1993 period.

The exchange rate reform in 1994, and depreciation of the official exchange rate discussed in Chapter 1, was another factor adding to inflationary pressures during 1993–1994. Meanwhile, the effects of the earlier 1988 fiscal pressures were exacerbated by panic buying and rising velocity in anticipation of the removal of remaining price controls over key commodities. Wu (2005, p. 368) observes that

the upward movement of prices that started with agricultural products in the fourth quarter of 1987 was spreading to other sectors; ... sporadic panic buying appeared everywhere ... [and] a negative growth rate of bank savings appeared in April [1988], indicating that the inflation expectation had begun to take shape.

relatively higher overall M2/output ratio to a less developed financial sector and smaller range of investment opportunities than those available in other neighboring economies.

[7] Baizhu Chen's (1997) long-run money demand estimates imply that broad money growth needed to be held to 28–29% in order to keep inflation below 10% – assuming a 10% rate of real output growth.

[8] Furthermore, under the Chinese definition of the deficit, debt issues are counted as part of total revenue. For consistency with the standard Western definition of the budget deficit, proceeds from debt issue should be subtracted from the officially stated budget balance (Wong, Heady, and Woo, 1995, pp. 23–25). This adjustment can only be performed through 1996, however, because official data on debt proceeds stopped being provided in

There were also major administrative price increases during each inflationary episode. Prices of pork, vegetables, sugar, and eggs were hiked by as much as 60% in April 1988 while, in 1994, food price inflation was fueled by a 40% rise in grain procurement prices (see Oppers, 1997, pp. 9–12). However, these administrative factors operated in conjunction with easier monetary policy and heightened deficit-monetization pressures.

Control Measures Old and New

Following in the footsteps of the "parity deposit system" of 1949, indexation of bank deposits was reintroduced in the face of the near 20% inflation of 1988. The buying panic that developed in that year saw the public pull their funds out of the banks and use the proceeds to stock up on durable goods. The M2/output ratio declined in 1988, after rising in every prior year in the reform period, and there was also a dramatic fall in China's historically high savings rate (see Song, 1995). To help combat this flight from financial assets, the government announced that savings deposits of three years or longer maturity would be eligible for a "subsidy interest rate" (SIR) based on the differential between the inflation rate and the interest rate on three-year savings deposits.[9] The SIR remained in double digits through the first three quarters of 1989, peaking at 13.64%. Adding the SIR to the base interest rate payable on three-year savings deposits yielded effective nominal returns above 20% in 1989, thereby keeping real returns positive despite the presence of 18% inflation. McKinnon (1994, p. 453) points to the importance of the 1988–1990 indexation in allowing the Chinese authorities to "preserve the incentives for the nonstate sector in general, and households in particular, to accumulate monetary assets." Meanwhile, Yi (1994, p. 70) documents the rapid rebound in bank deposits:

The time deposit increased rapidly in 1989 and 1990. By the end of 1989, the total deposit reached 514.69 billion yuan, which was 134.54 billion yuan higher than the year before... This trend continued in the early 1990s. At the end of 1991, the total residential deposits was 911 billion yuan, which was 46% of the gross national product (GNP) in that year (1985.5 billion).

the *China Statistical Yearbook*. Unadjusted figures are reported in Table 3.3 so as to at least achieve consistency across time. By way of comparison, however, the adjusted deficit was 2.5% of output in 1988–1989 as compared to an unadjusted total below 1% – while the 1994–1996 adjusted deficit reached 3.8% as compared to an unadjusted total that never exceeded 1.2% (Burdekin, 2000, p. 224).

[9] The price index used to calculate the value of the SIR was an unpublished "Total Commodity Retail Price Index" that included retail commodities, service products, and producer goods (see Burdekin and Hu, 1999, for further details).

Indexed government bonds with a three-year maturity were also introduced in late 1988. These indexed bonds offered returns tied to the SIR and proved very popular. The value of indexed bond issuance was RMB 12.5 billion in 1988 followed by another RMB 12.2 billion in 1989, with a three-year maturity. By comparison, only RMB 5.6 billion of same-maturity non-indexed bonds, themselves offering an interest rate of 14%, were issued in 1989 (Burdekin and Hu, 1999). Had the SIR remained at peak 1989 levels, the indexed bonds would have yielded nominal returns as high as 26%. However, by the time the indexed bonds matured in 1991–1992, the inflation rate was below the three-year savings deposit rate of 8.28% and the SIR was zero.[10]

The holders of the indexed bonds would have received only 9.28% in 1991–1992 (the 8.28% savings deposit rate plus 1%) had the authorities not retroactively hiked the payout to match the 14% coupon paid on the nominal bonds. This move was followed by renewed indexation of government bonds in 1993. Yet the outcome was quite different in that inflation was not controlled before the bonds matured and actual payouts did exceed 25%. The March 1996 SIR of 11.29%, for example, coupled with a base rate of 13.96%, yielded a total return of 25.25%. On April 1, 1996, the authorities announced a permanent end to the indexation policy. Nevertheless, the indexed bond issues formed an integral part not only of the Chinese government's anti-inflation program but also of the attempt to replace the prior system of "induced" bond subscriptions – whereby payments were deducted from salaries and operated like a withholding tax – with voluntary purchases. With indexation, bond holders now had a ready-made hedge against inflation, making the bonds a potentially attractive alternative to simply hoarding durable goods. This new policy was accompanied by mushrooming bond trading volumes (Burdekin and Hu, 1999).

More drastic palliatives than indexation, however, had received serious consideration as the gradual removal of price controls was met by run-ups in commodity prices. Indeed, the Chinese Academy of Social Sciences' own Research Group of Price Reform (1987, p. 139), called for: (1) the establishment of a price ceiling/protection price; (2) organizing a special (procurement) market for trading key commodities; (3) adjusting demand and supply indirectly via monetary and fiscal policy; and (4) using state trading companies to stockpile commodities and release them onto the market.

---

[10] Under the system adopted in China – contrary to the usual practice in, for example, Canada, the United Kingdom, and the United States – the inflation compensation payment, if any, is made at maturity based on the SIR at the end of the three-year holding period.

Although no such widespread intervention was actually implemented, the authorities have, at times, continued to resort to administrative measures of price control during the reform era.[11] For example, in the second half of 1995, the municipal government in Chongqing introduced a set of administrative and economic controls aimed at reining in the city's inflation rate (*Shijie ribao* [*World Daily*], 1996). Chongqing had had the worst inflation performance in 1994 of all the 35 largest cities in China. Focusing on basic foods, the municipal government increased their stocks of grain, oil, and meat and intervened aggressively to offset upward pressure on the market price of stocked meat. Although these measures were accompanied by resumption of a rationing system, the policy of unleashing a large supply of a key commodity (in this case, 500 metric tons of stocked meat) onto the market to drive down urban prices remains reminiscent of the 1949–1950 initiatives.[12]

Meanwhile, in 2005 China's State Reserve Bureau – after copper prices spiked upward on rumors that one of their own traders had accumulated a huge short position – "tried to cool the market by announcing it would sell 20,000 tonnes of copper... [the next day] and saying it held 1.3m tonnes of copper in stockpiles" (McGregor, Bream, and Morrison, 2005, p. 17). Even the United States jumped into this game, with President Bill Clinton employing a portion of the United States' Strategic Petroleum Reserve (SPR) in a similar fashion in 1996, ordering the sale of a portion of these reserves in an attempt to combat rapidly rising gasoline prices. The use of the SPR in a similar fashion in the face of the 2004 run-up in oil prices was the subject of much debate (see, for example, Yardeni, 2004). Although pressures for intervention were initially resisted by the Bush administration, continued oil price shocks did elicit limited intervention in 2005.[13]

However, the Chinese authorities have, for the most part, had no need for such measures in recent years. Underlying domestic inflationary pressures have been greatly reduced by enhanced fiscal discipline since the early 1990s, and the People's Bank has increasingly relied upon more conventional

[11] Moreover, although the government did not adopt the Price Reform Research Group's proposals, price controls were kept in place on a subset of key commodities such as cotton, fertilizers, oil, and grain. Higher prices for these items remained available on the black market, with resistance to government attempts to control China's cotton crop culminating in a so-called "market rebellion" in Fall 1994 (see Kahn, 1994).

[12] More recently, stocked meat was released onto the market on a national scale in September 2007 as the government tapped a "strategic pork reserve" to combat inflationary pressures associated with pork shortages (McGregor, 2007).

[13] China began development of its own strategic oil reserve in 2004 – with its oil reserve base in Zhenhai the first of four planned installations (*People's Daily Online*, October 10, 2004).

monetary policy tools like open market operations to stabilize prices. This major change from past practice has occurred in the aftermath of the 1994 Budget Law, which prohibits the government from borrowing from the People's Bank of China.[14] As noted by the World Bank (1996, pp. 10–11), following the passage of this Budget Law, "1994 and 1995 saw a contraction in borrowing from the central bank and a shift toward commercial bank financing, and direct borrowing from the public (using treasury bonds.)" Monetary policy remained relatively tight even as the budget deficit expanded after the Asian financial crisis, when the government launched a fiscal stimulus program aimed at combatting slowing economic growth. Spending on pump-priming measures immediately jumped to $12 billion in 1998. Such higher government spending was itself a response to rising unemployment and weak consumer spending, with China's growth rate declining from around 10% in 1995–1996 to 7.1% in 1999.

The (unadjusted) budget deficit's share of the economy rose to 3% in 2002 before dropping back to 1.5% in 2004 and 1.2% in 2005. Neither this deficit level nor China's debt-to-GDP ratio of around 25% would normally be considered worrisome in themselves. Both figures are considerably better than the norm for developing economies and better than recent US performance – not to mention Japan, with a debt-to-GDP ratio well above 100% and rising. Nevertheless, China's official fiscal position excludes an array of large, and likely mounting, implicit government obligations. As Bergsten et al. (2006, p. 37) point out, these include debts incurred by provincial and subprovincial authorities and unfunded state pension liabilities. Moreover, while direct finance of loss-making state-owned enterprises has been reined in since the mid-1990s, the bad loans previously made to these enterprises remain as a huge potential future fiscal drain. Much of this bad debt, which was acquired by the asset management companies set up to relieve the balance sheets of the large state-owned banks in 1999, had still not been disposed of by 2007. The government is ultimately responsible for covering the difference between the relatively high price paid for this debt and the much lower yield actually received by the asset management companies (see Chapter 7).

In addition, the cost of government-funded bank recapitalizations in 1998, 2003, and 2005 together amounted to 20% to 24% of China's 2004 GDP. The question is not whether more such infusions will be required

---

[14] The Budget Law has been accompanied by a variety of other financial reforms that include the creation of three new "policy banks" and increased autonomy for state commercial banks (see Chapter 7).

in the future but rather just how much bigger they will need to be. There remain serious sources of current and future fiscal burdens not adequately reflected in the rather benign official budget deficit data for China. As discussed earlier, this was true in the past as well. Increased off-budget loans apparently played an important part in fueling rising fiscal pressures at the time of the 1988 and 1993 inflation jumps (World Bank, 1995). Such off-budget loans also seem to have been a factor in the pre-reform period with People's Bank loans supplying 100% of working capital needs in the run-up to the 1961 inflation spike (Hsiao, 1971). Although the available data are insufficient to quantify a causal relationship between fiscal pressures and inflation in China, history does suggest that the potential for new fiscal strains should not be taken lightly.

Confronting Deflation and the Asian Financial Crisis in the Late 1990s

In contrast to the short-lived monetary tightening that helped reverse the 1988–1989 inflation surge, the contractionary policy initiated to combat the later 1993–1994 episode was followed by an extended downtrend in money supply growth. M2 growth actually declined continuously from 42.8% in 1993 to 12.3% in 2000. 1998 was the first full year of deflation. Meanwhile, output growth appeared to flatten out after 1994 and China's sharp monetary tightening was also accompanied by a sizeable stock market decline in that same year. The cumulative overall consumer price deflation of approximately 10% between 1998 and 2002 occurred even as the price of services rose by more than 50% (Zheng, 2002). On the other hand, the rate of decline of commodity prices and production materials outstripped the relatively mild descent of consumer prices – falling by average rates close to 2% and 4%, respectively, in the first half of 2002 even while consumer prices declined by an average of less than 1% (Yuan, 2002). The considerably sharper decline in producer prices, both in 1998–1999 and 2001–2002 is evident in Figure 3.1, which compares the growth rates of consumer and producer prices over the 1997–2007 period.

The continued price declines after the initial monetary tightening in 1994–1995 may have been exacerbated by the banking sector problems discussed in Chapter 7 – with bank reluctance to lend reflected in an excess of savings over lending of approximately RMB 3.65 billion by 2002 (Zhu, 2002). Consumer spending also lagged behind income, consistent with the standard tendency under deflation for consumers to put off purchases of nonessential goods that they expect to be able to buy at still cheaper prices

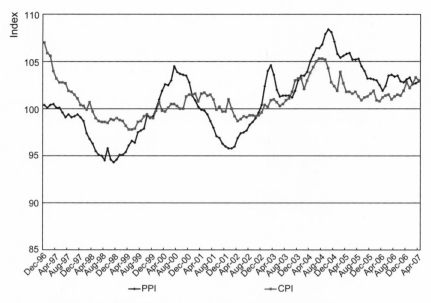

Figure 3.1. Annualized Growth Rates of China's Producer and Consumer Prices, 1997–2007. *Note:* PPI denotes Producer Price Index and CPI denotes Consumer Price Index. *Source:* Great China Database.

in the future (cf. Burdekin and Siklos, 2004, chapter 1). In China's case, concerns about the future direction of the economy also helped explain rising savings rates even in the face of successive interest rate cuts (Zhu, 2002).

The fact that deflation, like inflation, is ultimately a monetary phenomenon seemed to be recognized by Chinese policymakers – with the People's Bank of China raising its money growth targets to combat deflation and eventually restoring positive inflation rates in 2003. The close relationship between inflation and M2 money growth since 1990 is itself particularly striking in the Chinese case. In Figure 3.2, the monetary tightening aimed at combatting the 1993–1994 inflation spike is seen to be accompanied by declining inflation rates and, eventually, outright deflation. However, holding the renminbi exchange rate fixed against the US dollar, in spite of the depreciation pressure associated with the Asian financial crisis (Chapter 1), effectively handcuffed monetary policy at this time. In an indication of how severe an impact the crisis had on the Chinese economy, export growth dropped precipitously from 21% in 1997 to just 0.5% in 1998 (Lin, Cai, and Li, 2003, p. 274). At the same time, bank lending was being further curtailed by the need to reduce bad debts that were still conservatively estimated at

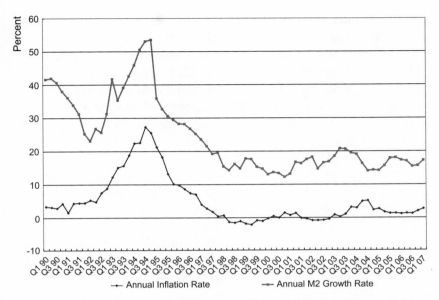

Figure 3.2. China's Inflation Rate vs. M2 Growth Rate, Quarterly Data, 1990Q1 to 2007Q1. *Note:* Inflation is measured by the year over year log difference in the Consumer Price Index. *Source:* Great China Database.

more than one-quarter of China's GDP – even *after* the removal of RMB 10 trillion in nonperforming loans transferred to the asset management companies (Chapter 7). This left expansionary fiscal policy to carry most of the burden in combatting the initial outbreak of deflation in China. In addition, in contrast to the policy reversals seen in Japan, for example, China's fiscal policy remained in a consistently expansionary mode even after the conclusion of the Asian financial crisis.

Deflation also emerged in Hong Kong, which, despite its return to Chinese rule in 1997, is treated as a separate economic entity.[15] Hong Kong consumer prices fell by an overall 12% between September 1998 and January 2002 (Schellekens, 2005, p. 244). In persevering with a fixed exchange rate policy during the Asian financial crisis, Hong Kong faced speculative attacks on the Hong Kong dollar and was forced into tight monetary policy that took a severe toll on the real economy. Hong Kong endured a 5.1% contraction in real GDP in 1998, for example (see Jao, 2001). Real exchange rate appreciation hurt Hong Kong's economy, just as it strained mainland China's, at a time when almost all other Asian currencies were undergoing

---

[15] The later deflation experienced in Taiwan, and the close economic ties between mainland China and Taiwan, are addressed in Part III of this volume.

large depreciation. Schellekens (2005) emphasizes that the parallel developments in mainland China and Hong Kong reflected their exposure to the same shocks and maintenance of similar fixed exchange rate regimes, rather than any mechanical price convergence effect.[16]

Hong Kong's deflation was worsened by the negative wealth effects of falling property and stock prices that reduced the collateral available for new loans, just as had been the case in Japan following the bursting of that nation's stock and land price bubble at the beginning of the 1990s (cf. Burdekin and Siklos, 2004). By comparison, the negative effects of China's own prior 1994 stock market decline were limited by the much lesser importance of mainland China's stock exchanges relative to the overall economy at that time.[17] The Hong Kong Monetary Authority itself resorted to direct stock purchases in 1998 as part of their attempt to ward off speculation against the Hong Kong dollar that was being spearheaded by short selling of Hong Kong stocks by a group of prominent hedge funds (see Krugman, 1999; Jao, 2001). This intervention did help Hong Kong maintain its currency peg but may have been rather a pyrrhic victory. Jao (2001, p. 205) concludes that, although the policy was "quite successful in protecting the integrity of the currency and the banking sector, a heavy price was paid, in terms of the worst recession in 40 years."

Expansionary policy to combat deflation in mainland China was not only fueled by the pressures of the Asian financial crisis but also the need to address the problems with the state enterprises sector and recapitalize the large state-owned banks that had accumulated vast bad debts from these same loss-making state-owned enterprises. After the 1997 15th Party Congress, for the first time, provided for the sale (or bankruptcy) of many of China's state enterprises, the authorities targeted 2,000 to 3,000 enterprises for bankruptcy, merger, or acquisition in 1998 – a year when 49% of large- and medium-sized state enterprises suffered losses (World Bank, 1999, p. 30). The layoffs associated with these moves certainly led to some worker unrest, however, and Kathy Chen (1997, p. A16) draws attention to the 50% increase in labor protests in 1997.[18] In June 1998, Jiang Zemin gave a speech

---

[16] Although Hong Kong, unlike mainland China, has a currency board rather than a true central bank, the key issue here was the simple fixity of the exchange rate throughout the Asian financial crisis and after.

[17] Although rising from 2.2% of household assets in 1992, stocks still enjoyed only a 7.7% share of household assets in 1997 – paling in comparison with the 67.1% of household assets still held in bank deposits (Lin, Cai, and Li, 2003, p. 263).

[18] In practice, layoffs quickly reduced the workforce in the state-owned enterprises by a total of 20 million through the end of 1998 (Lau, 1999, p. 76). Overall, employment in the

urging "caution in the sell-off of small state-owned companies, which were perceived as disturbing the orderly redeployment of laid-off state workers and harming workers' interests" (World Bank, 1999, p. 31).[19]

The financial weakness of the state enterprises prior to the 1997 initiative was reflected in an officially reported ratio of liabilities to assets that reached 85% in 1995. Lardy (1998, pp. 39–43) argues that this ratio was actually considerably understated and equivalent to a better than 500% debt-to-equity ratio. The upshot of this is that, as state-owned enterprises borrowed up to the hilt, the state banks that lent them the money were faced with vast levels of nonrecoverable loans. The financial burden on the economy arising from the state-owned enterprises was characterized by Dorn (1998, p. 133) in terms of a "terminal disease . . . eating up China's scarce capital." As discussed in more detail in Chapter 7, the Chinese government issued $32.5 billion in bonds in 1998 to help recapitalize the four state-owned banks and in 1999 the government established four financial asset management companies to purchase and manage bad loans from these banks.

From Deflation to Renewed Inflationary Pressures After 2002

Dollar depreciation set in after 2001 and, as discussed in Chapter 1, lowered the renminbi's value against other world currencies due to the exchange rate peg maintained until July 2005. The resulting decline in the real exchange rate added to the competitiveness of Chinese exports and gave a boost to China's economy. China's growth rate rose above 9% in 2002–2005 and reached 10.7% in 2006 (see Table 3.3). Moreover, with the renminbi now linked to a weakening US dollar, monetary policy could be loosened without putting pressure on the renminbi to fall relative to the pre-July 2005 pegged 8.28:1 exchange rate level. Broad money growth rose from 14.4% in 2001 to 19.6% in 2003, subsequently rebounding to 17.6% in 2005 and 16.9% in 2006 after a retrenchment to 14.4% in 2004. The pronounced acceleration in 2003 occurred as the People's Bank of China raised its money growth rate target to 18% in the first quarter of that year. Lardy (2005a, p. 44) argues that this 2003 easing was influenced by government fears that the

state-owned enterprises fell by 45 million – or approximately 40% – between 1996 and 2006 (Bergsten et al., 2006, p. 24).

[19] Meanwhile, Lin, Cai, and Li (2003, p. 275) stress the importance of excess capacity in making the subsequent deflation so hard for the government to reverse – arguing that even very large increases in the government's infrastructure investment could not combat excess capacity running at perhaps 30% or more.

outbreak of SARS would severely slow the economy – even though the actual effects, although dramatic at first, proved to be short-lived. Credit growth eventually reached an all-time high of RMB 2.99 trillion, or 25% of China's GDP (Lardy, 2005a, p. 45), and the ballooning lending rates may well have been associated with a renewed upsurge in bank nonperforming loan levels (Chapter 7).

Capital inflows into mainland China began to accelerate in 2001 and the buildup of foreign exchange reserves averaged $US 110 billion during 2001–2004, equivalent to 8% of China's GDP (He et al., 2005, p. 1). Reserve growth continued to accelerate after 2004, with foreign exchange reserves rising by $US 207 billion in 2005 and then by $US 247 billion in 2006. In response, as detailed in the next chapter, the People's Bank sought to sterilize the effects of the reserve inflows by selling government bonds and raising reserve requirements. He et al. (2005, p. 5) calculate that 42% of the overall domestic liquidity effects of the reserve growth were offset over the 2001–2004 period. However, continued concerns with overheating prompted new attempts to slow the economy via administrative controls on bank lending rates. Just prior to the May holidays in 2004 the central government

promised to choke investment in "overheated" sectors such as property and ordered the dramatic arrest of officials for building an unauthorized steel mill near Shanghai . . . The measures the government then implemented were straight from the tool kit of the planned economy, with blunt orders going out to state banks to restrain lending to targeted sectors.[20]

China's economy seemed to largely shrug off such efforts. Although money growth rates did drop back from the near 20% level reached in 2003, export growth ended up more than compensating for some temporary slowing in domestic investment. After lending and fixed asset growth reaccelerated in 2005–2007, notwithstanding the exchange rate appreciation implemented in July 2005, even more tightening attempts were made – with the People's Bank implementing a series of hikes in its benchmark lending rate from April 2006 on. However, accelerating asset prices were not initially accompanied by any similar explosion in consumer prices. The annualized rate of consumer price increase did see a ten-year high of 6.5% in August 2007, but almost all of the pick up in inflation through the summer appeared to derive from food price hikes exacerbated by flood damage to

[20] See McGregor (2006a, p. 6).

crops – with nonfood prices up by only 0.9%.[21] Although it remains to be seen whether the latest round of contractionary policy will be any more effective than the administrative measures imposed in 2004, additional perspective is offered in the next chapter in the form of a detailed analysis of the monetary strategy adopted by the People's Bank of China over the post-1990 period.

[21] The rising inflation was accompanied by bank withdrawals, including an RMB 278.4 billion decline in bank deposits in May 2007 when inflation began to exceed the benchmark annual interest rate on deposits (which stood at 3.06% prior to the hike to 3.33% on July 20). This likely reflected the attraction of the stock market as much as any concerns about ongoing inflation, however, and bank deposits rose again as the stock market corrected in June 2007, for example (*People's Daily Online*, August 11, 2007c).

FOUR

People's Bank of China Policymaking
and External Pressures

with Pierre L. Siklos[1]

In the first quarter of 2007, . . . the PBC [People's Bank of China] broadly sterilized the total liquidity from the RMB counterpart of foreign exchange assets supported with open market operations and reserve requirement policies in an effort to drain the liquidity in the banking system.

(People's Bank of China, 2007, p. 15)

Introduction

Chapter 1 discussed the more flexible renminbi policy adopted in 2005, and the ongoing gradual appreciation following the initial 2.1% move on July 21, 2005. In addition to the external effects of this policy move, allowing some freedom from the fixed exchange rate constraint promised to increase the People's Bank of China's scope for effective monetary control. Ba Shusong, deputy director-general of the Finance Institute of the State Council's Development Research Center, for example, emphasized that the fixed exchange rate had "jeopardized" the independence of Chinese monetary policy.[2] However, the People's Bank seems, in practice, to have been quite successful in containing the inflationary consequences of the continued buildup of foreign exchange reserves. Although the movement away from the old fixed exchange rate policy undoubtedly helped, the development of more market-orientated policy instruments also significantly benefited the People's Bank's monetary control.

This chapter begins with an overview of the changing techniques employed by the People's Bank over the years. The evolving role of open

---

[1] Pierre Siklos is Professor of Economics at Wilfrid Laurier University and Director of the Viessmann Research Centre (psiklos@wlu.ca). The authors are grateful to Yeqin Zeng, Nancy Tao, and Yanjie Feng Burdekin for translation help.
[2] Quoted in *People's Daily Online*, July 25, 2005a.

market operations is discussed in conjunction with the emergence of a liquid interbank bond market with a market-determined interest rate. Empirical modeling of People's Bank policy over the 1990–2006 period relates money supply growth to domestic output growth, growth in foreign exchange reserves, and the real exchange rate – as well as allowing for a shift in policy after the Asian financial crisis. The results yield some evidence of a countercyclical (stabilizing) response to real exchange rate movements and also are consistent with other studies suggesting that the People's Bank has, in fact, been successful in neutralizing the liquidity effects of faster rates of reserve accumulation. Although People's Bank policies definitely remained pressured by such external forces, the central bank did not show any signs of being overwhelmed by even the very large reserves inflows seen in early 2007.

Evolution of the People's Bank and Its Monetary Policy Tools

Although the People's Bank of China was founded in December 1948, it did not function as a true central bank until after September 1983. It was previously a "monobank," responsible for commercial banking as well as central banking functions, and essentially serving as the instrument for carrying out the government's credit plan for the economy (see Chapter 7). Indeed, according to Jao (1991, p. 16), during the monobank era the People's Bank "acted more like a cashier of the State Planning Commission and the Ministry of Finance." The People's Bank's subsequent embrace of traditional Western instruments of monetary control began in 1984 with the levying of reserve requirements to constrain lending by commercial banks. Contrary to the usual practice in the West, however, these reserve deposits were interest bearing – a feature that prevailed into the 2000s. Discount window lending also got underway in the 1980s. Yet interest rates remained essentially dictated by the People's Bank rather than being market determined. Meanwhile, conventional open market operations were deemed infeasible "because of the lack of a 'broad, active and resilient' market in government securities" (Jao, 1991, p. 17).

Passage of the Law of the People's Bank of China on March 18, 1995 helped make clear the People's Bank's responsibility for monetary policy and financial regulation, and provided for the setup of a monetary policy committee. Importantly, this 1995 law was preceded by the 1994 Budget Law, which, as discussed in Chapter 3, prohibited the government from borrowing from the People's Bank. This 1994 law helped weaken the link between fiscal and monetary policy and was followed by increased government reliance on debt finance rather than money finance. Market-based monetary policymaking remained handicapped by limited interest rate liberalization, however, and only since 2004 have commercial banks been able to set their lending rates free of any upper limit above the People's Bank's benchmark rate (Geiger, 2006, p. 8). The People's Bank also continued to enforce lower limits on lending rates and restrictions on bank deposit rates. For example, when the People's Bank announced a rise in loan and deposit rates on October 28, 2004, the communiqué provided no scope for banks exceeding the basic deposit rate that was laid down (People's Bank of China, 2004).

Experimentation with open market operations began as early as 1993 but were handicapped by the lack of a proper interbank market, prompting their temporary suspension in 1997 (see Geiger, 2006, p. 13). The reintroduction of open market operations in May 1998 proved to be much more successful, though, with the range of the operations extending from short-term government securities to a wider set of government instruments, policy financial bonds, and central bank bills (Xie, 2004, p. 4). Central bank bills are short-term debt instruments issued by the People's Bank itself. Their issuance was significantly expanded on September 24, 2002, when the People's Bank converted all repurchase contracts signed since June 25, 2002 into equivalent central bank bills (Xie, 2004, pp. 4–5). The People's Bank had begun making increasing foreign exchange purchases on the open market to offset upward pressure on the renminbi exchange rate with the dollar. In 2002, these repurchase agreements assumed an increasingly important role in offsetting the tendency for rising reserve inflows to boost overall monetary base growth in China. The problem was that the scale of these activities was threatening to produce a shortage of bonds in the market, hence the need to develop and expand central bank bills as an alternative liquid instrument.

Most central bank bills have carried maturity dates of one year or less. Central bank bills became the People's Bank's major weapon in offsetting the liquidity effects of China's huge reserve buildup in the 2000s. The bills began to be tradable on the interbank bond market in April 2003, and have since achieved a dominant position in this market. Their growing issuance is documented in Table 4.1 and by 2006 central bank bills enjoyed a 64.43% market share (Li and Du, 2007, p. 131). Central bank bills' share of the total monetary base exceeded 45% by June 2006 and total outstanding bills reached RMB 3,900 billion at the end of the first quarter of 2007

Table 4.1. *The Growing Importance of Central Bank Bills, 2002–2006*

| Year | Issue Volume of Central Bank Bills (in billions of renminbi) | | | | |
	3 Months Maturity	6 Months Maturity	1 Year Maturity	3 Year Maturity	Total
2002	40.0	108.8	45.0	0	193.8
2003	415.0	258.8	90.0	0	763.8
2004	564.9	184.0	737.2	30.0	1,516.1
2005	943.0	237.2	1,211.0	355.0	2,746.2
2006	1,015.0	95.0	2,542.3	0	3,652.3

Source: Li and Du (2007, p. 131).

(Kwan, 2006b; People's Bank of China, 2007, p. 15).[3] Issuance has been by continuous rolling competitive bidding and the active secondary market for these bills gave rise to a market-determined benchmark interest rate. A United States–style tender offering system was introduced in March 2006 and central bank bills have become significant not only as a monetary policy tool but also in furthering the ongoing movement toward interest rate liberalization. Although the liquidity of the interbank bond market has yet to be matched by the short-term interbank market (bank-to-bank loans ranging from overnight to four months), the bond repo market (short-term borrowing via repurchase agreements) has been another area enjoying increased liquidity – with the repo rate being market-determined since 1997 (Laurens and Maino, 2007, p. 16).

The People's Bank has not only used open market operations but also increased reserve requirements in the attempt to contain the extra liquidity generated by inflows of funds from abroad in recent years. In this way, the People's Bank has endeavored to keep money growth rates from rising too rapidly. Money supply targets were first introduced in 1986 and the elimination of credit ceilings in 1998 left money supply, principally M2, as the sole intermediate target officially directed toward achieving the ultimate goal of price stability (Laurens and Maino, 2007, p. 10) – with People's Bank Monetary Policy Director Dai Genyou (Dai, 2002), for example, stressing the steady growth achieved in M2, in the 14% to 15% range, over the

---

[3] Kwan (2006b) calls attention to the costs associated with this rapid growth in central bank bills, however, with People's Bank borrowing costs being exacerbated by the increased emphasis on longer maturities above one year as well as by rising yields at issue – going up from around 1.9% to nearly 2.8% between January 1, 2006 and August 15, 2006 alone.

1998–2001 period. M2 growth in turn relies upon monetary base growth, or high powered money, produced via the People's Bank's open market operations. The People's Bank's targets for M1 and M2 growth have at times been breached to the upside, as in 2002–2003, for example, but deviations from targeted growth rates have been reduced since the late 1990s – especially for M2 (see Geiger, 2006, p. 29). Whereas Geiger (2006) suggests that the central bank relied upon wage and price controls and window guidance to contain inflation despite missing the announced money growth targets, the fact remains that the lowered money growth targets after 1996 were accompanied by *both* sharply declining rates of money growth and declining inflation (see Chapter 3). Indeed, actual M2 growth rates tended to be *lower* than the targets over the 1997–2001 deflationary period – when an overly tight monetary policy appeared to facilitate the outright declines in prices that emerged over this interval.

The government and the central bank seem, for the most part, to have shared a similar concern with limiting the inflationary consequences of the reserve buildup in the early 2000s – although Lardy (2005a, pp. 44–46) does point to the hiking of money supply targets in 2003 being prompted by the government's concerns about growth prospects in the midst of the SARS epidemic.[4] Certainly, even though the December 27, 2003 amendment of the Law of the People's Bank of China offered some enhancements to central bank autonomy, the government retains significant scope for influencing the course of monetary policy.[5] The People's Bank's focus on purely monetary policy issues was admittedly enhanced by the March 2003 establishment of the China Banking Regulatory Commission, which was charged with the financial industry supervision that had previously fallen under the purview of the People's Bank. Nevertheless, the formal independence of the People's Bank remains quite limited. The central bank's monetary policy committee is still technically no more than an advisory committee and, as it stands, incorporates several government officials, including the deputy Minister of Finance (see Zhou and Li, 2007, pp. 80–84). Goodfriend and Prasad (2006) stress the need for proper operational independence of the People's Bank and advocate a move away from money supply targeting in favor of inflation targeting, with an explicit inflation objective to help anchor inflation expectations.

---

[4] This followed an increase in the People's Bank's M2 growth target from 14% to 17% in the fourth quarter of 2002, at a time when deflationary concerns were still prevalent ("China Still Troubled by Deflation in October," 2002).

[5] On the potential importance of this issue, see, for example, Banaian, Burdekin, and Willett (1995).

Upward pressure on money supply growth has been fueled by rapidly growing inflows of foreign exchange reserves in the 2000s (Chapters 1 and 2). This reserve buildup directly adds to monetary base, which comprises the sum of foreign and domestic assets, requiring the central bank to bring about an offsetting reduction in domestic assets if overall money growth rates are not to expand. The contractionary policies aimed at achieving such offsetting reductions in the domestic component of the monetary base are also known as "sterilization" measures. In the face of reserve growth of 40.8% in 2003, the rate of M2 money growth spiked up to 19.6% in that year. Money growth rates were subsequently brought back down during 2004–2006 following a battery of tightening measures initiated by the People's Bank of China (2005a, p. 126):

In response to overheating, the PBC mainly resorted to economic management efforts to contain the particularly large increase in the credit and monetary supply. This included open market operations to drain liquidity, higher reserve requirements, window guidance and structural adjustments (for instance, intensified regulation of lending to the real estate sector and a clampdown on illicit real estate loans).

The People's Bank carried out 110 open market operations in 2004 alone, selling securities, chiefly central bank bills, to withdraw liquidity from the economy. He et al. (2005) calculate that these interventions brought the monetary base growth rate down from 30% to 11.4% in 2004. Overall, He et al. (2005) find that the effects of increases in foreign assets were essentially fully offset by an equal reduction in domestic assets over the 1998–2004 period, implying complete sterilization. Ouyang, Rajan, and Willett (2007) find near-complete sterilization over the 1999–2005 period, with typically 90% of the reserve inflows being sterilized.[6] Meanwhile, less than full offset of increases in foreign assets over the 1997–2006 period is suggested by Bouvatier (2007) – while Burdekin and Siklos (2008) find negative effects of foreign reserve growth on total monetary base growth combined with positive effects on M2 growth during 1990–2003. Although all of these studies indicate that the buildup of foreign reserves had a major impact on People's Bank policy, the available empirical estimates suggest that the People's Bank remained largely successful in insulating overall money growth from the effects of these reserve inflows. Further analysis of this relationship is provided in the econometric work presented later in the chapter.

[6] As a cautionary note, similar sterilization levels were, in fact, recorded by a number of East Asian countries in the run-up to the Asian financial crisis (cf. Cavoli and Rajan, 2006).

Table 4.2. *Successive Hikes in the Required Reserve Ratio,*
September 2003–June 2007

Jan-03	6	Jan-04	7	Jan-05	7.5	Jan-06	7.5	Jan-07	9.5
Feb-03	6	Feb-04	7	Feb-05	7.5	Feb-06	7.5	Feb-07	10
Mar-03	6	Mar-04	7	Mar-05	7.5	Mar-06	7.5	Mar-07	10
Apr-03	6	Apr-04	7.5	Apr-05	7.5	Apr-06	7.5	Apr-07	10.5
May-03	6	May-04	7.5	May-05	7.5	May-06	7.5	May-07	11
Jun-03	6	Jun-04	7.5	Jun-05	7.5	Jun-06	7.5	Jun-07	11.5
Jul-03	6	Jul-04	7.5	Jul-05	7.5	Jul-06	8		
Aug-03	6	Aug-04	7.5	Aug-05	7.5	Aug-06	8.5		
Sep-03	7	Sep-04	7.5	Sep-05	7.5	Sep-06	8.5		
Oct-03	7	Oct-04	7.5	Oct-05	7.5	Oct-06	8.5		
Nov-03	7	Nov-04	7.5	Nov-05	7.5	Nov-06	9		
Dec-03	7	Dec-04	7.5	Dec-05	7.5	Dec-06	9		

Source: Great China Database (http://www.finasia.biz/tejonline/tejonline.htm).

In addition to open market operations, the People's Bank launched a succession of hikes in the minimum reserve requirement ratio, forcing banks to hold onto more funds to back the loans that they issue. An initial full percentage point increase in the ratio was imposed in September 2003, followed by a half percentage point increase in April 2004 and then eight more half percentage point increases in just eleven months, starting from July 2006. These increases took the reserve requirement ratio up from 6% in August 2003 to 11.5% in June 2007 (see Table 4.2).[7] Other measures included hikes in the People's Bank's benchmark lending and deposit rates in both 2004 and 2007 and more administrative measures like the directive to state banks to refrain from lending to targeted sectors, such as real estate, ahead of the May 2004 holidays (McGregor, 2006a). The People's Bank of China (2007, p. 16) has also not hesitated to issue "special" central bank bills

to commercial banks with relatively rapid credit growth and sufficient liquidity. This measure not only withdrew liquidity but also served as a warning to banks with high credit growth.

Modeling People's Bank of China Policymaking

The People's Bank's focus on money supply growth begs the question of exactly what role money supply movements have played in the Chinese

[7] The reserve requirement ratio remained below the 13% level maintained from 1988–1998, however, prior to the reduction to 6% in just two steps in 1998–1999 following the outbreak of the Asian financial crisis (see Figure 4.1).

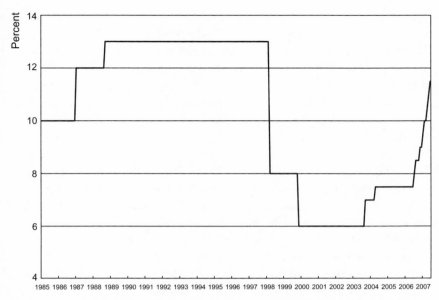

Figure 4.1. People's Bank Required Reserve Ratios, 1985–2007. *Source:* Great China Database.

economy in recent years. The existing evidence on this point is mixed. For example, while Sun and Ma (2004) and Zhang and Wan (2004) each identify a link between money movements and the price level, there is some ambiguity as to whether prices respond to money supply changes or, rather, monetary policy simply accommodates existing price trends – whereby it is price movements that drive money supply movements rather than the other way around.[8] However, a consistent, long-run response of inflation to different rates of monetary expansion over the 1990–2004 period is identified by Gerlach and Kong (2005).[9] In addition, Zhang and Wan (2004), while finding a key role for price expectations in influencing money, prices, and output alike, point to greater stability in the relationship between M2 (the aggregate emphasized by the People's Bank) and both output and prices in China. They also find evidence of a long-term, cointegrating relationship among M2, prices, and output.

[8] As noted by Zhang and Wan (2004), the earlier literature using pre-1990 data yields similarly mixed evidence on the causality issue.

[9] In an estimation extending back into the pre-reform period, Chow and Shen (2005) also find a consistent long-run relationship between money and prices in China. Over the 1952–2002 interval, money shocks are found to produce short-lived output effects combined with enduring effects on prices.

Potential structural breaks pose an additional complication, though. Even restricting attention to just the 1990–2002 period, Sun and Ma (2004) find that the effect of the different monetary aggregates (monetary base, M1 and M2) on prices disappears after the onset of deflation in 1998. This deflation, emerging in the midst of the Asian financial crisis, was, in fact, accompanied by a marked acceleration in savings growth relative to consumption (see Xu, 2002). The decline in the consumer price index was itself driven by a sharp drop in food prices that averaged −3.2% in 1998 and −4.2% in 1999 (Wu, 2004, p. 37). Elimination of tariffs as China joined the World Trade Organization (WTO) may also have extended the deflationary trend, as well as helping to account for the fact that wholesale prices dropped so much more than consumer prices in 2001–2002 (Dai, 2002). Meanwhile, the People's Bank's scope for expanding the rate of monetary expansion to ward off deflation was limited by the need to simultaneously offset downward pressure on the renminbi (Chapter 1). Supporting the currency meant selling dollars and buying renminbi, thereby tending to reduce the domestic money supply at the very time when output and price conditions would normally have called for more expansionary policy.

In the empirical work discussed later, this chapter seeks to capture People's Bank policy responses over the 1990–2006 period that surrounds the 1998–2002 deflationary episode. By far the most popular way of capturing central bank policymaking in recent years has been through estimation of the "Taylor rule" (Taylor, 1993). This approach, which appeared to be an especially good fit with US Federal Reserve policy during the Alan Greenspan era, explains central bank interest-rate setting as a function of the gap between inflation and its target value and the gap between actual real output and its potential level. Countercyclical policy suggests that the central bank will raise rates when either inflation or real output rises above target so as to cool the economy off and help move the future realizations of these variables downward. However, lack of flexibility in interest rates poses potential problems for the Taylor rule. When interest rates are already very low, falling inflation and/or output levels may well leave the Taylor rule calling for negative interest rates that cannot be delivered in practice. Moreover, in situations like mainland China, where interest rate liberalization remains incomplete, interest rates may simply not be a meaningful target variable.[10] Nor are interest rates an actual target variable in China's case.

---

[10] Estimation of the real output gap embodied in the Taylor rule would also be problematic in China's case.

McCallum's (1988) alternative rule, under which movements in a monetary aggregate represent the central bank's policy variable, is therefore almost certainly more applicable to China. McCallum's original formulation expressed monetary base growth as a function of nominal output (that is, the product of real output and the price level) and velocity growth. Given that the People's Bank has often emphasized M2 growth rates, M2 is entered as a dependent variable in the ensuing empirical work in addition to the monetary base series originally suggested by McCallum (1988). A velocity term is included in the specification so as to allow money supply growth to adjust upward in the face of the rising money demand implied by declining velocity of circulation. Otherwise, excess money demand would put upward pressure on interest rates and likely exert deflationary effects on the economy. Such monetary expansion would not be inflationary as the central bank would simply be providing people with the extra money they want to hold and, insofar as money supply and money demand grow together, there would be no extra spending pressure. Finally, in the event that nominal output growth is exactly on target and velocity is constant, the rule allows for a benchmark monetary expansion that is one-for-one with the target growth rate of nominal output. This essentially yields Friedman's famous x% rule for monetary policy modified to allow for responses to persistent velocity movements and deviations from the (presumed sustainable) target rate of output growth.

With nominal GDP as the output measure, the basic McCallum rule has the following form:

$$\Delta m_t = \Delta x^* - \Delta v_t + 0.5(\Delta x^* - \Delta x_{t-1}) \tag{1}$$

where Δm_t is the growth of the monetary aggregate,
  Δx_t is the growth rate of nominal GDP,
  Δx^* is the target growth rate of nominal GDP, and
  Δv_t is the average growth rate of velocity over the same period.

In applying the McCallum rule to China, we augment the specification to allow for People's Bank responses to growth in foreign exchange reserves and the real exchange rate of the renminbi as well as a possible shift in policy following the onset of the Asian financial crisis and initial deflationary pressures. Just as the surge in M2 growth to nearly 20% in 2003 drew attention to the potential importance of exchange rate movements and reserve inflows, these same factors (in reverse) may have been important contributors to deflationary pressures in the late 1990s.[11] Meanwhile, even though we cannot fully account for such "structural" factors as WTO accession, our allowance for a parameter shift after 1997 shows this particular effect to be highly significant.[12] We assess People's Bank policy over the 1990–2006 period, thereby including the 1993–1994 inflation spike, the subsequent anti-inflationary policy, the attempts to reflate the economy after the 1997–1998 Asian financial crisis, the more recent pressures for renminbi appreciation that emerged after 2001, and the first year of the new exchange rate regime announced in July 2005.

Estimation Results

Our application of the McCallum rule to China utilizes quarterly data on money supply series, nominal GDP, foreign exchange reserves, and the real exchange rate that are drawn from the Great China Database and the International Monetary Fund's *International Financial Statistics*. The real exchange rate series is the International Monetary Fund's real effective exchange rate index for China – as previously depicted in Chapter 1. Meanwhile, velocity is calculated for each monetary aggregate by dividing the monetary variable into nominal GDP – with the implied growth rate smoothed by taking a moving average. However, a key empirical problem is the absence of a regularly provided official target for nominal GDP growth. Chinese officials have at times referred to targeted real growth in the high single digits and, even in the face of the Asian financial crisis, stuck to a 9% target for real growth (Wong, 1998, p. 38). Combining that with single-digit inflation suggests an implicit target nominal GDP growth rate in the range of 10% to 20%, depending upon exactly how much attempted restraint is to be imposed on inflation. The targets for 2006, the last year in our sample period, of 8% real growth and 3% inflation (People's Bank of China, 2006, p. 50) implied an 11% target rate of nominal GDP growth. Actual nominal GDP growth rose above 30% in the face of the 1993–1994 inflation spike, however, before dropping to around 10% at the end of the 1990s and then rising again toward the end of our sample period.

---

[11] Even for an earlier data set ending in the first quarter of 2003, forecasting analysis in Burdekin and Siklos (2008) already pointed to a new rise in inflationary pressures. (The potential impact of capital inflows under a fixed, undervalued exchange rate remains exemplified by the earlier period of Chinese history analyzed in Chapter 6).

[12] This is in line with the 1998 shift noted by Sun and Ma (2004) but seemingly inconsistent with Cargill and Parker's (2004) finding that deflation exerted no significant effects on Chinese money demand.

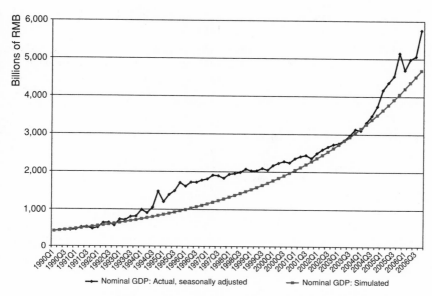

Figure 4.2. Actual vs. Simulated Values of Nominal Output, 1990–2006.

In our analysis, the unobservable target nominal GDP growth is modeled based on the trend properties of the raw data, which is not only required by the absence of a consistent series of official target values but also in keeping with the long-standing Friedmanite rationale for linking money growth to trend growth in output. A quarterly 3.75% growth rate, with a stochastic component around this growth rate, appears to best capture the underlying properties of the data (as detailed in Burdekin and Siklos, 2008). The resulting series, together with actual GDP, is plotted in Figure 2. The results of implementing equation (1) in the original form specified by McCallum are included in Burdekin and Siklos (2008). Relative to the indicated McCallum rule, monetary policy was found to be too loose until about 1996 since actual M2 growth and monetary base growth far exceeded predicted money growth. This indicated period of monetary excess naturally coincides quite closely with the 1993–1994 inflation spike discussed in Chapter 3. With regard to the post-1996 experience, the basic McCallum rule implied that M2 growth tended to be too tight but monetary base growth, on the other hand, remained more or less in line with the rule's predictions.

In reapplying the McCallum rule to an extended 1990–2006 dataset, the estimates reported in this chapter not only allow the response to the nominal GDP output gap to be determined by the data but also simultaneously allow for money supply reactions to the rate of change of foreign exchange reserves,

Table 4.3. *Money supply reactions based on extended McCallum Rule Estimates,*
1990–2006

Right-hand-side Variables	Ordinary Least Squares (OLS) Estimates		Generalized Method of Moments (GMM) Estimates	
	M2 Growth	Monetary Base Growth	M2 Growth	Monetary Base Growth
Constant	6.55	5.78	6.43	5.69
	(0.50)***	(0.59)***	(0.28)***	(0.32)***
Nominal output gap	−0.02	−0.01	−0.04	−0.02
	(0.03)	(0.04)	$(0.02)^a$	(0.03)
Post-Asian financial crisis dummy	−2.74	−3.42	−2.55	−2.87
	(0.66)***	(0.79)***	(0.37)***	(0.42)***
Rate of change of foreign exchange reserves	−0.07	−0.01	−0.05	−0.01
	(0.04)*	(0.05)	(0.02)**	(0.03)
Rate of change of the real exchange rate	−1.38	−3.47	−2.08	−4.17
	(1.43)	(1.69)**	(1.05)*	(0.89)***
R^2 overall goodness of fit	0.38	0.37	0.37	0.36
J-test for over-identifying restrictions	–	–	6.24 $(p = 0.86)^b$	8.15 $(p = 0.61)^b$

Notes: Standard errors are reported beneath the coefficients; ***, **, and * indicate significance at the 99%, 95%, and 90% confidence levels, respectively.
[a] Denotes significance at the 89.5% confidence level.
[b] Denotes the exact significance level for the *J-test* statistic – with the insignificant values implying that the over-identifying restrictions required for the GMM estimation could not be rejected (see text under equation (2) for the list of instruments).

the rate of change of the real exchange rate, and a post-Asian financial crisis dummy set equal to one after 1997. The estimation period is from the second quarter of 1991 through the second quarter of 2006. Table 4.3 reports a series of regressions of the form:

$$\Delta m_t = \beta_0 + \beta_1(\Delta x^* - \Delta x_{t-1}) + \beta_2 D_t + \beta_3 \dot{f}_t + \beta_4 \dot{r}_t + e_t \qquad (2)$$

where D_t is the post-Asian financial crisis dummy,
　　$\dot{f}_t$ is the rate of foreign exchange reserves,
　　$\dot{r}_t$ is the rate of change in the real exchange rate,
　　e_t is an error term,
and all other variables are as previously defined.

　　Ordinary least squares (OLS) estimates are reported first. These estimates may not accurately reflect the People's Bank of China's true reaction to the right-hand-side variables in equation (2), however, as OLS estimation co-mingles the central bank's policy response with more general economy-wide reactions. This is due to the endogeneity, or non-predetermined nature, of the right-hand-side variables. Hence, the final two column of Table 4.3 show the results of reestimation using the Generalized Method of Moments (GMM) procedure to correct for this endogeneity issue. The constant, post-Asian financial crisis dummy, two lags of each of the variables in the equation, and two lags of export growth were used as instruments to apply the GMM procedure.[13]

The 0.5 coefficient value for β_1 hypothesized by McCallum (1988) is not supported in the Chinese case, and the GDP gap is generally statistically insignificant – in the one case where it is marginally significant, the negative sign actually implies an accommodative, procyclical response to nominal output movements.[14] The post-Asian financial crisis dummy is negative and highly significant for both M2 and the monetary base across each of the two estimation procedures. Monetary policy may well have remained tighter after 1997 in the face of pressures arising, first, from the need to support the exchange rate in the immediate aftermath of the Asian financial crisis, and, second, the need to offset incipient inflationary pressures arising from the reserve buildup later on. There is also some evidence of a tendency for M2 growth to slow as foreign exchange reserve growth accelerates, although this effect is neither very strong nor very highly significant. Meanwhile, the fact that the monetary base shows no significant reaction to reserve growth remains consistent with People's Bank success in sterilizing reserve inflows.

Insulating the overall level of the monetary base from the effects of reserve inflows requires that the domestic component of the base be reduced, on a one-to-one basis, when the foreign component is forced up by new reserve accumulation. Complete, or near-complete sterilization, as discerned by both He et al. (2005) and Ouyang, Rajan, and Willett (2007), implies the overall monetary base remaining invariant to increased reserve inflows,

---

[13] The GMM sample period begins in the third quarter of 1991. *J*-test statistics, as reported in Table 4.3, support the appropriateness of the overidentifying restrictions required to produce the GMM results.

[14] Similar findings were obtained by Burdekin and Siklos (2008) based on other alternative extensions of the basic McCallum rule. Consideration of lagged values of the right-hand-side variables did not affect the generally accommodative pattern (in line with that observed by Zhang and Wan, 2004).

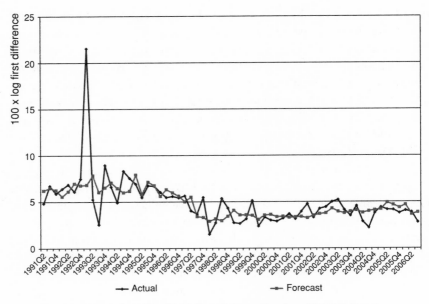

Figure 4.3. Actual vs. Fitted M2 Growth Rates Based on GMM Estimation.

therefore, consistent with the present findings.[15] On the other hand, failure to fully sterilize reserve inflows should be associated with a positive monetary base reaction to higher rates of reserve accumulation. Finally, there is evidence of a negative reaction to the real exchange rate in three cases out of four, indicating a countercyclical (stabilizing) response to real exchange rate appreciation. Real exchange rate appreciation, as experienced during much of the 1990s (Chapter 1), can arise when Chinese prices are rising faster than prices abroad. Tighter monetary policy that reduced Chinese inflation rates would tend to offset such real exchange rate appreciation.

Our final exercise is to compare the predicted values from the regressions reported in Table 4.3 to actual money growth rates observed over the 1991–2006 period. Given that forecast values from the alternative OLS and GMM regressions for both M2 and the monetary base proved to share almost identical trends, Figures 4.3 and 4.4 simply compare M2 and monetary base fitted values from the GMM estimation to the actual money growth rates. Figure 4.3 points to M2 being, as one would have suspected, generally too

[15] Examination of the effects of foreign exchange reserves over the shorter 1991–2003 sample period considered in Burdekin and Siklos (2008), without allowing for the post-Asian financial crisis dummy, had actually suggested "over-sterilization" in that monetary base growth appeared to elicit an overall negative reaction to faster rates of reserve accumulation.

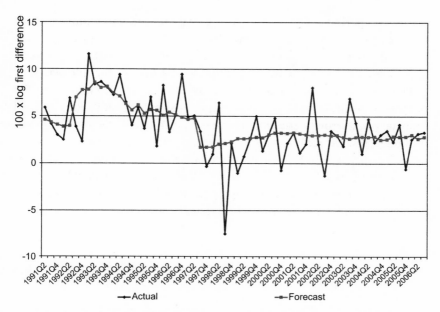

Figure 4.4. Actual vs. Fitted Monetary Base Growth Rates Based on GMM Estimation.

loose during the 1993–1995 inflation spike – but otherwise shows actual M2 growth according quite well with the forecast values implied by the extended McCallum policy rule. Meanwhile, Figure 4.4 suggests a more moderate, but also more extended, tendency for overly high growth rates for the monetary base during 1993–1998. After that, monetary base growth looks to have become too tight in 1998–1999, at the time that the Chinese economy entered deflation, but subsequently follows a similar trend to the forecast values. Overall, the strong suggestion of overly loose policy in the early to mid-1990s followed by indications (from the performance of monetary base growth) of overly tight policy at the end of the 1990s seems quite consistent with actual experience. It is also interesting to see that sustained deviations from forecast values were generally avoided after 2000 in spite of the pressures arising from record rates of foreign reserve accumulation and the claimed undervaluation of the renminbi.

Conclusions

Increased sophistication of People's Bank monetary policy since the 1990s appears to have been accompanied by smaller deviations from the forecast values generated by an extended McCallum-type rule estimated over the

1991–2006 period. There is evidence of a significant, and enduring, step-down in the rate of both monetary base and M2 growth since the Asian financial crisis combined with some evidence of a countercyclical response to movements in the real exchange rate. Examination of the role played by growth in foreign exchange reserves suggests that reserve accumulation did not lead to any loss of control over the money supply through 2006. Overall monetary base growth appears to have remained unaffected by rising rates of foreign reserve accumulation, consistent with People's Bank success in offsetting increases in foreign assets with decreases in domestic assets. The expanding market for central bank bills has provided a valuable weapon for such sterilization measures, helping the People's Bank withdraw greater amounts of liquidity in the face of heightened rates of reserve accumulation.

PART II

THE IMPORTANCE OF INTERNATIONAL
FACTORS, PAST AND PRESENT

FIVE

US Pressure on China and Hong Kong
in the 1930s

At a time when other countries have been depreciating their monetary units..., China, whose currency is on a metallic basis, has seen the value of its monetary unit steadily appreciate... If the Chinese exporter is to retain his markets, it must be by marking down prices, thereby communicating the evils of deflation to producers throughout the country... Furthermore, heavy exports to silver have seriously contracted currency and credit in China, which makes for higher exchange and lower prices.

(Dr. H. H. Kung, China's Minister of Finance, October 10, 1935)[1]

Introduction

Although the post-2001 dollar depreciation discussed in Chapters 1 and 2 was not part of any officially declared government policy, the 40% devaluation of the dollar against gold in 1933–1934 reflected US policymakers' determination to free the economy from persistent deflationary pressures and was accompanied by a rapid acceleration of domestic money supply growth (cf. Friedman and Schwartz, 1963; Bernanke, 2002). This US monetary expansion was fueled by large-scale silver purchases, under which the US government issued silver certificates in exchange for the newly purchased silver – with these silver certificates then circulating as currency and adding to the nation's money supply. The US silver purchases had major implications for China as well. In the early 1930s, China and the British crown colony of Hong Kong were essentially alone in still linking their currencies to silver. As the world price of silver rose in response to the US silver

---

[1] As quoted in T'ang (1936, pp. 76–77).

The author is indebted to Warren Bailey for supplying monthly data on the Hong Kong and Shanghai Banking Corporation, is most grateful to Marc Weidenmier for his helpful comments and suggestions, and thanks Nancy Tao for her research assistance and Yanjie Feng Burdekin for her translation help.

purchase program, these silver-based currencies appreciated in value. This, in turn, made China and Hong Kong's exports more expensive abroad and less competitive in world markets.

China experienced a large outflow of silver in 1934 that led to a liquidity shortage in Shanghai late in the year and exacerbated the pressures associated with the appreciating value of the national currency. The Chinese authorities came under increasing pressure to offset deflationary pressures and imposed administrative measures in October 1934 to try and limit the outflow of silver. Following these measures, price deflation was slowed relative to that endured by Hong Kong but smuggling activities still produced sizeable silver outflows. In November 1935, China broke entirely from the silver standard and Hong Kong immediately followed suit, in each case adopting a new exchange rate peg with the pound sterling. Whereas Hong Kong's exchange rate peg was sustained until the outbreak of World War II, the new Chinese currency, the *fapi*, did not fare so well. The *fapi*, in fact, underwent a seventeen-hundredfold depreciation over the eight years of the 1937–1945 Sino-Japanese War before (literally) disappearing during the ensuing Chinese Civil War. Although China's suffering in the early 1930s was not entirely caused by US policy actions, the short-term and long-term damage arising from sudden upward pressure on the external value of its currency is likely a lesson that is hard to forget.

China's Vulnerability

Even after China's imperial era ended in 1912 with the abdication of the Qing dynasty in favor of a new republic, the authorities maintained a similar currency system based on silver coins. The new Republican dollar became the legal standard, with the distribution of these standardized coins expanding after the Nationalist government established itself in Nanking in 1927 (see T'ang, 1936, chapter II). The Nationalists, under Chiang Kai-shek, gradually extended their control over the economy until the "Nanking decade" was ended by all-out war with Japan in July 1937.[2] The "yuan" currency units referred to in this chapter reflect the silver coin standard that was maintained until November 1935. With other major world economies having moved away from silver and tied their currencies to gold by the end of the nineteenth century, China, like Hong Kong, enjoyed a flexible exchange

---

[2] See Fenby (2004) for a detailed account of the complex series of events that culminated in Civil War and Chiang Kai-shek's defeat at the hands of the Communists. The inflationary pressures accompanying the ensuing Nationalist exodus to Taiwan at the end of the 1940s are assessed in Chapter 6.

rate with the "gold bloc." This flexibility ended up being a double-edged sword, however, as it tied the currency to a commodity whose price was not only determined abroad but, after 1933, strongly driven by the actions of the United States. China had got a boost from a depreciating exchange rate during the early years of the Great Depression as silver prices fell, automatically pulling China's currency lower relative to the gold bloc countries (see, for example, Friedman, 1992; Lai and Gau, 2003). However, these benefits dissipated as, following the United Kingdom's exit from the gold standard in 1931, the old gold bloc started adopting floating, and rapidly depreciating, exchange rates. The US Silver Purchase Act of June 19, 1934 then put sudden additional upward pressure on China's silver-based currency.

The scale of the US silver purchases was such that, by May 31, 1935, the Treasury had accumulated over 421 million ounces of silver – 283 million of which came from open-market purchases coupled with 25 million ounces of newly produced domestic silver and nearly 113 million from nationalization of preexisting silver stocks (Blum, 1959, p. 194).[3] The US price of silver bottomed out in December 1932, briefly falling below 25 cents an ounce (Westerfield, 1936, p. 26). The silver price then more than doubled between December 1933 and April 1935, peaking at 81 cents an ounce on April 26, 1935 (Friedman, 1992, p. 67). The sharply rising monthly closing price of silver in New York is shown in Figure 5.1. As silver rose, the value of China's currency rose too and the declining number of yuan required to purchase each US dollar over this period of rising silver prices is shown in Figure 5.2. The approximate 40% rise of China's currency against the US dollar in 1933–1935 was accompanied by a near 50% rise against the pound sterling and a 177% rise against the Japanese yen from 1931 to 1935 (Chung-kuo k'o-hsüeh yüan, 1958, p. 112).

Friedman (1992, p. 76) draws attention to the fact that, in the face of all this currency appreciation, China suffered an accelerating decline in imports, in both nominal and real terms, over the 1933–1935 period. The import decline peaked in 1934 (Table 5.1) and, in real terms, Chinese imports fell by an overall 39.3% between 1930 and 1935 while exports fell by 12.9%.[4] The sharp fall in imports in 1934 was accompanied by a sudden increase in

---

[3] The Silver Purchase Act's domestic effects on the US economy are analyzed in Burdekin and Weidenmier (2008).

[4] Although the overall estimated ratio of imports to GDP in China was 6.8% during 1931–1935 and the export ratio just 4.7% (Yeh, 1979, p. 116), this belies the importance of international trade to the key city of Shanghai, which served not only as China's financial center but also its main manufacturing hub and port – leaving China's response to "international demands mediated through Shanghai-based traders" (Rawski, 1989, p. 235).

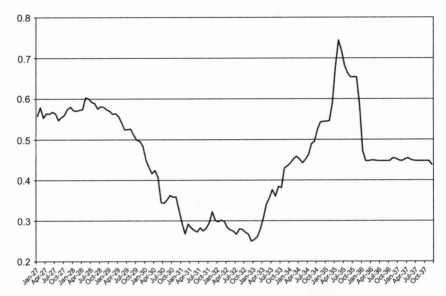

Figure 5.1. Silver Price in New York, January 1927–December 1937 (end-of-month $US closing prices).

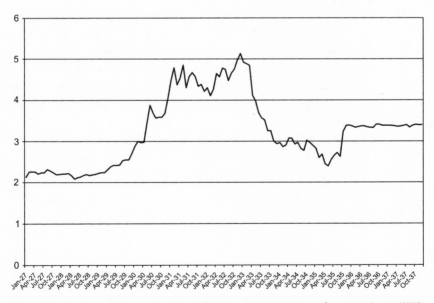

Figure 5.2. Exchange Rate vs. the US Dollar, January 1927–December 1937 (yuan/$US, end-of-month closing prices).

Table 5.1. *China's Imports, Exports, and Silver Flows, 1926–1936*

Year	Import Quantity Index	Export Quantity Index	Percentage Change in Imports	Official Percentage Change in Exports	Estimated Net Outflow of Silver[a]	Clandestine Exports of Silver[a]
1926	100.0	100.0	–	–	−82,891	–
1927	82.3	98.9	−17.7%	−1.1	−101,400	–
1928	100.7	107.4	22.4	8.6	−165,764	–
1929	107.2	108.4	6.5	0.9	−164,877	–
1930	98.2	94.6	−8.4	−12.7	−104,395	–
1931	99.1	92.0	0.9	−2.7	−70,803	–
1932	81.3	69.9	−18.0	−24.0	+11,444	–
1933	79.1	82.9	−2.7	18.6	+14,122	–
1934	64.4	83.1	−18.6	0.2	+256,728	+23,214
1935	59.6	82.4	−6.8	−0.8	+59,397	+230,117
1936	55.0	81.7	−7.7	−0.8	+249,623	+40,041

[a] Denominated in thousands of Chinese yuan.

Source: Cheng (1956, pp. 70, 263); Chung-kuo k'o-hsüeh yüan (1958, pp. 108–109); and author's calculations.

the outflow of silver from China, rising from 14 million yuan in 1933 to over 256 million yuan in 1934.[5] China had previously enjoyed an inflow of silver, and the switch from inflows to modest-sized outflows in 1932 coincided with the second largest import decline over the 1926–1936 period. The 1934 outflow was comprised primarily of silver shipments by foreign banks in Shanghai. As shown in Table 5.2, the foreign banks' aggregate silver holdings dropped from 275.7 million yuan in December 1933 to just 54.7 million yuan in December 1934, with over 80% of the decline occurring after July 1934. Over 30% of the December 1933 silver stock was held by a single bank, the Hongkong and Shanghai Banking Corporation (HSBC), which cut its own silver holding from 83.9 million yuan to 7.5 million yuan in 1934 alone (see Tamagna, 1942, p. 104; King, 1988, p. 408). Meanwhile, Chinese banks' silver holdings actually held relatively steady at 280.3 million

---

[5] Furthermore, after large-scale silver purchases got underway, US exports to China *fell* by 38% between September 1934 and September 1935 even as US exports to the rest of the world actually increased over this same period (Westerfield, 1936, p. 112). China's historical sensitivity to the world silver price is also evident in the longer-run time series analysis of Bailey and Bhaopichitr (2004), which suggests a consistent link between the world silver price and China's own exports over the 1866–1928 period. Meanwhile, empirical analysis presented in Burdekin (2008) confirms a close link between silver prices and Chinese exchange rate and price levels from 1927 through China's exit from the silver standard in 1935.

Table 5.2. *Silver Stock Positions in Shanghai, 1931–1935*

Date	Chinese Banks	Foreign Banks	Total
December 1931	179,117	86,883	266,000
June 1932	–	–	369,000
December 1932	252,955	185,045	438,000
June 1933	–	–	447,000
December 1933	271,800	275,660	547,500
July 1934	330,600	232,200	562,800
December 1934	280,300	54,702	335,000
June 1935	–	–	341,000
September 1935	293,400	42,700	336,100

Notes: Figures are in thousands of Chinese yuan.
Sources: Tamagna (1942, p. 104); Cheng (1956, p. 79); Young (1971, p. 200); and author's calculations.

yuan, down 15% from the July 1934 level but still up 3% from December 1933. The drain of funds associated with the silver outflow appears to have generated significant liquidity problems, as evidenced by rising interest rates and declining stock values in Shanghai. In addition, as demonstrated later on, HSBC's large silver sales did not prevent its own share price from suffering in the midst of the worsening conditions that followed the US silver purchases.

Deflation persisted in China from 1932 until 1935 as reflected in Figure 5.3, which plots Shanghai wholesale prices from 1927 until the outbreak of open warfare with Japan in July 1937. This deflationary trend got underway after the initial appreciation of China's currency against the pound sterling and the Japanese yen in 1931 was followed by a rapid rise against the US dollar once the United States exited the gold standard in early 1933 (Figure 5.2). The financial center of Shanghai was initially cushioned from the contractionary effects of China's currency appreciation, however, benefiting from an inflow of silver from China's interior that more than offset the external outflow in 1932–1933 (see Burdekin, 2008). Total Shanghai silver stocks steadily increased from 266 million yuan at the end of 1931 to over 560 million yuan in mid-1934 (Table 5.2).[6] Unfortunately, this favorable position quickly evaporated in the second half of 1934 once large-scale US silver purchases got underway. Shanghai suffered a double blow from not

---

[6] The absolute peak level of 594 million yuan was reached in April–May 1934 (Young, 1971, p. 200n).

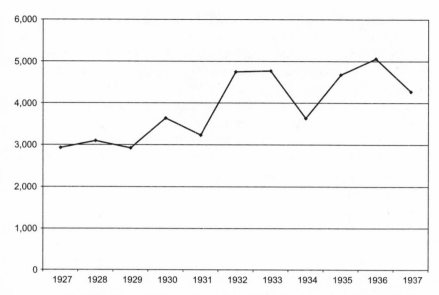

Figure 5.3. Shanghai Stock Market Index, 1927–1937 (end of year value-weighted series denominated in yuan).

only large outflows of silver abroad but also an abrupt reversal of the internal flow of silver into the city. T'ang (1936, p. 109) attributes the sudden reversal of the internal flow of silver into Shanghai in September 1934 as being

due not to internal conditions, but mainly to external. Most of the silver shipped from Shanghai to the interior found its way out of the country, and was ultimately purchased by the United States Government.

The significance of the shift in the internal flows of silver at this time is noted by Friedman (1940, p. 53), who also documents the sharp acceleration in the rate of business failures in 1934 and a more than 50% decline in property values within Shanghai's foreign enclave:

Shanghai, center of British interests, was seriously affected . . . The monthly average of reorganizations in 1933 was 5.08, by 1934 it was 107.50, and for the first six months of 1935, 155.17. The monthly average number of failures was 17.83, 30.50, and 41.67 for 1933, 1934, and 1935, respectively. The number of new buildings constructed in the International Settlement fell from 8,699 in 1931 to 4,571 in 1934, while the assessed value of these buildings fell from Ch.$ 64,466,532 to $27,600,350.

The volume of real estate transactions in Shanghai fell by over 92% between 1931 and 1934 and then declined by a further 42% over the first ten months of 1935 (Lin, 1936, p. 64). With much bank lending tied to real estate, loan activity dried up as well and bank runs emerged in May 1935 in the face of the failure of the American-Oriental Banking Corporation and two other major financial corporations (Leavens, 1939, p. 307; Ji, 2003, pp. 189–190; Burdekin, 2008). King (1988, p. 409) links the problems directly to the drain of silver insofar as "the silver had become the basis of multiple credit expansion, and its export undermined the stability of the banking system." By June 1935, 13 of Shanghai's traditional, or "native," banks had entered liquidation proceedings, while as many as 148 native banks across thirty-one Chinese cities went bankrupt during 1935 (Tamagna, 1942, p. 83).[7]

The tightening credit conditions were reflected in an upward surge in interest rates in late 1934. Shen (1941, p. 29) notes that interest rates charged by Shanghai's native banks quadrupled between October 1934 and December 1934, rising from an annualized average rate of approximately 2.6% in October to 12.0% in December – with a high of 21.9% being recorded in that month.[8] Rates remained at elevated levels in January 1935 before declining in February 1935 when government banks stepped in and "provided funds to ease the adjustments among the native banks, which were handicapped by frozen assets even more than the modern-style commercial banks" (Young, 1971, p. 222). The accompanying sharp decline in share prices in 1934 is evidenced in Figure 5.4, which depicts end-of-year value-weighted Shanghai Stock Exchange indices denominated in yuan.[9] At year-end 1934, the market index stood at 3631.573, down 23.9% from its year-end 1933 level of 4769.799. This decrease followed increases of 47.0% in 1932 and 0.45% in 1933,[10] and is indicative of a sudden decline following a period of relative prosperity. Market difficulties continued into the early months of 1935, when "trading on the Exchange almost came to a halt because of the extreme tightness of money" (Young, 1971, p. 221). Meanwhile, the ongoing

---

[7] The native banks coexisted with foreign banks and the more Western-orientated "modern banks," which granted loans based on collateral in contrast to the native banks' emphasis on personal connections and trust (cf. Ji, 2003, p. 107).

[8] All of the city's various banking institutions relied upon the Shanghai Native Bankers Guild for interbank clearing, leaving the native interest rates fixed by the Guild as the chief benchmark "generally regarded by bankers and merchants as a safe guide for conducting business transactions" (Chang, 1938, p. 32). The rates were originally reported in terms of cents per thousand yuan per day – and the implied daily rate has simply been multiplied by 365 to obtain the annualized rates referred to in the text.

[9] These stock exchange data are drawn from the Shanghai Stock Exchange Research Project of the International Center of Finance at Yale University (http://icf.som.yale.edu/sse).

[10] Alternative equal-weighted and price-weighted indices also evidence this pattern.

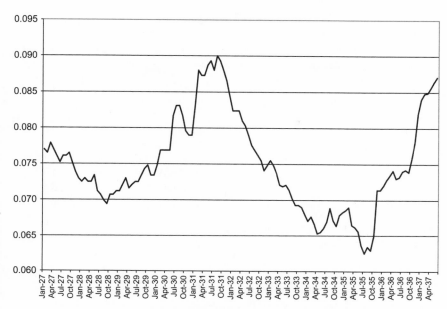

Figure 5.4. Shanghai Wholesale Prices, January 1927–June 1937.

importance of both real estate and the banking sector is suggested by the leading shares of land companies and banks and finance companies in the Shanghai Stock Exchange index (see Table 5.3).

The Chinese and Hong Kong Experiences Compared

On October 15, 1934, the Chinese authorities attempted to limit the outflow of silver by levying an export duty and equalization charge on all new silver exports. The duty charged was 10%, less an allowance for minting charges paid in the case of silver dollars and mint-issued silver bars. Meanwhile, the equalization charge was set "equal to the deficiency, if any, existing between the theoretical parity of London silver and a rate of exchange officially fixed by the Central Bank of China, after making allowance for the export duty" (Young, 1971, p. 215). The intention was to stop China's currency from automatically appreciating in step with world silver prices. If world silver prices rose, making silver more valuable abroad than in China, the incentive to ship silver out of the country would, in theory, be nullified by an offsetting increase in the equalization charge. Although the official net outflow of silver did slow greatly, legal exports were augmented by large-scale smuggling. Bank of China estimates, as reported in the last column of

Table 5.3. *Shanghai Stock Exchange Components in 1934*

Market Sector (with number of listings in parentheses)	Year End Paid Up Value of Issued Shares (denominated in $US)	Percentage of the Total
Lands (14)	$18,851,262.68	18.1%
Banks & Finance Companies (10)	17,105,955.79	16.5
Plantations (37)	12,556,077.41	12.1
Utilities (8)	10,402,019.62	10.0
Cotton (4)	6,241,100.00	6.0
Docks, Wharves & Transport (6)	6,163,242.44	5.9
Insurance (5)	5,122,050.00	4.9
Miscellaneous (24)	27,474,635.70	26.4
TOTAL	103,946,343.60	

Note: Totals exclude bonds and preference issues.
Source: International Center of Finance at Yale University (http://icf.som.yale.edu/sse) and author's calculations.

Table 5.1, imply that the total outflow of silver may even have been slightly higher in 1935 than in 1934. The smuggling was aided and abetted by the Japanese, who had seized China's northeastern province of Manchuria in September 1931, creating the puppet state of Manchukuo. The illegal silver flow in that area may have reached 15 million yuan a month and the Japanese authorities "were reported to have put a branch office of the Manchukuo Central Bank at the Manchurian border to pay a good price for smuggled silver" (Young, 1971, p. 216). Significant quantities of silver were also smuggled out via Hong Kong. King (1957, p. 107) states:

During the first six months of 1935, the Colony exported $24,156,038 worth of silver bullion and specie; during the second six months, $150,661,908. Most of this represented re-exports, since the Colony's silver was mainly in the form of reserves against the note issue, but what free silver was in existence was exported. Coins were melted down and there was a shortage of circulating media.

After the October 1934 measures were imposed, a considerable gap opened between the foreign exchange value of China's currency and the actual value of its silver content on world markets. Young (1971, p. 217) notes that, with US silver prices near $US0.55 per ounce in October 1934, "the silver content of the Chinese dollar was worth abroad about one-fourth more than in China." Although reduction of the equalization charge beginning October 19, 1934 allowed renewed appreciation of China's currency relative to the US dollar, the accelerating rise in silver prices in April–May 1935 gave rise to as much as a 50% gap between the internal and external value of China's silver (Young, 1971, p. 218). Despite the obvious stimulus

Table 5.4. *Monthly Silver Outflows and Wholesale Prices in Shanghai, Tianjin, Guangzhou, and Hong Kong, January 1934–December 1935*

| Year and Month | Net Silver Outflow from China[a] | Wholesale Price Indices (1926 = 100) | | | | Hong Kong Dollar Exchange Rate[d] |
		Shanghai	Tianjin[b]	Guangzhou[c]	Hong Kong	
1934						
January	−1,783	97.2	91.6	99.8	97.8	90.250
February	+1,567	98.0	92.1	100.4	96.1	90.125
March	−867	96.6	91.1	100.1	92.9	89.500
April	+14,764	94.6	89.2	98.6	92.6	89.500
May	+2,147	94.9	89.4	98.0	95.6	89.500
June	+12,936	95.7	89.5	92.5	97.4	90.500
July	+24,308	97.1	90.9	92.5	93.0	90.250
August	+79,094	99.8	94.8	94.6	95.3	90.250
September	+48,140	97.3	92.5	91.6	91.2	90.250
October	+56,332	96.1	92.3	90.4	92.0	85.375
November	+11,328	98.3	93.0	87.0	91.3	81.000
December	+11,975	99.0	95.0	86.2	88.2	80.500
1935						
January	−2,709	99.4	96.1	86.4	83.4	80.000
February	−550	99.9	96.9	87.2	84.3	81.500
March	−987	96.4	95.8	85.5	76.1	79.500
April	−2,430	95.9	95.3	83.8	77.9	74.000
May	+1,043	95.0	95.1	81.1	73.1	68.000
June	−48	92.1	93.4	80.2	71.1	69.000
July	−97	90.5	91.8	80.8	73.4	73.000
August	−229	91.9	91.2	81.7	69.4	72.000
September	−737	91.1	90.7	82.0	73.3	73.750
October	−55	94.1	94.2	81.9	72.6	73.500
November	−111	103.3	100.9	92.3	85.4	80.000
December	+66,542	103.3	102.5	94.0	94.2	90.000

[a] Denominated in thousands of Chinese yuan.
[b] Formerly known as Tientsin.
[c] Formerly known as Canton City.
[d] Number of Hong Kong dollars per 100 Chinese yuan (*fapi* from November 1935).
Sources: Chung-kuo k'o-hsüeh yüan (1958, pp. 109–110, 112–113); Young (1971, pp. 477–478, 480).

to smuggling activities, the Chinese policies do appear to have been effective in slowing the rate of currency appreciation and, in turn, limiting the degree of deflation experienced in China. Up until the Chinese authorities' intervention in October 1934, the rate of exchange with the Hong Kong dollar remained steady at around 0.9 Hong Kong dollars per Chinese yuan (Table 5.4). However, the Hong Kong dollar then appreciated by 25% until the exchange rate reached 0.68 Hong Kong dollars per Chinese yuan in May 1935. At the same time, Hong Kong's deflation worsened relative to that experienced in Shanghai and other Chinese cities (also shown in Table 5.4). Hong Kong wholesale prices dropped by 25% between October 1934 and August 1935, while Shanghai wholesale prices dropped by just 4% over the same period – and Tianjin and Guangzhou recorded declines of approximately 1% and 10%, respectively.

The underlying problem of soaring silver prices remained unsolved, however, and Chinese pleas for moderation in the scale of US silver purchases failed to bring about any significant change in US policy (cf. Young, 1971, pp. 223–229). The continued silver drain from China was reflected in British imports of over 85 million troy ounces of silver from Japan and approximately 73 million ounces from Hong Kong during 1935 (T'ang, 1936, p. 115). Given that Japan's own silver production was negligible, and Hong Kong's nonexistent, the lion's share of this silver almost certainly originated in China[11] – with the United Kingdom then shipping the silver on to the United States.[12] As if the silver drain, deflation, and business slowdown were not enough, further pressure on the government stemmed from a renewed rise in bond yields in 1935 as the sustainability of China's financial situation became increasingly in doubt. Most bond sales were financed by direct sale to the banks, which paid out cash based on the market value of the bonds. As the market price of government bonds declined, the cash supplied by the banks in return for new bond issues also fell, pushing up even the nominal financing cost of the new 6% bond issues to as much as 10% in the midst of the deflation (Salter, 1934, p. 64). Young (1971, p. 222) encapsulates the government's problem in early 1935 of "trying to sustain confidence while maintaining the internal convertibility of bank notes into silver despite the drain abroad."

China's Minister of Finance Dr. H. H. Kung had recognized "at the outset that the remedy adopted in October 1934 could only be temporarily effective; it was not a fundamental solution."[13] In an attempt to finally bring the deflationary silver drain and its accompanying financial pressures to an end, the Chinese government delinked its currency from silver. Under the

---

[11] According to a contemporary account, "[w]hile some 7 millions of [the silver imported from Japan] may have come from Japanese mines, the bulk of it is silver smuggled out of China" (see T'ang, 1936, p. 115).

[12] Foreign banks operating in China appear to have contributed to this smuggling of silver. In the face of rising opportunity costs of maintaining a silver reserve against note issues, HSBC Deputy Manager E. J. Davies wrote in November 1934 that "foreign banks were busy smuggling large quantities of mainland silver via Hong Kong, and that the British-run Chartered Bank was prominent amongst the offenders" (see Horesh, 2008).

[13] As quoted by Shen (1941, p. 16).

terms of the decree of November 3, 1935, all silver in circulation was nation-alized and new notes issued by the three government banks (the Central Bank of China, Bank of China, and Bank of Communications), with only limited silver backing, became legal tender. The three government banks were authorized to buy and sell foreign exchange in unlimited quantities in order to maintain exchange rate stability relative to the pound sterling and the US dollar, assisted with the boost to foreign exchange reserves arising from the sale of 50 million ounces of nationalized silver to the United States between December 21, 1935 and January 7, 1936 (Young, 1971, p. 241). The stability in the exchange rate with the US dollar through mid-1937 can be seen in Figure 5.2, before war with Japan initiated an ever-worsening spiral of currency depreciation.

China's final break from the silver standard was quickly followed by Hong Kong. The Colonial Government imposed an embargo on silver exports on November 9, 1935, and, on December 5, 1935,

the Hongkong Legislative Council passed an Ordinance providing for the with-drawal of all silver money in the Colony, for the creation of an exchange fund, and for the amendment of the law relating to legal tender. (T'ang, 1936, p. 93)

Hong Kong's note issuing banks were required to surrender all silver coin and bullion that they had been holding to back their note issue, receiving in exchange certificates of indebtedness equal to the face value of the notes covered. The currency was henceforth backed by the pound sterling rather than by silver, with the Exchange Fund holding a fixed amount of sterling credits against the issue of paper currency by HSBC, the Chartered Bank of India, Australia, and China, and the Mercantile Bank of India.[14] The Hong Kong dollar and the new Chinese *fapi* were both, in fact, pegged against the pound sterling in December 1935.[15] As shown in Table 5.4 and 5.5, the Hong Kong dollar was initially set at an approximate 10% premium to the Chinese *fapi*, following which the Hong Kong authorities made a series of adjustments aimed at bringing the two neighboring currencies

---

[14] These credits included the aforementioned certificates of indebtedness issued in exchange for the banks' silver holdings plus sterling certificates deposited with the Crown Agent (Tamagna, 1942, p. 115).

[15] With the *fapi* also pegged against the US dollar, this left the central bank responding to divergent trends in the pound versus the dollar by widening the spreads between its selling and buying rates in September 1936. The authorities had successfully weathered a speculative attack against the central bank's twin exchange rate bands earlier in the year, with government banks selling approximately $US 40 million in support of the Chinese currency between mid-May and the end of June 1936 – following which bond yields retreated as capital began to flow back into China (Young, 1971, pp. 247–248).

Table 5.5. *Monthly Silver Outflows and Wholesale Prices in Shanghai, Tianjin, Guangzhou, and Hong Kong, January 1936–June 1937*

Year and Month	Net Silver Outflow from China[a]	Wholesale Price Indices (1926 = 100)				Hong Kong Dollar Exchange Rate[d]
		Shanghai	Tianjin[b]	Guangzhou[c]	Hong Kong	
1936						
January	+15,416	104.3	104.1	95.6	97.4	91.500
February	−572	105.6	107.1	98.3	97.7	90.500
March	−677	106.4	110.5	99.4	101.8	91.250
April	−92	107.3	111.5	100.9	102.2	91.250
May	+16,472	105.8	109.1	102.3	103.3	91.000
June	+69,244	106.1	108.1	110.5	100.9	92.500
July	+10,926	107.2	109.6	112.9	106.8	92.500
August	+11,603	107.4	109.3	109.5	104.4	96.000
September	+90,918	107.0	108.7	108.9	103.0	96.000
October	+35,914	109.7	111.5	108.7	106.9	96.500
November	+474	113.0	115.1	109.6	103.7	96.500
December	−1	118.8	122.8	111.3	109.1	96.750
1937						
January	0[e]	121.6	126.3	115.7	114.5	–
February	−139	122.9	128.9	118.0	117.3	–
March	−40	123.0	129.7	117.5	122.0	–
April	−28	123.9	134.1	119.8	127.4	–
May	+8	125.1	130.4	119.8	128.1	–
June	−124	126.1	130.4	118.7	131.2	–

[a] Denominated in thousands of Chinese yuan.
[b] Formerly known as Tientsin.
[c] Formerly known as Canton City.
[d] Number of Hong Kong dollars per 100 Chinese yuan (*fapi* from November 1935).
[e] Actual value limited to +226 yuan.
Sources: Shen (1941, p. 32); Young (1971, pp. 478, 480); Chung-kuo k'o-hsüeh yüan (1958, p. 113).

closer to parity (Tamagna, 1942, p. 115). The premium was down to around 3% at year-end 1936.

Deflation ended in both China and Hong Kong soon after the abandonment of the link with silver. As shown in Table 5.5, Hong Kong wholesale prices, after remaining below their 1926 base of 100 throughout 1934 and 1935, finally rose above that level in March 1936 as part of an ongoing reflationary trend. The three Chinese cities depicted in Table 5.5 also evidenced gradual, but sustained, upward price movements between November 1935 and the outbreak of war in mid-1937. Interestingly, however, wholesale prices in Guangzhou, which is located in the southern Chinese province of

Guangdong (formerly Canton) neighboring Hong Kong, appear to follow a trajectory more similar to Hong Kong's wholesale price series than to those of the other more northerly Chinese cities. Guangzhou experienced steeper deflation than the other Chinese cities in 1934–1935, and, like Hong Kong, its wholesale price index did not return above its 1926 base until several months into 1936 – in April for Guangzhou versus March for Hong Kong.[16]

Causal Effects of the Silver Purchase Program on China

The data and anecdotal accounts of China's situation in the 1930s reviewed earlier seemingly make it hard to escape the conclusion that US silver purchases, and associated pressures for currency appreciation, did significant damage to the Chinese economy. If this perspective is correct, there should be a consistent tendency for the Chinese price level to fall as the currency strengthened against the dollar and for the currency appreciation to be linked to silver prices and/or the onset of the US silver purchase program. Econometric analysis in Burdekin (2008) suggests a statistically significant effect of silver prices on China's exchange rate, and a significant deflationary effect of exchange rate appreciation, over the 1928–1937 period. Moreover, historical decompositions of price level and exchange rate movements over this same sample period point to a major impact of silver price shocks on both these key Chinese variables. Elsewhere, Lai and Gau's (2003) vector autoregressive analysis also identifies significant effects of silver on China's prices and exchange rates over the 1929–1935 period.

In this section, the causal relationship between silver prices and Chinese price and exchange rate series is examined through a series of Granger-causality tests. This procedure sheds light on whether past movements in one variable exert significant effects on another. In this way, we can see if silver price movements, for example, played a significant role in accounting for movements in the Chinese variables. We can also see whether the underlying relationships changed, as one would expect, after China made the final break from silver in November 1935. This exercise employs monthly data on the Shanghai wholesale price index, the yuan/$US exchange rate, and the New York silver cash price drawn from the Global Financial

---

[16] Later on, the widespread circulation of Hong Kong dollars in Guangdong produced what was tantamount to a *de facto* common currency area (see Schenk, 2000, and Chapter 10). The Hong Kong dollar offered an appealing stable value alternative to the rapidly depreciating Nationalist currency of the 1940s as well as, following Nationalist defeat in the Civil War, the relatively untried renminbi issues in the early days of the People's Republic.

Database (http://www.globalfindata.com). In order to allow for effects of the purchasing power of silver rather than the absolute silver price (cf. *Silver and Prices in China*, 1935), a real silver price series is constructed by deflating the silver price by the US producer price index. To assure stationarity, all series were converted to growth rate form by taking the log first difference of the raw data. The data set covers the "Nanking decade" of Nationalist rule in China, running up until the outbreak of all-out war with Japan in July 1937.[17]

Causality testing reveals that US silver prices Granger-cause Chinese inflation over the January 1928 to October 1935 period but not over the full sample ending in June 1937 (Table 5.6). This is consistent with significant effects of silver price movements on China over the period preceding the November 1935 currency reform. China's November 1935 break from the silver standard was intended to end its vulnerability to swings in silver prices, and the results are consistent with this goal being achieved. It is, unfortunately, not possible to examine the post-November 1935 period in isolation as there are simply insufficient observations available prior to the July 1937 outbreak of war. Meanwhile, the exchange rate Granger-causes inflation over the whole period, suggesting that exchange rate movements were consistently important over the Nanking decade – and in line with the deflationary effects of currency appreciation discussed in the preceding sections. The conclusions drawn from Table 5.6 are also supported when the equations are reestimated using the real silver price in place of the nominal silver price (Table 5.7).[18]

Silver Shocks and Stock Price Movements

The Granger-causality effects discussed earlier remain limited to the effects of silver prices on nominal variables, owing to the absence of usable series on real variables like output. Although annual estimates by Yeh (1979, p. 97) do suggest that an 8.7% drop in China's real GDP accompanied the

---

[17] Loss of territorial control as well as competing money issues by Japanese puppet banks and other local issuers make all national economic data for this period problematic even prior to 1937 – hence the reliance on a Shanghai, rather than national, price index and an international exchange rate measure. Output data are especially complicated by the loss of Manchuria to the Japanese in 1931. Available real GDP and money supply series (Yeh, 1979; Rawski, 1989) are, in any event, annual estimates only and cannot be used here.

[18] The only seemingly spurious result is the finding that the exchange rate Granger-causes the silver price rather than the other way around. This is almost certainly a figment of the contemporaneous, rather than lagged, relationship between these two variables identified in the regression analysis performed in Burdekin (2008).

Table 5.6. *Granger-Causality Tests on inflation, the exchange rate, and silver prices*

Causal Relationship Tested	F-Statistic
1928:01 – 1935:10	
US Silver Price → Inflation	**3.27****
	[0.0152]
Inflation ↛ US Silver Price	0.87
	[0.4854]
Exchange Rate → Inflation	**7.23*****
	[0.0000]
Inflation ↛ Exchange Rate	0.81
	[0.5241]
Exchange Rate → US Silver Price	**4.55*****
	[0.0022]
US Silver Price ↛ Exchange Rate	1.43
	[0.2323]
1928:01 – 1937:06	
US Silver Price ↛ Inflation	1.79
	[0.1356]
Inflation ↛ US Silver Price	0.88
	[0.4770]
Exchange Rate → Inflation	**10.14*****
	[0.0000]
Inflation ↛ Exchange Rate	0.62
	[0.6507]
Exchange Rate → US Silver Price	**5.21*****
	[0.0007]
US Silver Price ↛ Exchange Rate	1.11
	[0.3568]

Notes: ***, **, and * denote significance at the 99%, 95%, and 90% levels, respectively; the figures in brackets are the exact significance levels (P-values); and four lags have been included in each of the test regressions.

onset of US silver purchases in 1934, Brandt and Sargent (1989) and Rawski (1989, 1993) point to Chinese banks' ability to expand their note issues sufficiently to offset the decline in silver money as world silver prices rose – thereby helping limit (or, much more arguably, eliminate) the negative deflationary effects discerned by Friedman (1992) and many contemporary accounts (see also Burdekin, 2008). In the absence of reliable and consistent data on Chinese real economic performance, monthly stock market data offer an alternative, relatively high-frequency window that could shed light on the real effects of silver price movements.

Table 5.7. *Granger-Causality with the real silver*
price in the three-equation system

Causal Relationship Tested	F-Statistic
1928:01 – 1935:09	
US Silver Price → Inflation	**3.00****
	[0.0229]
Inflation → US Silver Price	0.57
	[0.6819]
Exchange Rate → Inflation	**7.23*****
	[0.0000]
Inflation → Exchange Rate	0.81
	[0.5241]
Exchange Rate → US Silver Price	**3.45****
	[0.0116]
US Silver Price → Exchange Rate	0.80
	[0.5266]
1928:01 – 1937:06	
US Silver Price → Inflation	1.97
	[0.1047]
Inflation → US Silver Price	1.26
	[0.2911]
Exchange Rate → Inflation	**10.14*****
	[0.0000]
Inflation → Exchange Rate	0.62
	[0.6507]
Exchange Rate → US Silver Price	**3.61*****
	[0.0085]
US Silver Price → Exchange Rate	0.65
	[0.6253]

Notes: ***, **, and * denote significance at the 99%, 95%, and 90% levels, respectively; the figures in brackets are the exact significance levels (P-values); and four lags have been included in each of the test regressions.

This section focuses on the evolution of the HSBC stock price over the 1927–1937 period, thereby taking advantage of a consistent data series on an institution that stood out as a major player in both Chinese and Hong Kong financial markets. HSBC actually operated as an official arm of Chinese monetary policy prior to the Nanking decade and remained "the most important foreign bank in China [that] had long dominated international finance there ... " (Schenk, 2002). HSBC has, of course, retained its position as a major international bank to this day. HSBC stock traded actively in London and Shanghai as well as in Hong Kong. Although the data employed

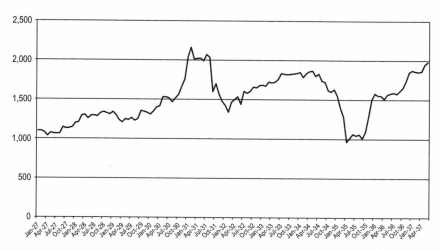

Figure 5.5. Hongkong and Shanghai Banking Corporation, January 1927–June 1937 (month-end closing share price in Hong Kong).

in this section are taken from the Hong Kong market, stock prices were generally very similar across markets, reflecting the availability of telegraph communications (Bailey and Bhaopichitr, 2004, p. 146). The HSBC data series spans the period both before and after China's monetary reform on November 5, 1935 that freed the note issue from its old link to the shrinking stock of available silver.[19]

HSBC's trading price over the January 1927 to June 1937 period is plotted in Figure 5.5, revealing sustained gains over the late 1920s followed by sharp declines in 1931 and 1934–1935. These declines themselves appear to coincide, first, with the British and Japanese break from gold – coupled with the September 1931 Japanese invasion of Manchuria – and, second, with the sharp rise in silver prices following the implementation of the US silver purchase program. Econometric analysis confirms that each of these declines represented a nonreversed "turning point" in the equity series. The HSBC stock price is initially simply modeled as a function of its own past history, with such series often displaying a certain degree of inertia whereby past movements, on average, help predict future movements. After converting the stock price series into log first difference form to assure stationarity, allowance was made for effects of lagged values going back four months together with a constant and a time trend. Only one lag, that is the

---

[19] This end-of-month series was collected from contemporary newspapers by Bailey and Bhaopichitr (2004) and kindly provided to the author by Warren Bailey.

prior month's value, was found to be significant, leading to the following basic specification:

$$\Delta HSBC = \underset{(0.010)}{0.004} + \underset{(0.090)}{0.172} \, \Delta HSBC(-1) - \underset{(0.0001)}{0.000005} \, TIME \qquad (1)$$

$$R^2 = 0.03$$

where $\Delta HSBC$ is the first difference of the natural logarithm of the HSBC series,

$\Delta HSBC(-1)$ is the lagged value,

TIME is a simple linear time trend,

Standard errors are given in parentheses below each estimated coefficient, and

R^2 denotes the coefficient of determination, or overall explanatory power.[20]

The results suggest that the effect of the lagged stock price change is positive and significant at the 94% confidence level. Although the overall explanatory power of the basic equation is low, the next step is to allow for additional dummy variables that can capture possible shifts in the equation over the sample period and, hence, better explain the major ups and downs. Following the general procedure suggested by Banerjee, Lumsdaine, and Stock (1992), the data were organized into a series of non-overlapping "windows," each being a year in length. Repeated estimation, progressively moving through the overall sample period, reveals those windows, or portions of the sample, where especially low R^2 values make the presence of a structural break most likely. Dummy variables are then defined successively for each week in the period surrounding the window in question, with these dummies taking on a value of one for that week and every week thereafter. The week for which this "rolling" estimation procedure yields the highest dummy variable significance level then forms our best estimate of the exact date at which a nonreversed "turning point" occurs.[21]

The most significant breakpoints for the HSBC series are presented in Table 5.8. The results suggest that negative turning points in the series occurred in March and September 1931. The latter downturn occurs in the same month as the United Kingdom's exit from the gold standard and Japan's

---

[20] None of the equations yields evidence of serial correlation based on application of the Breusch-Godfrey LM test.

[21] For more details on the empirical procedure, and an analogous application to asset prices during World War II, see Brown and Burdekin (2002).

Table 5.8. *Potential Turning Points in the Hong Kong and Shanghai Bank Corporation Stock Price Series*

Date	t-Statistic
March 1931	−2.557***
September 1931	−2.151**
February 1932	2.055**
March 1932	3.922***
June 1934	−2.622***
August 1934	−2.061**
May 1935	1.849*

Notes: The t-statistics reflect the sign and significance of the coefficient attached to a dummy variable defined for the month in question, and ***,**, and * denote significance at the 99%, 95%, and 90% confidence levels, respectively.

invasion of Manchuria. The UK policy action gave rise to depreciation of the pound against the Chinese currency whereas the loss of Manchuria deprived China of a key source of industrial production and 15% of its overall customs revenues (Young, 1971, p. 200). The earlier turning point indicated for March 1931 appears to coincide with a correction from the sharp share price advance that began during the summer of 1930, but is not obviously tied to major historical events. Meanwhile, the positive turning point suggested for March 1932 saw HSBC's stock price begin a partial recovery from the steep downturn initiated in September 1931. The gains continued until 1934 and perhaps reflect the fact that business conditions in Shanghai were not, at first, so adversely affected by the 1931 events, with inflows of silver from China's interior more than compensating for the outflow abroad (as discussed earlier).

Successive negative turning points are indicated for June 1934 and August 1934. The first negative turning point coincides with the passage of the US Silver Purchase Act on June 19, 1934. Although large-scale purchases did not get underway until the following month, the act clearly presaged new upward pressure on silver prices and hence additional upward pressures on China's currency. Meanwhile, August 1934 stands out as the month with the most dramatic increase in the silver drain prior to China's November 1935 break from silver (see Table 5.4). Both June 1934 and August 1934 were therefore months that contained plenty of bad news for business interests in Shanghai and for the silver-standard economies generally. The specific dates of the negative turning points appear to point, rather unambiguously, to a negative reaction to the initiation, and effects, of the US Silver Purchase Act. HSBC's stock price certainly dropped precipitously after the act was passed, falling by over 46% between June 1934 and April 1935 – at the very least suggesting that the act was not favorably received by the bank's investors.

After bottoming out in April 1935, HSBC's stock price enjoyed a limited "bounce" followed by accelerating gains after the November 1935 currency reform. HSBC's share price rose by just under 13% between April and October 1935 before embarking on a near 82% advance between October 1935 and June 1937. The significant positive turning point identified for May 1935 coincides with the initial recovery from the low recorded in April 1935 but precedes the larger advance that, based on the raw data displayed in Figure 5.5, appeared to correspond with the November 1935 break from silver. The turning point procedure is, unfortunately, often unable to distinguish breaks in nearby months, and identification is further hampered when proximity to the end of the sample leaves little time for the turning point to be established in the data. The bottom line is that we see evidence that the stock price recovered in 1935, even though the empirical procedure cannot precisely tie the recovery to the actual month of the currency reform.

Overall, the turning point analysis, first, offers empirical confirmation of the negative effects generally attributed to the United Kingdom's exit from the gold standard and the Japanese invasion of Manchuria. Following partial recovery in 1932, renewed successive negative turning points arise just when the US Silver Purchase Act was passed and large-scale silver purchases began. HSBC's stock plunged after these latter events, and, although there is evidence of a positive turning point as early as May 1935, large gains were postponed until after China's break from silver later in the year.

Conclusions

The sharp decline in HSBC stock during 1934, coupled with causal effects of silver prices on Chinese wholesale prices prior to the November 1935 currency reform, simply offers further confirmation of the picture arising from available descriptive data and anecdotal accounts. Evidence ranging from share price movements, to interest rates, and business and bank failures, suggests that the silver drain from Shanghai in 1934 exerted negative effects on real variables. Liquidity shortages appear to have been particularly stringent near the end of the year. Although China and Hong Kong both entered deflation well before the US silver purchases began, these large-scale purchases exacerbated the deflationary pressures and forced even sharper appreciation on the silver-based currencies. The deflationary effects were even worse in Hong Kong than in China, implying that at least some tangible benefits derived from the October 1934 measures aimed at holding currency appreciation in China below the rate of increase in world silver prices. However, only the complete abandonment of the silver standard in November 1935 ended the deflation.

China's exit from the silver standard in November 1935, although offering relief from silver-induced deflationary pressures, also put an end to any limit on Chinese money issuance and arguably may have speeded China's eventual descent into hyperinflation (Friedman, 1992).[22] The initial application of a pegged exchange rate policy appears to have been relatively successful, however, and likely would have remained tenable for much longer had it not been for the Japanese invasion. Hong Kong certainly appeared to fare quite well after abandoning silver, and confidence in the Hong Kong dollar was established through maintaining a peg with the pound sterling, at sixteen Hong Kong dollars per pound, until the outbreak of World War II in 1939 (Schenk, 2000, p. 743). It is unclear whether the lesson to be drawn from this 1930s episode is the danger of unbacked paper currency or the danger of excessive currency appreciation. The additional currency appreciation that followed the implementation of the US Silver Purchase Act certainly did appear to be more than China's own economy could bear at the time, producing a seemingly immediate, and severe, reversal of Shanghai's prosperity and producing still more severe deflation in the neighboring economy of Hong Kong. The US silver purchases were not the sole source of the problem, but they may well have been responsible for causing the appreciation pressures to, if not spiral out of control, at least push the degree of economic strain beyond the breaking point.

---

[22] The relevance of basic monetary relationships even in the face of the rising threat to national sovereignty after 1937 in China is itself echoed also in the Confederate civil war experience (Burdekin and Weidenmier, 2001).

SIX

Inflation Transmission to Taiwan in the 1940s

with Hsin-hui I. H. Whited[1]

As hyperinflation spiraled upward, the Chinese people lost all confidence in the Nationalist government... The issuance of gold yuan notes heralded the last curtain call of the Nationalist government on the mainland of China.

(Ji, 2003, p. 229)

Introduction

Whereas the preceding chapter considered the deflationary damage exerted by an artificially overvalued exchange rate in the 1930s, Taiwan's experience at the end of the 1940s offers a vivid illustration of the inflationary pressures that can be generated by an excessively undervalued exchange rate. Resisting upward pressure on the currency in such a case fuels inflation, *inter alia*, as undervaluation of the domestic currency triggers capital inflows that drive up the money supply. As discussed in Chapter 1, there were fears that central bank loss of control over the money supply in the face of surging capital inflows would lead to this scenario being repeated in mainland China in 2004. "Hot flows" of funds into China appeared to subside in the face of the gradual appreciation effected during 2005–2007, however, and the actual degree of recent renminbi undervaluation remained subject to considerable doubt (Chapter 1). China's accelerating accumulation of foreign exchange reserves has nevertheless required massive sterilization efforts by the People's Bank of China (Chapter 4), and

[1] Hsin-hui I. H. Whited is an Associate Professor at Colorado State University–Pueblo (ida.whited@colostate-pueblo.edu). This chapter is adapted from an article (Burdekin and Whited, 2005) published in the *China Economic Review*, Copyright Elsevier, and is reprinted with kind permission of the publisher. The authors thank Tom Willett, Marc Weidenmier, Kerry Odell, Eric Helland, Greg Hess, and two anonymous referees for their helpful comments and are grateful to Munir Quddus for kindly furnishing the data employed in Quddus, Liu, and Butler (1989).

ongoing concerns about imported inflationary pressures prompted a variety of tightening measures, including a succession of reserve requirement increases and interest rate hikes. This chapter uses an example from China's own history to demonstrate how dangerous such imported inflation can be – albeit under circumstances far more extreme than anything that is likely to unfold today.

During the twilight of Nationalist rule in mainland China in 1947–1949, there was a large outflow of funds from mainland China to Taiwan as excess money supply growth on the mainland was translated into excess money growth in Taiwan. A fixed exchange rate between mainland China's new "gold yuan" and Taiwan's currency, coupled with Nationalist control over both the Central Bank of China and the Bank of Taiwan, created an almost ideal vehicle for massive capital flight. Rising capital inflows into Taiwan reflected not only the deteriorating conditions on the mainland but also excess money growth that had, as a major outlet, the exit strategy offered by the fixed exchange rate imposed by Chiang Kai-shek's Nationalist regime. Holders of gold yuan took advantage of the fact that the Bank of Taiwan was forced to accept the weakening Nationalist currency and exchange it for the separate Taiwanese currency at an artificially overvalued rate – that is, seriously overvaluing the gold yuan while undervaluing the Taiwanese currency. Indeed, the worse conditions became on the mainland, the greater the incentive to capitalize on the fixed exchange rate and move funds into Taiwan.

One way of assessing the magnitude of the overvaluation of the gold yuan against the Taiwanese currency is to consider how the gold yuan fared in black market trading. On October 15, 1948, the US Ambassador to China, John Leighton Stuart, observed that the US dollar was exchanging for 16 gold yuan in Beijing even though the official rate was only 4:1 – whereas an ounce of gold was selling for 1,000 gold yuan, similarly up dramatically from the official rate set at 200 gold yuan per ounce.[2] The fixed rate of exchange with the Taiwanese currency remained available through the fall of 1948, however, in spite of rapidly accelerating money growth on the mainland reflected in the plunging black market currency values. The resultant exporting of hyperinflation to Taiwan suggests that the policies of

---

[2] Letter from Ambassador Stuart to Secretary Marshall (US Department of State, 1949, p. 879). Tallman, Tang, and Wang (2003) find a strongly significant effect of the black market exchange rate in the formation of expectations over the late 1940s in China, but do not consider the potential impetus to capital flight arising from the growing gap between the black market rate and the fixed official exchange rate in the aftermath of the August 1948 reform.

Table 6.1. *Nationalist Government Finances, 1936–1949*

	Expenditure	Revenue	Budget Deficit	Note Issue Outstanding
1936–1937	1,894	1,972	−78	1,410
1937–1938	2,091	815	1,276	1,730
1939	2,797	740	2,057	4,290
1940	5,288	1,325	3,963	7,870
1941	10,003	1,310	8,693	15,100
1942	24,511	5,630	18,881	34,400
1943	58,816	20,403	38,413	75,400
1944	171,689	38,503	133,186	189,500
1945	2,348,085	1,241,389	1,106,696	1,031,900
1946	7,574,790	2,876,988	4,697,802	3,726,100
1947	43,393,895	14,064,383	29,329,512	33,188,500
Jan–July 1948	655,471,087	220,905,475	434,565,612	374,762,200
Aug 1948	–	–	–	890,400,000
Sept 1948	1,030,242,000	326,562,000	703,680,000	3,606,000,000
Oct 1948	848,499,000	435,270,000	413,229,000	5,550,000,000
Nov 1948	2,024,832,000	517,230,000	1,507,602,000	10,182,000,000
Dec 1948	7,948,827,000	1,340,241,000	6,608,586,000	24,960,000,000
Jan 1949	–	–	–	62,466,000,000
Feb 1949	–	–	–	178,932,000,000
Mar 1949	–	–	–	588,207,000,000
Apr 1949	–	–	–	15,483,720,000,000

Notes: All numbers are given in millions of *fapi*. Data from August 1948 forward have been converted by applying the official three-million-to-one exchange rate between *fapi* and the gold yuan. Note issues outstanding are end-of-period values.

Sources: Chang (1958, pp. 16, 40, 51, 71, 84, 124, 168); Wu (1958, p. 122); and authors' calculations.

Nationalist leader Chiang Kai-shek might well have the dubious, and quite possibly unique, honor of being responsible not just for one hyperinflation but rather for two. The initial hyperinflation in mainland China was itself fueled by wartime expenditures, with the Sino-Japanese War that began in 1937 melding into World War II and then, with no respite, an escalating civil war against the Communist forces of Mao Tse-tung. The associated massive budget deficits and increasing reliance on the printing press are clearly evident in Table 6.1 However, it is the interrelationship between inflation in mainland China and inflation in Taiwan that adds a most unusual, and novel, twist to this hyperinflation experience. Capital inflows from mainland China played a key role in the process by which Taiwan's resources and the Bank of Taiwan's printing press were used to help finance the failing Nationalist war effort.

Formal tests of how Taiwan's inflation was affected by events on the mainland have been surprisingly sparse. However, the single study by Lin and Wu

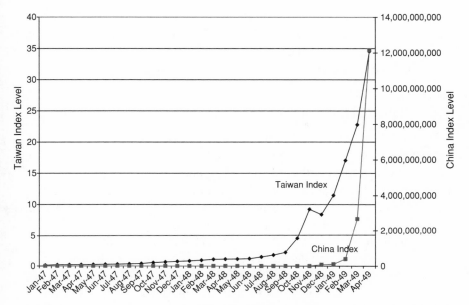

Figure 6.1. Price Indices for Taiwan and Mainland China, January 1947–April 1949.

(1989) does find that mainland inflation (as measured by the inflation rate in Shanghai) Granger causes Taiwanese inflation over the January 1946–April 1949 period.[3] This chapter assesses both the importance of mainland Chinese variables to Taiwan's inflation and the effects of capital inflows from mainland China to Taiwan over the 1947–1949 period. We also allow for a structural break following the monetary reform in mainland China in August 1948 that is thought to have spurred capital inflows and inflationary pressures in Taiwan.[4] The acceleration in Taiwanese prices following this reform is shown in Figure 6.1, which plots Taiwan and mainland China price movements over the 1947–1949 period (based on wholesale price indices from the cities of Taipei and Shanghai). Our empirical work confirms the importance of the August 1948 reform to Taiwan and shows Taiwanese

---

[3] Meanwhile, Lin and Wu (1989), Makinen and Woodward (1989), and Quddus, Liu, and Butler (1989) all test causality between money growth and inflation in Taiwan but Lin and Wu's conclusions are opposite to the other two studies.

[4] Quddus, Liu, and Butler (1989) previously found that truncating the sample period at August 1948 had a significant effect on their results – eliminating the bidirectional feedback between inflation and money growth in mainland China that applies if the sample is extended into 1949 (see also Tang and Hu, 1983). Meanwhile, our own prior analysis of inflation and the growth rates of money balances in Taiwan over the 1945–1953 period (Burdekin and Whited, 2001) suggests that the August 1948 reform coincides with the beginnings of an extended period of instability in Taiwanese currency and inflation processes that continues into 1949 and 1950.

inflation rates to be significantly affected by capital inflows and mainland China inflation and money growth rates. Taiwanese money growth is itself driven by such external factors, leaving it with no apparent independent role in the inflation process.

Imported Inflation and Mainland China's Currency Reform

Taiwan was returned to Chiang Kai-shek's Nationalist government by the Japanese on November 1, 1945. The Bank of Taiwan then set up a special deposit program to withdraw the old Japanese notes and prohibited the circulation of notes issued after the Japanese surrender. By the beginning of December 1945, the money issued had decreased 20% from the level in October and this deposit program seemed to be effective in reducing the pressure to print money for deficit finance. However, the Bank of Taiwan was soon faced by new loan demands from China's Nationalist Government. In May 1946, the loans debited to the Taiwan Provincial Government equaled 62.8% of the Bank of Taiwan's total loans. On May 22, 1946, the Bank of Taiwan was authorized by the Nationalist Government to issue a new local currency, called the *taipi*, in an amount equivalent to 5.3 billion *fapi*. There were no reserves for the *taipi* and its circulation was limited to Taiwan with issuance remaining subject to Nationalist government approval. Makinen and Woodward (1989, p. 91) state that, after this point, "the public finance practices of the Taiwanese government paralleled those on the mainland in that a major source of revenue was derived from the inflation tax." Not only did the Bank of Taiwan face the huge burden of financing the expenses of two governments (the Taiwanese Provincial government and the Nationalist government on the mainland) but also loans to the government were augmented by unsecured loans to state-owned enterprises (Lin and Wu, 1989, pp. 932–933).

The monthly rate of inflation gradually increased during 1947 and early 1948 before accelerating dramatically in the second half of 1948 to over 107% in October and November. This dramatic change was a direct consequence of the August 19, 1948, monetary reform in mainland China that replaced the old *fapi* currency with the "gold yuan" as the official currency on the mainland. Under this reform, private holdings of gold and silver were prohibited and all specie had to be turned into the central bank in exchange for gold yuan notes. Gold yuan notes could not be converted back into gold, however, and even the promised partial gold backing evaporated as increasingly large note issues were undertaken well in excess of the promised 2 billion yuan maximum.

Prices and exchange rates in mainland China were initially frozen at the August 19 levels, and extreme penalties were adopted against hoarders and black marketeers. In Shanghai, Chiang Kai-shek's eldest son stringently enforced these restrictive measures using the secret police. However, the government's perilous financial and military position fueled ever-increasing inflationary pressures. Losses to Mao Tse-tung's Communist forces had severely disrupted production and transportation and depleted the government's tax revenue. Spurred also by rising military spending, the budget deficit rose from 29 thousand billion *fapi* in 1947 to 434 thousand billion *fapi* in January–July 1948, while the money supply soared by 1,029% between December 1947 and July 1948 (Table 6.1). Notwithstanding the Minister of Finance's August 1948 announcement that the budget deficit "would be reduced from 70 per cent to 30 per cent of government expenditure" (Chang, 1958, p. 80), the actual reliance on deficit spending reached 75% of spending in November 1948 and 83% of spending in December 1948 (Table 6.1). It was soon obvious that there were no grounds for confidence in the new monetary standard. Whereas deposits in private banks in Shanghai initially rose after the reform, and the velocity of circulation of money declined, Chang (1958, p. 274) states that by

the end of October the index of the note issue was four and a half times that of August, price and wage ceilings were in the process of disintegration, and it was abundantly clear that inflation could no longer be contained by the expedient of the currency change... In November the value of checks cleared in Shanghai rose to more than three times the note issue, and the velocity of circulation of money jumped nearly six times the October figure... The black-market rate of interest leapt to 120 per cent per month ...

Besides simply unloading unwanted gold yuan notes by purchasing goods and services, mainland Chinese sought to transfer funds to South China en route to Hong Kong.[5] However, the exchange rate arrangements adopted in August 1948 gave a special impetus to capital flight to Taiwan. Prior to August 19, the exchange rate system adopted between the *fapi* and *taipi* currencies was an adjustable (or managed) exchange rate system. On August 18, 1948, the exchange rate between these two currencies was 1:1,635 (one *taipi* was equal to 1,635 *fapi*). On August 19, 1948, the exchange rate between the gold yuan notes and *fapi* was set at 1:3,000,000 (one gold yuan note was equal to 3 million *fapi*). The official exchange rate between the *taipi* and the gold yuan thus became 1,835:1 (1,835 *taipi* equal to one gold yuan note).

---

[5] The total capital flight from China to Hong Kong between 1947 and 1949 has been estimated at around 500 million Hong Kong dollars (Chang, 1958, p. 320).

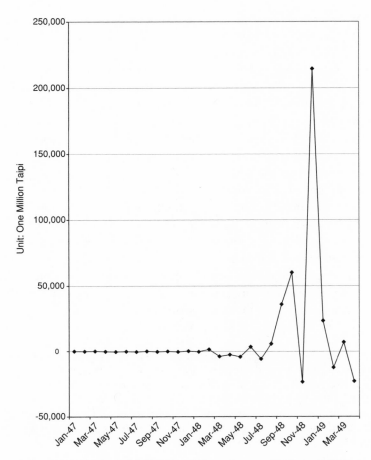

Figure 6.2. Net Capital Inflow into Taiwan, January 1947–April 1949.

With the official exchange rate between the gold yuan and the *taipi* held unchanged in spite of the growing loss of confidence in the gold yuan, the attraction of exchanging gold yuan for *taipi* was obvious.[6] The accelerating net capital inflows into Taiwan after the August 1948 reform are depicted in Figure 6.2. Perhaps reflecting the fact that the "failure of the monetary reform seemed to be anticipated by the public" (Li and Wu, 1997, p. 7), the net capital inflow over August, September, and October 1948 amounted to close to 100,000 million *taipi*. This capital inflow was the major force

---

[6] Wu (1997, p. 535) also points out that, with the artificially high rate of exchange for the gold yuan against the Taiwanese *taipi* after August 1948 making Taiwanese exports cheaper in gold yuan terms, the exchange rate policy provided price subsidization for Shanghai.

causing the money supply to double over this same period, accounting for 86.8% of the M1 money supply increase in September 1948 and 97.9% of the October increase (Lin and Wu, 1989, pp. 935–936). The Bank of Taiwan finally stopped accepting deposits in gold yuan notes from the mainland on October 23, 1948. And, on November 1, 1948, the Nationalist government belatedly adjusted the exchange rate between the *taipi* and the gold yuan – quickly adjusting it again on November 11. Also, from November 12, the exchange rate was allowed to change more often in response to market forces (Li and Wu, 1997). The exchange rate adjustment was accompanied by a capital outflow that grew 8.8-fold between October and November 1948 and created the first net capital outflow since the August 1948 reform was enacted. Deflation of −9.01% was recorded in Taiwan during December 1948, showing how sensitive inflation rates were to the Nationalist government's exchange rate policy at that time.

However, Taiwan's respite at the end of 1948 was short-lived. Capital flight to Taiwan reaccelerated in the face of the Nationalists' crumbling military position on the mainland and the Nationalist government itself began to transfer its remaining resources to Taiwan. In the face of mounting deficits on the mainland, the 2 billion yuan maximum for the gold yuan notes was formally set aside on November 11, 1948. Meanwhile, the price controls in Shanghai unraveled during the middle of October 1948 in the midst of panic buying when retailers "withheld their goods from sale rather than sell them at official prices, and even the restaurants refused to do business" (Chang, 1958, p. 80). Prices were formally freed on November 1, 1948 under a Financial Emergency Executive Order. Although nearly 3.4 billion gold yuan (equivalent to more than 10,182 thousand billion *fapi*) were in circulation on November 30, 1948, by the end of April 1949 total note issue had risen to more than 5 thousand billion gold yuan (equivalent to a staggering 15,483,720 thousand billion *fapi* – see Table 6.1). Shanghai wholesale prices rose 59,374 times between September 1948 and April 1949 before rising a further 85 times between April and May 1949 on the eve of the fall of that city to the Communists on May 27, 1949.

On July 3, 1949, the director of the People's Bank of China at Shanghai claimed that the total issue of gold yuan notes had actually reached 60,000 billion on May 25, 1949 – equivalent to 180,000 quadrillion *fapi*, or 11.6 times larger than the April 1949 figure given by the Nationalist central bank (Table 6.1). Although not coming close to the inflationary spiral under the Nationalists, the Communist takeover still saw the beleaguered city of Shanghai endure a further tenfold increase in wholesale prices before stabilization was finally achieved in March 1950 (Chapter 3). Although

Nationalist forces remained on the field in mainland China until 1950, Chou (1963, p. 27) states that after the fall of Shanghai "the gold yuan notes were rejected by the public." Attempts to replace the gold yuan notes with a new "silver yuan" standard on July 1, 1949 were an utter failure. Reportedly, the budget deficit in the second half of 1949 totaled 88% of expenditures – a deficit that "had to be met with gold, silver, and foreign exchange since bank notes no longer enjoyed the people's acceptance" (Chang, 1958, p. 169).

Taiwan's November 1948 net capital outflow of −23,277 million *taipi* reversed to a capital inflow of 214,495 million *taipi* in December 1948. And this December capital inflow amounted to 73.4% of the total increase in currency in that month (Li and Wu, 1997, p. 8).[7] The Taiwanese money supply grew 1.27-fold between November and December 1948. Pressures on the money supply increased when many divisions of the Nationalist army began moving to Taiwan in 1949. The overall growth rate of the money supply increased to 37.3% in January 1949 and then, after settling back to 8.4% in February, rose again to 19.5% in March, 17.2% in April, and 39.5% in May. Inflation reaccelerated during this period, reaching 36.2% in January, 48.7% in February, 33.9% in March, 51.4% in April, and 102.1% in May. This increase, however, still paled in comparison to the depreciation of the gold yuan. By late April and early May 1949, the gold yuan's initial official exchange ratio of 4 gold yuan to the US dollar had fallen to the point that open market quotations ranged from 5 million to 10 million gold yuan per US dollar (US Department of State, 1949, p. 401).

Time Series Analysis

This section employs data on the Taiwanese money supply and the Taipei wholesale price index from Liu (1970) along with data on capital inflows into Taiwan from mainland China given by Lin and Wu (1989, p. 934). The mainland Chinese money supply and inflation series are based on the currency series and Shanghai wholesale price data provided by Quddus, Liu, and Butler (1989). As depicted in Figure 6.3, inflation in mainland Chinese and inflation in Taiwan appear to track each other quite closely over the January 1946–April 1949 period except for the interval between August and December 1948, that is, immediately after the implementation of the August

---

[7] Even if the adoption of a more flexible exchange rate policy did "succeed in reducing the *taipi* value of these inward remittances, and therefore their inflationary effect on the island's economy" (Chou, 1963, p. 37), the available data suggest that the impact on Taiwanese money growth remained potentially very powerful.

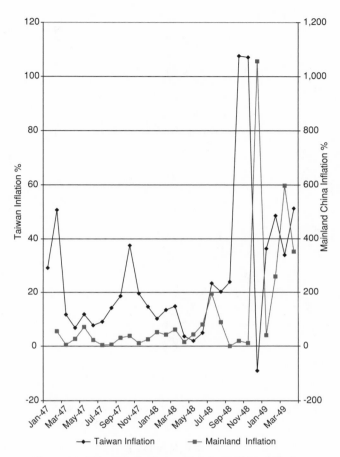

Figure 6.3. Taiwan Inflation vs. Mainland China Inflation.

1948 currency reform and the imposition of a fixed rate of exchange for the new gold yuan. The soaring Taiwanese inflation in September–November 1948 occurs even though mainland Chinese price rises are temporarily restrained. Figure 6.4, however, shows the inflationary surge in Taiwan to immediately follow the surge in capital inflows from August–October 1948. Moreover, the temporary drop in Taiwanese inflation in December 1948 is immediately preceded by the temporary reversal of the capital inflow from mainland China in November. Figures 6.3 and 6.4 are therefore very much consistent with generally close ties between mainland Chinese and Taiwanese inflation in the late 1940s supplemented by a seemingly leading role played by capital inflows during the fixed exchange rate period.

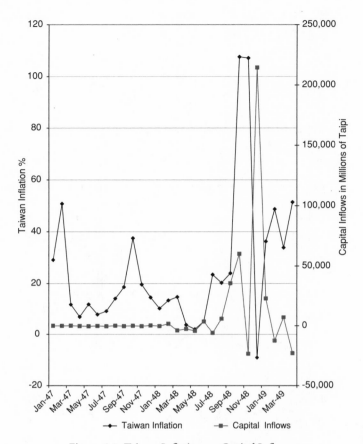

Figure 6.4. Taiwan Inflation vs. Capital Inflows.

The apparent impact of mainland Chinese inflation and capital inflows on Taiwanese inflation seen in Figures 6.3 and 6.4 receives confirmation in the formal time series analysis that we performed. Although limited by the short length of the estimation period, this empirical work serves to corroborate the inferences drawn from the graphical display.[8] Taiwanese

[8] Formal tests for stationarity of the series are compromised both by the small sample and the presence of additive outliers associated with the spikes in both capital inflows and inflation near the end of the sample. As discussed later, these spikes appear to follow a structural break in August 1948, biasing the results of conventional unit root tests against stationarity. The Phillips-Perron test (which unlike the basic Augmented Dickey-Fuller test corrects for both heteroskedasticity and autocorrelation of unknown form – see, for example, Holden and Perman, 1994) fails to confirm stationarity in only one out of five cases, however. As reported in the Appendix Table A6.1, the only series in question is Chinese money growth. Following Gujarati (2003), the Appendix table also reports Ljung and Box

inflation and money growth are regressed on their own past values, past values of mainland Chinese money growth and inflation, and the level of capital inflows. This method allows us to assess the role played by external monetary conditions in the hyperinflation process in Taiwan while also allowing for the potential role played by domestic rates of monetary expansion. We also examine the determination of the capital inflows themselves and regress the inflows on the difference between mainland Chinese and Taiwanese money growth and inflation rates. Increases in these inflation and money growth differentials could be expected to fuel capital outflows from mainland China to Taiwan through increasing the degree of overvaluation of the gold yuan exchange rate.

According to the literature on exchange market pressure (see, for example, Girton and Roper, 1977; Burdekin and Burkett, 1990), excess money growth and excess inflation in mainland China vis-à-vis Taiwan should be reflected in some combination of currency depreciation and international reserve losses. If the exchange rate is held constant, loss of international reserves, or capital outflow from mainland China, becomes the only outlet for the exchange market pressure. A number of Latin American countries experienced this phenomenon in the run-up to the debt crisis of the 1980s, where "the general tendency toward overvaluation fueled massive capital flight... In country after country, the public speculated against the central bank by acquiring foreign exchange and moving it abroad" (Edwards, 1995, p. 23).

Inflation, money growth, and capital inflow equations were estimated over monthly data from 1947 through April 1949 (the last month prior to the fall of Shanghai).[9] Empirical results from this short available sample period help confirm the international transmission of inflation from China to Taiwan already suggested by the descriptive data, charts, and anecdotal accounts. We tested for shifts in the relationships at the time of the August 19, 1948 reform in mainland China and, given evidence that such a shift occurred, also reestimated the equations with the sample truncated at July 1948. Although this further cuts into the already highly limited number of observations, the finding of a break in itself offers some corroboration of the importance of the currency reform and the temporary fixed exchange rate that accompanied it.

(1978) Q-statistics based on the correlogram of the data series. These Q statistics support stationarity of all five series. Besides capital inflows, the addition of contemporaneous values of the other variables was always rejected on the basis of an F-test.

[9] The exact lag order of the variables was determined – from a maximum of four lags – by applying the Akaike information criterion (AIC).

Table 6.2. *Regression Results for Taiwanese Inflation and Taiwanese Money Growth*

Right-hand-side Variables	Taiwanese Inflation		Taiwanese Money Growth	
	1947:6–1949:4	1947:6–1948:7	1947:6–1949:4	1947:6–1948:7
Constant	2.765	4.506***	3.733	−11.640
	(1.34)	(3.11)	(0.56)	(−1.74)
Taiwanese Money Growth (−1)			0.230	0.608#
			(0.89)	(1.89)
Taiwanese Money Growth (−2)			0.456	−0.054
			(1.41)	(−0.51)
Chinese Inflation (−1)	−0.043***	0.087***		
	(−11.20)	(9.15)		
Chinese Money Growth (−1)	0.310***	0.126**	−0.147**	0.326
	(18.09)	(3.13)	(−2.78)	(1.56)
Chinese Money Growth (−2)			0.205***	0.478
			(2.95)	(1.47)
Capital Inflow	−0.067***	0.411***	0.420***	1.550**
	(−13.19)	(6.26)	(6.82)	(2.98)
Capital Inflow (−1)	0.730***	2.410***	−0.138	−2.050***
	(13.33)	(26.98)	(−0.95)	(−5.14)
Capital Inflow (−2)			−0.213	4.830***
			(−1.27)	(7.97)
Estimation Method	Generalized Method of Moments		Two-Stage Least Squares	
Adjusted R	–	–	0.87	0.82
J-Statistic/F-Statistic	0.175	0.262	21.81***	9.51***
Chow Test for August 1948 breakpoint	–	–	4.83**	–

Notes: The numbers in parentheses after the independent variables denote the lag order (if any); ***, **, *, and # denote significance at the 99%, 95%, 90%, and 89% levels, respectively; *t*-statistics are in parentheses; and the J-statistic is an alternative goodness-of-fit diagnostic for the generalized methods of moments case (the lower the value, the better).

The results for the Taiwanese inflation and money growth equations are presented in Table 6.2 Lagged Chinese money growth, and contemporaneous and lagged values of the capital inflows from mainland China, are significant in each equation. Lagged Chinese inflation is also significant in the inflation equation. The money growth equation is estimated using a two-stage least squares (2SLS) method[10] – incorporating an autoregressive

[10] Additional lagged values of the variables included in the equations were used to form the instruments in the estimation. In the inflation equation the instruments used were lags

term – while the inflation equation is estimated using the generalized method of moments (GMM) so as to correct for possible non-normality of the residuals.[11] The full sample results are followed by results for a shortened 1947:6–1948:7 subsample that stops just prior to mainland China's August 1948 monetary reform.

The inflation equation reveals the expected positive effects of higher Chinese money growth and rising capital inflows (the positive coefficient on lagged inflows being ten times larger than the negative coefficient on the contemporaneous value). Lagged Chinese inflation also has the expected positive, and significant, effect in the pre-August 1948 subsample. Just as Taiwan's inflation seems to have been essentially imported from mainland China, Taiwanese money growth is seen to be endogenously driven by the mainland Chinese variables and capital inflows. Indeed, lagged Chinese money growth and capital inflows are the only significant variables in the money growth equations for Taiwan.[12]

The Table 6.2 results clearly corroborate the important role played by capital inflows in the Taiwanese inflation process. An important motivation behind these capital flows was undoubtedly flight from the political and military risks on the mainland to the relative safety of Taiwan. Yet these capital inflows were also likely responsive to exchange rate overvaluation associated with any worsening of inflationary pressures in mainland China over and above the levels prevailing in Taiwan. Accordingly, we next examined whether the volume of inflows can be explained by the differential between

two through four of Chinese inflation, Chinese money growth, and capital inflows. In the money growth equation the instruments were lags three through five of Taiwanese money growth, Chinese money growth, and capital inflows.

[11] In applying a battery of specification tests to the equations, Q-tests and LM tests for serial correlation, the White test for heteroskedasticity, and Ramsey's RESET test always indicated that the null hypothesis of no specification error could not be rejected. The Jarque-Bera normality test suggested, however, that the residuals from the initial 2SLS estimates of the inflation equation were significantly non-normal.

[12] Application of a Wald test showed the overall positive effect of Chinese money growth in the full-sample results to be significant only at approximately the 87% level. There are also partially offsetting effects for the capital inflows variable but neither of the negative coefficients on the lagged terms is significant at even the 80% level. Reestimating the equation over the full-sample with the statistically insignificant lagged Taiwanese money growth and lagged capital inflow deleted actually improves the overall goodness of fit and, for comparison, the results are:

$$\text{Taiwanese money growth} = 13.812^{***} - 0.096^{**}\text{Chinese Money Growth}(-1)$$
$$+ 0.135^{**}\text{Chinese Money Growth}(-2)$$
$$+ 0.422^{***}\text{Capital Inflow}$$
$$\text{Adjusted } R^2 = 0.88; \text{ F-Statistic} = 49.71^{***}; \text{ Chow Breakpoint Test} = 2.4^*$$

Table 6.3. *Regression Results for Capital Inflows into
Taiwan from Mainland China*

Right-hand-side Variables	Capital Inflows	
	1947:8–1949:4	1947:7–1948:7
Constant	−5.010*	0.275
	(−1.78)	(0.23)
Inflation	0.151***	−0.027
Differential	(4.49)	(−0.91)
Inflation	−0.090**	0.023
Differential (−1)	(−2.89)	(0.33)
Inflation	−0.114***	−0.058
Differential (−2)	(−7.51)	(−1.46)
Money Growth	0.506***	0.026
Differential (−3)	(3.94)	(0.25)
Estimation Method	Two-Stage Least Squares	
Adjusted R^2	0.92	0.22
F-Statistic	26.94***	1.76
Chow Breakpoint Test	92.99***	

Notes: "Inflation Differential" is the difference between the inflation
rate for mainland China and the Taiwanese inflation rate, and "Money
Growth Differential" is the difference between the money growth rate
in mainland China and the Taiwanese money growth rate. (See also
the explanatory notes to Table 6.2.)

mainland Chinese and Taiwanese money growth and inflation rates. We
would expect any such relationship to be strongest after the August 1948
reform when the rate of exchange between the *taipi* and the new gold yuan
was fixed notwithstanding a tremendous surge of inflationary pressure on
the mainland. In Table 6.3, we examine the effects on capital inflows of
money growth and inflation differentials between mainland China and Taiwan over the full sample and over the pre-August 1948 subsample. Although
the indicated effect of the inflation differential on capital inflows is actually
ambiguous given the mixed significant negative and positive coefficients,
the lagged money growth differential is significant at the 99% level with the
expected positive sign.[13]

---

[13] The results are undoubtedly compromised by including observations both before and after
the August 1948 reform – but reestimation over the pre-August 1948 subsample yields a
poor fit with no significant coefficients. The relative quiescence of capital inflows prior to

The overall dependence of the Taiwanese variables on mainland Chinese "forcing variables" receives further confirmation if we apply Granger-causality tests to our set of five variables (details provided in Burdekin and Whited, 2005). As discussed in Chapter 5, these tests examine the extent to which movements in one variable can be explained by past movements in another – in this case yielding results in line with the inferences drawn from Table 6.2 earlier. First, capital inflows exert causal effects on both Taiwanese inflation and Taiwanese money growth. Second, Chinese money growth and Chinese inflation also Granger-cause Taiwanese inflation, as suggested in Table 6.2[14] Third, Taiwanese money growth does not Granger-cause Taiwanese inflation. The only differences from the implications derived from Table 6.2 are that there is no confirmed causal effect of Chinese money growth on Taiwanese money growth in the Granger tests and that there is a suggested causal effect of Taiwanese inflation on Taiwanese money growth that was not indicated in the prior regression results.[15]

In general, we find considerable support for Taiwan's inflation at the end of the 1940s being driven by imported inflationary pressure from mainland China. The overvaluation of the gold yuan relative to the Taiwanese *taipi* after the August 1948 reform helped encourage the flow of excess money from mainland China to Taiwan. The importance of this reform is indicated both by the graphical display and by the identification of an August 1948 structural break in our empirical testing. We also find evidence that the inflows into Taiwan were themselves responsive to the money growth

the August 1948 reform, in contrast to the very sharp movements later on (Figure 6.2), likely lies behind this result.

[14] Further estimation of impulse response functions confirms that the suggested causal effects of the Chinese variables on Taiwanese inflation and the effects of capital inflows are economically significant in terms of their magnitudes. One standard deviation shocks to Chinese money growth and Chinese inflation produce an up to 10% shift in Taiwanese inflation across the different lag orders. Similar-size shifts in Taiwanese money growth and Taiwanese inflation follow a one standard deviation shock to the level of capital inflows. (The impulse responses were calculated using the Monte Carlo method with 100 repetitions and are robust to changes in the ordering of the variables.)

[15] The implication that Taiwanese inflation Granger-causes Taiwanese money growth but that Taiwanese money growth does not Granger-cause Taiwanese inflation matches the conclusions drawn by Makinen and Woodward (1989) and Quddus, Liu, and Butler (1989) based on their bivariate causality testing with these two variables. This is also consistent with the potential feedback from inflation to future rates of money growth in high inflation episodes emphasized by Sargent and Wallace (1973). Surprisingly, Lin and Wu (1989) reach opposite conclusions even though they, like us, control for the role played by the mainland Chinese variables in their causality testing. Lin and Wu's other finding, however, that Chinese inflation Granger-causes Taiwanese inflation remains in line with our results.

differential between mainland China and Taiwan – that is, the more money growth in mainland China exceeded that in Taiwan, the greater the extent to which this excess money seems to have flowed into Taiwan through capital inflows.

Concluding Comments

The late 1940s episode seems to be a textbook case of the exporting of inflation from the fading Nationalist regime on the mainland to their new power base on Taiwan. This process was facilitated by the August 1948 fixed rate of exchange for the new gold yuan against the Taiwanese *taipi* that left the *taipi* dramatically undervalued.[16] The endogeneity of Taiwan's money supply at the time naturally represents an extreme case where the domestic monetary authority loses all control over the rate of credit creation. Extraordinarily rapid rates of monetary expansion in mainland China coupled with the fixed exchange rate regime forced on Taiwan produced this outcome. Much lesser external pressure on mainland China today, as well as additional policy options for combatting inflationary pressures through such measures as bond sales and interest rate hikes, ensures that the scale of the danger faced by China today is obviously in no way comparable to Taiwan in the late 1940s. The basic mechanism laid bare in the earlier historical case does remain quite relevant, however, as reflected in the challenges faced by Chinese authorities' in offsetting the effects of the post-2000 rise in reserve inflows.

---

[16] The inflationary spiral in Taiwan continued into 1950 when it was finally stopped with the help of a deposit program designed to draw currency out of circulation and with the arrival of US aid (see, for example, the discussion and references in Burdekin and Whited, 2001).

Appendix Table A6.1. *Stationarity Test Results*

Variables	Phillips-Perron Statistics			Ljung-Box Q Statistics
	Lag Order 1	Lag Order 2	Lag Order 3	Up to Lag Order 12
Taiwanese Inflation	−3.47**	−3.36**	−3.39**	5.70**
Chinese Inflation	−4.33***	−4.34***	−4.42***	5.33**
Taiwanese Money Growth	−4.46***	−4.44***	−4.45***	2.57***
Chinese Money Growth	3.34	4.02	5.09	0.63***
Capital Inflow	−5.23***	−5.23***	−5.25***	2.21***

Notes: *** and ** denote that the null hypothesis of a unit root is rejected at the 99% and 95% levels, respectively, and the Ljung-Box Q statistics also reject non-stationarity at each individual lag order from 1 through 12.

SEVEN

WTO Challenges and China's Banking Sector Today

with Emily Kochanowicz[1]

[T]he State must take a dominant controlling share in the State-owned commercial banks in order to keep the economic lifeline of the country in state's hands and fending off financial risks.

(Chinese Premier Wen Jiabao, 2006)[2]

Introduction

When China's economic reforms began in 1978, government control over banking activities was absolute. The People's Bank of China functioned not only as a central bank but also as a loan-issuing bank. There was no real banking system in place outside the People's Bank and no established markets for bonds or stocks. However, the dismantling of the old "monobank" system has been followed by some dramatic changes following China's World Trade Organization (WTO) entry in December 2001. Joint-stock ownership was established in three of the largest state banks, coupled with foreign ownership stakes and the gradual opening of China's market to foreign banks. The government still exercises dominant control over the banking system, though, and the major banks required government injections of funds to shore up their balance sheets. This chapter considers the evolution of China's state-owned banks since the reforms of the 1990s and the actual and potential impact of China's WTO membership. Despite the improvements that have been made, we argue that freer foreign

[1] Emily Kochanowicz is an Associate with Houlihan Lokey Howard & Zukin Europe, Ltd. (ekochano@gmail.com). This chapter owes its origins to her senior thesis at Claremont McKenna College. The authors thank Jim Dorn for his exceptionally helpful comments on an earlier version of this chapter and are grateful to Nancy Tao for her extensive assistance in updating the data and to Yeqin Zeng for his translation help.
[2] Quoted in *People's Daily Online*, March 15, 2006c.

competition may be needed to bring about a more market-oriented lending system and promote adequate funding opportunities for China's rapidly growing private sector.

Overview of the Banking Landscape

After the People's Bank's responsibility for lending to state-owned enterprises was transferred to the newly formed Industrial and Commercial Bank of China (ICBC) in 1984, it gradually moved to exercise monetary control through such Western mechanisms as setting reserve requirements and managing credit funds (Chapter 4). Newly separated specialized state-owned commercial banks began directing lending activities in their particular sphere of influence – with ICBC, the China Construction Bank (CCB), and the Agricultural Bank of China (ABC) handling domestic transactions, and the Bank of China (BOC) specializing in international transactions. Commercialization of the big four state-owned commercial banks (SOCBs) was fostered by the creation of three new policy banks in 1994: the State Development Bank of China, the Import-Export Bank of China, and the Agricultural Development Bank of China. Policy loans were transferred to these new institutions while the big four banks now became accountable for their own profits and losses.[3]

A growing number of joint-stock commercial banks have also been established subject to People's Bank approval, with majority government ownership. Beginning with the Shenzhen Development Bank in 1991, minority share holdings of the joint-stock banks have been listed on Chinese stock exchanges (Fu and Heffernan, 2007, p. 37). They were allowed to expand nationwide in 1993. The largest such institution, the Bank of Communications, enjoyed a very successful initial public offering (IPO) on the Hong Kong Stock Exchange on June 23, 2005. The Bank of Communications was subsequently reclassified as a "large state-owned bank" in April 2007 – although, despite rapid growth, it remained at only approximately one-quarter the size of the others in terms of total assets (see Tucker and Anderlini, 2007). The following analysis is focused primarily on the largest, original four SOCBs for which longer, more consistent data series are available. The big four SOCBs still accounted for more than half of total assets in

---

[3] The actual assistance rendered by the new policy banks remained in question, however. Most of their bond issues aimed at supporting lending were actually being purchased by other banks, with the big four state-owned banks in the lead (Barth, Koepp, and Zhou, 2004).

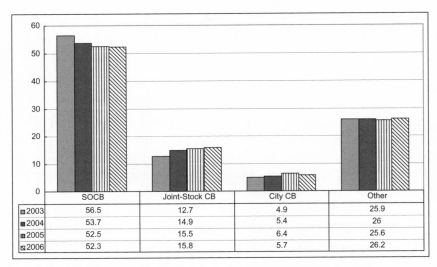

	SOCB	Joint-Stock CB	City CB	Other
2003	56.5	12.7	4.9	25.9
2004	53.7	14.9	5.4	26
2005	52.5	15.5	6.4	25.6
2006	52.3	15.8	5.7	26.2

Figure 7.1. Average Share of Total Industry Assets by Type of Commercial Bank, 2003–2006. *Source:* China Banking Regulatory Commission (CBRC website).

China's banking system during 2006, albeit with a 52.3% share compared to 56.5% in 2003 (Figure 7.1). The joint-stock banks and city commercial banks each registered gains in recent years, reaching 15.8% and 5.7% of total assets, respectively, in 2006. The SOCBs' share of total new loans issued did drop below 50% by 2005, however, with an overall share of 47%, compared to 23% for the joint-stock banks (including Bank of Communications). Rural credit cooperatives, city commercial banks, and three policy banks account for most remaining loan issuance (Figure 7.2).

Among the four main SOCBs, ICBC stands out as the biggest of the big, with over 30% of total SOCB assets, deposits, and loans at year-end 2005 (Table 7.1). The other three SOCBs were of approximately equivalent size in terms of assets and deposits but ABC had a proportionately larger share of loans (26.2%) and also considerably more branches than even ICBC. As discussed in more detail later, in 2007 ABC was the only SOCB yet to undergo restructuring and the only one not to be publicly listed. It stood in need of a substantial injection of funds before being a viable candidate for an IPO. Until quite recently, however, the other three SOCBs shared ABC's ongoing weak balance sheet and large percentage of nonperforming loans (NPLs). This situation stemmed from their common history of supporting China's largely loss-making state enterprise sector. Only in the second half of the 1990s did the government at last take steps to address the losses in the state enterprise sector, issuing $32.5 billion in bonds in 1998 to help

Table 7.1. *Relative Size of the Big Four State-Owned Banks, as of December 31, 2005*

Bank	Assets Billions of Yuan	Assets Percent of Total	Deposits Billions of Yuan	Deposits Percent of Total	Loans Billions of Yuan	Loans Percent of Total	Approximate Number of Branches
Agricultural Bank of China (ABC)	4,771.0	23.3	4,036.9	23.2	2,829.3	26.2	28,234
Bank of China (BOC)	4,742.8	23.2	3,703.8	21.3	2,235.0	20.7	11,618
China Construction Bank (CCB)	4,585.7	22.4	4,006.0	23.0	2,458.4	22.7	14,250
Industrial and Commercial Bank of China (ICBC)	6,373.8	31.1	5,660.5	32.5	3,289.6	30.4	18,870
TOTALS	20,473.3	100.0	17,407.2	100.0	10,812.3	100.0	72,972

Note: Loans are stated before allowance for impairment losses.
Source: Dobson and Kashyap (2006, p. 108); author's calculations.

recapitalize the four big SOCBs. The government also indicated that market discipline would begin playing at least a tentative role in the banking system. For the first time, a regional commercial bank, Hainan Development Bank, was closed by the People's Bank in June 1998 following a payments crisis.

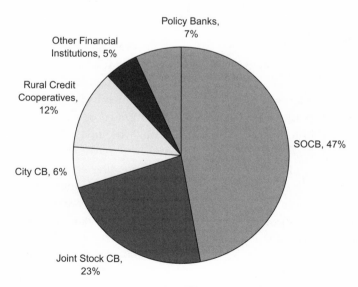

Figure 7.2. State-Owned Commercial Banks' Share of New Loans Issued in 2005. *Source:* People's Bank of China.

Table 7.2. *Nonperforming Loan Levels of the Big Four State-Owned Banks*

NPL%	2005	2004	2003	2002	2001	2000
BOC	4.6	5.1	15.9	22.4	27.5	26.5
CCB	3.8	3.7	9.1	15.4	19.4	19.9
ICBC	4.7	19.1	21.3	25.5	29.8	34.4
ABC	26.3	26.8	30.7	36.7	41.4	
SOCB aggregate	10.5	15.6	17.8	23.1	25.4	

Note: The NPL figures reflect the five-level reporting standard adopted in 1998.
Source: 2001–2005 data are as listed in Barth and Caprio (2007, p. 43) and the China Banking Regulatory Commission website (http://www.cbrc.gov.cn); 2000 figures are *Bankscope* data given by García-Herrero, Gavilá, and Santabárbara (2006, p. 350).

However, full repayment of foreign creditors and domestic depositors was guaranteed by the national government (Guo, 2004, p. 282).

The earlier financial weakness of the state enterprises has been well documented by Lardy (1998). Forced lending to these enterprises caused non-recoverable loans to continually build up on bank balance sheets, with vast levels remaining even after the 1998 bailout. To address this problem, a system of asset management companies (AMCs) was set up to absorb the SOCBs' NPLs and then package these loans for sale on the market. In this respect, their function was rather like that of the Resolution Trust Corporation, set up in 1989 to sell off the assets of defunct US savings and loan institutions, and continuing its operations until 1995. China's first AMC, China Cinda, was founded in Beijing on April 20, 1999, and three more AMCs were established later in the year. The system of AMCs had the twin goals of strengthening the banks' balance sheets while also reducing the state enterprises' debt burden. New oversight came from the China Banking Regulatory Commission (CBRC) in 2003. The AMCs disposed of an aggregate RMB 866.3 billion in nonperforming loans through the first quarter of 2006 – with an overall cash recovery rate of 20.8% (http://www.cbrc.gov.cn).

When consistent series on SOCB NPL ratios first became available in 2000, the lowest ratio was 19.9% for CCB – whereas BOC and ICBC reported 26.5% and 34.4%, respectively (see Table 7.2). The first available number for ABC, as of 2001, showed a 41.4% NPL ratio. All four banks fell well below the international capital adequacy standard of 8%. Each bank reported profit increases and lower NPL ratios from 2002 onward, however – with the reported aggregate NPL ratio down to just 8.20% of total loans as of March 31, 2007 – but the bulk of these improvements were achieved only after additional large government bailouts in 2003 and 2005. Moreover, external NPL estimates typically remain much higher than the official CBRC figures. For example, Setser (2006, p. 384) suggests that, for China's banking system as a whole, NPLs may have reached $US 470 billion in 2006 – representing 16.6% of all loans and 17.7% of China's GDP. There have also been fears that recent high lending rates, spurred in part by the liquidity-enhancing reserve inflows discussed in Chapter 4, may have given rise to further new NPL growth. If just 15% of the loans issued during the post-2002 lending boom ended up going bad, which would be considerably lower than the historical percentage under past lending booms,[4] this would suggest additional NPLs amounting to around 8% of China's GDP (Setser, 2006).

A key milestone and challenge for China's banking system was the provision for foreign banks being able to compete directly with domestic banks under the terms of China's WTO membership. Although China joined the WTO in December 2001, the WTO granted China a five-year "buffer period" ending in December 2006, prior to which foreign entry remained limited. The scope for foreign banks serving as an alternative source of capital for China's growing private sector was consequently delayed. Yet foreign financial institutions were allowed to purchase minority stakes in local banks even prior to China's December 2001 membership, beginning with smaller institutions but extending in 2005–2006 to the SOCBs themselves. Interest rate liberalization is being implemented (even though banks initially seemed to make relatively little use of the recent freedom to charge higher rates to weaker borrowers according to Podpiera, 2006) as the authorities seek to transition away from the old situation where deposit and loan rates were simply set by the People's Bank. Although it remains to be seen whether China's large state banks can successfully prevail as internationally competitive, independent financial institutions, CCB's 2005 IPO, and those of BOC and ICBC in 2006, were at first very well received.

The Changing Role of the Big Four State-Owned Banks

The four SOCBs had historically specialized lending practices that continue to be reflected in their loan portfolios to this day. For example, BOC has much more foreign exposure owing to its responsibility for a large share of China's foreign exchange business whereas ABC's loans still primarily support rural agricultural and industrial development. The SOCBs have,

---

[4] Lardy (2005a, p. 46) notes that, during the 1994–1996 downturn, 40% of the loans extended during the preceding 1989–1993 credit boom "become nonperforming, even on the rather lax loan classification criteria prevailing at the time" (see also Ma, 2006; Podpiera, 2006).

however, become less exclusive over time in the face of new entrants. For example, after BOC lost its monopoly of the foreign exchange business, its market share dropped to two-fifths in 1996 (Lardy, 1998, p. 65) and the bank responded by broadening its financial role and developing its branch network to encourage regional deposit collection. With these adaptations, BOC became China's third largest bank in asset size, a position that it maintained into 2005 (Table 7.1). ABC, BOC, and CCB have been operating in their current form since 1979, with CCB being granted the primary role of funding new investment projects. ICBC was founded only in 1984 but, from the outset, became the largest SOCB in terms of asset size. It subsequently grew at an extraordinary rate, increasing its assets by 460% between 1989 and 2001,[5] and achieving registered capital of RMB 248 billion by the time it was transformed into a joint-stock company in October 2005.

Until 1998, the central government incorporated the four SOCBs into its credit plan to finance its state-owned enterprises (SOEs). This move left the SOCBs with no real scope for taking into account the creditworthiness of policy borrowers or questioning the loans they were directed to make for politically motivated projects. The practice of assigning loan quotas to every region under each year's credit plan further prevented the allocation of credit from being determined by market forces. For example, regions with low growth potential tended to receive relatively large amounts of loans because of their dependence on SOEs. Such forced emphasis on the weaker economic areas was hardly conducive to determining loans on the basis of standard risk and return criteria. Although the credit plan techni-cally became "voluntary" in 1998, BOC in 2000, for example, deliberately increased its lending capacity so that its loan portfolio was more in line with the state's economic policy. This increase included the granting of substantially more infrastructure loans even though BOC infrastructure loans already accounted for 45% of its portfolio in 1999 (*China Daily*, Feb-ruary 11, 2000).

Under the credit plan, policy lending quotas had been set without any reference to the banks' ability to meet the quotas. In high-growth areas where deposits were high, bank lending options were constrained and they did not have sufficient interest income to pay depositors. To make payments they kept large (interest-bearing) excess reserves with the People's Bank. Low growth areas, meanwhile, tended to have high quotas that the banks could not meet through their deposits alone. Therefore, they had to turn to the People's Bank for funds, leaving the central bank redistributing funds from

---

[5] *Almanac of China's Finance and Banking,* 2002, p. 435.

high-deposit areas to low-deposit areas. The old central bank role as the provider of SOE working capital needs (Chapter 3) was therefore simply being carried on indirectly by using the banking system as a conduit for these same central bank funds.

In a testament to the forced nature of SOCB lending during the days of the credit plan, ABC, for example, did not even establish a preferred creditor list until 1999 – at which time the then-president of ABC stated that, for the first time, "ABC will pay more attention to the quality of the loans than the quantity" (*China Daily*, January 21, 1999). This change, however, did not mean that the SOCBs were entirely freed from government pressure for high levels of loans to spur growth. Indeed, the "new" ABC credit list still reflected the long-standing government emphasis on putting livestock farmers in a position to consume excess grain, thereby supporting higher agricultural product prices. Moreover, the historical burden of prior bad loans plus ongoing protection of many SOEs continued to hamper full commercialization of the four major banks. Even in 1998, little was done to increase accountability of the SOEs, whose nonrepayment of SOCB loans was the fundamental cause of the whole NPL problem. With the banks lacking the authority to independently cut off new lending to defaulting SOEs, they were essentially forced to make new loans to cover the defaulted interest payments, reporting phantom interest profits in the process. The Ministry of Finance continued to forbid increased loan loss provisions until 2000. Its reluctance stemmed from the fact that, as such loan loss provisions are deducted from profits, they reduce the amount of taxable income that the ministry can collect. As recently as 1997, banks were allowed to classify only 1% of their portfolio as NPLs. Thus, the government not only forced the banks to make bad loans but also would not let them write them off.

Although almost all domestic banks in China are still at least partially state-owned, only the four largest were ever part of the credit plan. The smaller banks historically were able to achieve greater profitability and efficiency levels because their loan portfolios contained more private or collective enterprises. The SOCBs continued to feature relatively low-profit efficiency over the 1994–2003 period (Berger, Hasan, and Zhou, 2008) while weaker SOCB prudential standards were reflected in lower excess reserves, lower deposit/loan ratios, and higher loan/asset ratios than for the smaller joint-stock banks, for example (Jia, 2008).[6] In the past, the government had deliberately restricted the smaller banks' growth so that they would not pull

---

[6] Lower efficiency levels for SOCBs than for the joint-stock banks are also identified by Fu and Heffernan (2007); Shih, Zhang, and Liu (2007); and Ariff and Can (2008).

deposit resources away from the specialized banks as they commercialized. Berger, Hasan, and Zhou (2008) identify benefits from the more recent government move to permit minority foreign ownership in the banks, however – leaving at least the hope that similar benefits will accrue from the prospective fuller opening up of the SOCBs to foreign ownership.

The earlier, pre-WTO exclusion of foreign banks from the domestic deposit and loan markets reflected the government's fears that more efficient foreign institutions would threaten the SOCBs. WTO entry essentially forced the authorities to commercialize the banks, however, so that they could be in a position to survive the new competition.[7] Although burdensome restrictions delayed the benefits of including more competitive, better-managed foreign banks in China's financial markets, the opening-up process accelerated considerably after the partial IPO of BOC in Hong Kong in 2002. By 2006 foreign investors had taken strategic positions in seventeen major Chinese banks in addition to their stakes in BOC, CCB, and ICBC (Ernst & Young, 2006, p. 11). The more promising banking landscape of the 2000s, however, would scarcely have been attainable without the reforms, and NPL reductions, initiated in the 1990s.

The 1997–1998 Reforms[8]

The SOE Bankruptcy Law of 1997, which preceded the abolition of the credit plan, seemed like an initial step in the right direction. If only profitable enterprises were to remain open, the share of profitable investments available to the banks looked set to rise as demand from inefficient borrowers fell away. Unfortunately, although the 15th Party Congress boldly defined new bankruptcy laws, enforcement remained an open question and no regulatory body was established to implement the law. Closing SOEs remained a very difficult and unpopular step because of the wide range of welfare support provided to their employees. As a result, SOEs have, in practice, typically been pushed to either go public or merge with healthier counterparts.[9] Nevertheless, the rate of reduction in total SOE employment

---

[7] For details on the evolution of China's banking laws, and its WTO commitments, see Barth et al. (2007).

[8] For analysis and discussion of the earlier policy changes and other developments, see, for example, Lardy (1998) and Park and Sehrt (2001).

[9] This pressure is somewhat reminiscent of the encouragement given to mergers between defunct savings and loans institutions and healthier partners in the United States during the 1980s. The abrupt 1989 cancelling of the special accounting benefits required to make such transactions tolerable to the acquiring institutions prompted lawsuits against the federal government that continue, with some success, to this day.

did accelerate after 1997 (Bajona and Chu, 2004, p. 9), with employment falling by approximately 40% – or 45 million – between 1996 and 2006 (Bergsten et al., 2006, p. 24). However, the intended liberalizing effects of the ensuing January 1998 lifting of the credit plan were rudely interrupted by the Asian financial crisis. The government demanded huge increases in lending to help offset the negative effects of the crisis, launching the Fixed Asset Investment Program that involved boosting the allocation of funds to SOEs through the SOCBs (Lardy, 1999, p. 19). At RMB 1 trillion, the 1998 loan targets, for example, were 25% above 1997 levels (Lardy, 1999, p. 20), thereby rather negating any real freedom for the SOCBs to get their own liability ratios under control.

There were some important increases in SOCB operational freedoms under the 1998 reforms, however, and bank managers were permitted to cut costs by laying off excess employees and closing redundant branches. Whereas previously the government always dictated the assignment of officials to bank posts, more and more control over hiring began being delegated to the banks directly. The banks were also able to make some headway in controlling their cost inefficiencies and improving profitability. Another significant development was the restructuring of the People's Bank's branch network, with its former thirty-one major branches being cut back in November 1998 to just nine high-level offices controlled from Beijing. This was intended to make the People's Bank "less vulnerable to provincial government pressure on provincial branches to expand bank credit to fund local projects" (Chiu and Lewis, 2006, p. 200), thereby, in turn, easing the pressure on the corresponding local SOCB branches.[10] Finally, in 1998, the NPL classification changed from the old four-level Chinese standard to a five-level accrual basis, similar to the international standard. This change eventually allowed for greater transparency in the market, even though it took some time for the SOCBs to retroactively report NPL data using the new classification. BOC, for example, initially reported its December 1999 NPL ratio at just 15% under the old system before disclosing the 39% ratio arising under the new system (*Asian Banker Journal,* June 19, 2001). The new system was not fully implemented until July 2001 (Guo, 2004, p. 277).

In 1998 the Ministry of Finance issued RMB 270 billion ($US 32.5 billion) in special bonds to recapitalize the SOCBs. This recapitalization effort, in itself, however, did nothing to stop the source of the nonperforming loans.

---

[10] Earlier limitations on relending by local People's Bank branches had been imposed in 1994 in an attempt to rein in excessive loan creation driven by pressure from local government officials (Park and Sehrt, 2001, p. 618).

As a result, the capital infusion that brought the banks closer to the 8% international standard for capital adequacy had to be followed by further substantial recapitalizations in 2003 and after. The 1998 bond recapitalization worked to raise total bank capital from RMB 208 billion to RMB 478 billion, while the 2003 infusion added another RMB 370 billion. At that time, $US 45 billion of China's official foreign exchange reserves were drawn upon to further recapitalize BOC and CCB in preparation for their IPOs. Yet another $US 15 billion in foreign exchange reserves was employed in recapitalizing ICBC in 2005. NPLs totaling RMB 705 billion were transferred to AMCs in May–June 2005 and, with essentially the full book value of the NPLs being replaced by new cash or by claims on the AMCs or the government itself, the total cost of the latest bailout likely exceeded $US 80 billion (see Podpiera, 2006, p. 8).

The Operations of the Asset Management Companies

The first AMC, China Cinda, was charged with purchasing CCB's bad loans and initially took in RMB 250 billion in NPLs in April 1999. The other three AMCs, China Orient, China Great Wall, and China Huarong, were established in October 1999 to manage the NPLs of BOC, ABC, and ICBC, respectively. The AMCs are state-owned but nevertheless enjoy independent legal status. When AMCs take over a loan, the enterprise in question is to pay dividends to the AMC instead of paying interest to the bank. Meanwhile, the bank receives an interest-paying bond for the face value of the debt. The AMC then seeks to recover the principal value by either an IPO or by transferring the ownership. In September 1999 Cinda undertook China's first ever debt-for-equity swap, offering a novel approach to addressing the debt restructuring problem. Previously, debt-equity swaps had not been viewed as a viable option because of limitations on how much equity banks could hold. Furthermore, no secondary loan workout market existed. Although the AMCs provided the needed secondary market, however, doubts remain as to the true value of their acquired equity holdings. Typically, repurchase agreements have limited the potential returns accruing to the AMCs on the upside, whereas AMCs still remain vulnerable to partial, or total, loss if poor SOE performance should lead the SOE managers, or associated local governments, to default.[11]

---

[11] McIver (2005, p. 21), in characterizing such SOE equity positions as risky subordinated bonds with attached and embedded options, concludes that their value cannot be expected to measure up to the market value of more standard equity holdings.

Each of the AMCs was granted RMB 10 billion in assets from the Ministry of Finance to run its operations and commercial banks were targeted to aid in funding. Ultimately the Ministry of Finance was to be responsible for their losses but the AMCs were monitored by the People's Bank prior to the 2003 establishment of the CBRC. AMC operations were restricted to more recent loans. No loans extended prior to 1996 were transferable because banks were not officially held responsible for their own profits and losses until the passage of the Commercial Banking Law of 1995. Moreover, only loans classified as doubtful could be put forward and no loans that were seen as a total loss were eligible for transfer onto the balance sheets of the AMCs. Nevertheless, dramatic initial NPL reductions were achieved. BOC's transfer of RMB 232.9 billion to Orient AMC in fiscal 2000 reduced its reported NPL level from 39% to 29% between December 31, 1999 and December 31, 2000 (*Asian Banker Journal*, June 19, 2001). And the CCB's initial disposal of RMB 250 billion in NPLs was followed by the auctioning off of further RMB 8 billion and RMB 4 billion loan parcels in 2002. In 2000 Cinda AMC boasted that it converted $US 20 billion of debt into equity holdings in 392 companies (*Almanac of China's Finance and Banking*, 2002), thereby reducing the debt-to-asset ratio of these companies from 70% to 40% (Clifford, Balfour, and Webb, 2001, p. 50).

In all, the AMCs began with RMB 1.4 trillion in NPLs to work out, equivalent to approximately 8% of China's GDP. They paid for these NPLs with a 2.25% ten-year bond for 83% of the total, paying cash for the remaining 17% (García-Herrero, Gavilá, and Santabárbara, 2006, p. 315). This arrangement had the effect of adding an interest-paying asset plus substantial cash to the SOCBs' balance sheets at the face value of the transfer.[12] However, the actual effectiveness of AMC operations remains somewhat unclear. In 1999, for example, the AMCs took over $US 160 billion in debt but resolved only 15% of this total. Moreover, embezzlement and accounting malpractices, both within the state enterprises and the state banks that provided them with loans, compounded the scale of the problem. The initial rate of return from AMC operations was confined to between 15% and 25% and the overall cash recovery ratio remained around 20% into 2006 according to CBRC reports (http://www.cbrc.gov.cn). Actual rates have varied greatly across the different AMCs, with Cinda AMC consistently achieving the highest recovery rates (31.56% in first quarter 2006) and Great Wall AMC consistently

---

[12] Subsequent asset transfers were handled via auction, however, with the AMCs no longer restricted to dealing with just their original "partner" bank but able to compete freely for all bank assets.

doing much worse than the others (10.28% in first quarter 2006).[13] Whereas Cinda was initially linked to CCB, Great Wall apparently continued to suffer from its ties to ABC, by far the weakest of the SOCBs.

Needless to say, these recovery rates imply that the AMCs have been operating with substantial losses, given that they purchased the NPLs from the SOCBs at no less than 50% of face value. This situation leaves the AMCs exposed to large accounting losses and Huarong AMC Vice President Ding Zhongchi explicitly called "on the government to provide financial help to cover the losses arising from the disposal of NPLs" (Guerrera and McGregor, 2005, p. 19).[14] The AMCs may well need a government bailout themselves to pay the principal on the bonds issued to the SOCBs in return for the NPLs – and there is already some doubt as to whether all the interest payments have actually been made (García-Herrero, Gavilá, and Santabárbara, 2006, p. 326–327). Indeed, McIver (2005, p. 15) suggests that the "AMCs represent a serious default risk to the SOCBs in their own right."

Although the AMCs have made efforts to attract the interest of foreign investors, sales to foreign entities have accounted for only a relatively small portion of the AMCs' overall NPL disposal. In the first NPL auction open to foreign investors, Huarong AMC succeeded in selling $US 1.2 billion worth of NPLs to a group led by Morgan Stanley. The magnitude of this "success" is rather qualified, however, by the fact that the actual proceeds realized from the sale were only $US 100 million, meaning that Huarong got just 8 cents on the dollar (Johnson, 2002, p. 26). Morgan Stanley did go on to establish a joint venture with Huarong to reorganize debt and to employ and train Huarong employees on how to work out loans independently. And Huarong later took the lead in aggressively competing with foreign investors in NPL auctions by the other three AMCs – as well as announcing ambitious plans to transform itself into an investment bank that could extend into brokerage activities and other financial services (Guerrera and McGregor, 2005). This transformation may be difficult unless Huarong first receives an injection of government funds to cover the large accounting losses undoubtedly sustained from its core NPL business – which

---

[13] In the face of an apparent slowing in the pace of NPL disposal, Cinda, having pioneered China's first debt-equity swap in 1999, announced innovative plans to issue the nation's first NPL-backed securities in 2006. It was hoped that the securitization of around RMB 4.75 billion in bad loans acquired from BOC would pave the way for more offerings of this type and help boost overall NPL disposal rates. Cinda's securities were backed by approximately RMB 21 billion in NPLs (see Yeh, 2006, p. 30).

[14] The initial underfunding of the four AMCs was reflected in initial capital of just RMB 40 billion (or $US 4.8 billion) for dealing with $US 480 billion in NPLs (Nanto and Sinha, 2002, p. 484).

would only add to the already high burden of bolstering the SOCB balance sheets.

The size of the NPLs transferred to the AMCs from the SOCBs certainly remains quite out of proportion to the funds realized as a result of their operations. Given an approximate 20% reported overall cash recovery rate, combined with the fact that only about 50% of the loans transferred had been restructured or disposed of through 2005, the true yield might more accurately be stated as 10% (García-Herrero, Gavilá, and Santabárbara, 2006, p. 315). Such low returns lend some support to early criticisms that the AMCs were doing little more then redistributing the NPL problem (Clifford, 2002, p. 18). Government-funded capital injections and not the AMCs operations themselves have certainly been the dominant factor in the improvement effected in SOCB balance sheets since 1998. Indeed, Ma (2006) estimates that total restructuring costs may have reached RMB 4,047 billion by the end of 2005 – after taking into account not only the losses on the NPL transfers but also SOCB equity write-downs and carving out of doubtful loans by the People's Bank, other costs born by bank customers and foreign investors, RMB 500 billion for city commercial banks, and RMB 35 billion for the Bank of Communications in 2004.

Future costs could be significantly exacerbated by new additions to the stock of NPLs, with investment in fixed assets that approached 50% of GDP in mid-2006 raising the "risk that wasteful investment could end up bloating the bad-loan portfolios of Chinese banks" (Browne, 2006).[15] It is, at this stage, unclear that the latest round of recapitilizations represents an end and not simply part of an ongoing process.[16] Lardy (2005a, p. 46) actually suggests that much of the existing government-funded capital infusions to the banking system could be "washed out by the new nonperforming loans that emerge in 2005–07." Any such developments could pose a real threat to China's economic stability, with Bergsten et al. (2006, p. 38) concluding that:

Banks cannot continue to absorb state capital at anything like the pace of recent years if China's fiscal position is to be sustained.

[15] CBRC Deputy-Chairman Jiang Dingzhi went on record stating that the situation was under control and that the regulatory agency had effectively "required the banks to change their attitude from pursuing asset growth and excessive expansion, and asked them to operate under capital constraints" (see McGregor, 2006b). However, the continued rapid pace of actual loan growth appeared to belie such restraint.

[16] Podpiera (2006) finds that SOCB lending was still being driven primarily by the availability of funds rather than by relative enterprise performance levels over the 1997–2004 period – pointing to an ongoing "system in which many investment decisions are based less on the price of credit than the pursuit of economic growth" (McGregor, 2006b, p. 6).

Did State-Owned Bank Behavior Really Change After 1998?

The old credit plan prescribed an essentially redistributive function for bank lending. This is in keeping with Park and Sehrt's (2001) finding that the banks did indeed lend more to poorer provinces, *ceteris paribus*, during the pre-1998 period. A more market-based approach, however, would almost certainly imply lending more to the stronger provinces. Park and Sehrt (2001) also find evidence that, again for the pre-1998 period, the SOCBs tended to allocate more funds to provinces where SOEs accounted for a larger share of provincial GDP. One way of addressing the question of whether overall loan allocation by the SOCBs did, in fact, change after the abolition of the national credit plan is to look at historical data on SOCB loan distributions. Table 7.3 divides China's thirty-one provinces, municipalities, and administrative regions into top, middle, and bottom tiers according to each year's per capita GDP of each region. The data suggest that loan allocation to the richest provinces remained relatively stable since 1994 for ABC and BOC, with ABC averaging close to 50% for this group and BOC near 65%. Meanwhile, ABC, not surprisingly given its rural base, continued to allocate the largest share of loans to the poorest provinces – typically providing more than 22% to this group.

However, more obvious changes are evident in the cases of CCB and ICBC. Each of these banks evinces an increase in lending to the richest provinces, and a decrease in lending to the poorest provinces, over the sample period. This behavior may reflect more market-based lending after the loosening of the old quota allocation controls. CCB features the most pronounced change in behavior, with its loan allocation to the wealthiest regions rising from 45.9% in 1994 to 57.9% in 2005 while the allocation to the poorest regions fell from 24.9% to 19.1% over that same period. Overall changes in lending patterns have remained quite mild, though, and the premise that SOCB lending may still not be in-line with the opportunities available in the richer regions is supported by Podpiera's (2006) finding that the big four banks lost market share to other financial institutions in those provinces featuring more profitable SOEs.

Another aspect of the 1998 reforms was a targeted maximum loan-to-deposit ratio of 0.75. The evolution of SOCB loan-to-deposit ratios shown in Figure 7.3 suggests that, while the ratio did decline for each of the SOCBs after 1998, this represents a continuation of a declining trend evident from the beginning of the data sample in 1994. Loan-to-deposit ratios do certainly converge to more similar levels by 2001, however, typically remaining within a 0.8 to 0.6 range from 2001 to 2005 – after ranging between 0.8 and 1.2 in 1994. ABC was the last to achieve the 0.75 target for its loan-to-deposit

Table 7.3. *Loan Allocation of the Big Four State-Owned Banks*

ABC	2005	2004	2003	2002	2001	2000	1999	1998	1997	1996	1995	1994
High Tier	52.3%	52.4%	52.2%	52.8%	50.9%	50.2%	48.2%	47.2%	53.4%	49.1%	47.5%	47.3%
Mid Tier	24.1%	24.7%	24.0%	21.0%	25.1%	27.0%	29.1%	29.7%	26.3%	31.1%	26.6%	28.7%
Low Tier	23.6%	22.9%	23.8%	26.2%	24.0%	22.8%	22.7%	23.1%	20.3%	19.8%	25.9%	24.0%
BOC	**2005**	**2004**	**2003**	**2002**	**2001**	**2000**	**1999**	**1998**	**1997**	**1996**	**1995**	**1994**
High Tier	–	66.5%	64.3%	64.2%	64.8%	67.4%	62.8%	63.0%	63.0%	63.0%	63.8%	62.2%
Mid Tier	–	19.5%	21.2%	20.8%	18.8%	20.6%	23.3%	23.3%	23.2%	23.3%	20.2%	22.2%
Low Tier	–	14.0%	14.5%	15.0%	16.4%	12.1%	13.9%	13.7%	13.8%	13.7%	16.0%	15.6%
CCB	**2005**	**2004**	**2003**	**2002**	**2001**	**2000**	**1999**	**1998**	**1997**	**1996**	**1995**	**1994**
High Tier	57.9%	61.4%	57.8%	58.4%	59.6%	58.8%	56.5%	54.0%	53.1%	50.9%	49.3%	45.9%
Mid Tier	23.0%	21.0%	21.4%	21.8%	20.4%	22.5%	23.9%	26.3%	26.8%	29.7%	25.9%	29.2%
Low Tier	19.1%	17.5%	20.8%	19.8%	20.0%	18.7%	19.6%	19.8%	20.0%	19.4%	24.8%	24.9%
ICBC	**2005**	**2004**	**2003**	**2002**	**2001**	**2000**	**1999**	**1998**	**1997**	**1996**	**1995**	**1994**
High Tier	–	57.8%	58.1%	56.3%	57.9%	57.6%	54.9%	54.0%	53.8%	51.9%	51.9%	47.7%
Mid Tier	–	23.3%	22.6%	23.2%	22.5%	24.6%	26.0%	26.8%	27.0%	28.3%	25.1%	29.4%
Low Tier	–	18.9%	19.3%	20.5%	19.6%	17.8%	19.1%	19.1%	19.2%	19.8%	23.0%	22.9%

Notes: China's thirty-one provinces, municipalities, and administrative regions are divided into three tiers according to their relative rankings based on each year's provincial nominal per capita GDP.

Foreign currency loans and deposits are included from 2000 with the $US amounts converted into RMB using the 8.28 fixed exchange rate that applied through 2004. The annual average exchange rate value was used for 2005.

Source: Almanac of China's Finance and Banking, Beijing, 1995–2006.

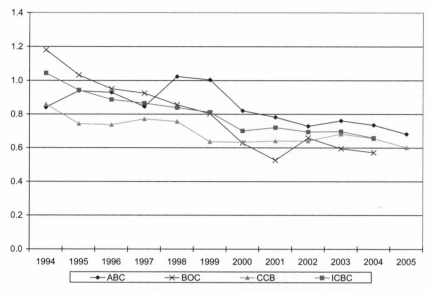

Figure 7.3. Loan-to-Deposit Ratios of the Big Four State-Owned Commercial Banks.

ratio, reaching this goal only in 2005, and also demonstrates the smallest change over the post-1994 period. Meanwhile, the most dramatic drop was enjoyed by BOC, with a halving of its loan-to-deposit ratio between 1994 and 2004. These data suggest that, even though changes in loan allocation across regions seem to have been more incremental in nature for most of the SOCBs, a meaningful change in total lending rates occurred since the mid-1990s and the ending of the credit plan. This result is consistent with Jia's (2008) empirical findings that identify an improving trend in SOCB loan/asset and deposit/loan ratios over the 1994–2004 interval.

Burdekin and Tao (2007) offer some additional empirical evidence on the extent to which the overall decline in loan-to-deposit ratios over the 1994–2005 period may have been influenced by such factors as the concentration of SOEs and the level of provincial prosperity as well as the banks' overall intake of deposits. This study allows for variations in bank behavior by province as well as over time. There is some support for CCB and ICBC being inclined to lend more to richer provinces over the sample period while lending by ABC and CCB may have become less redistributive over time. In ABC's case, however, evidence of continued SOE lending implies that any evolution in bank business practices remained, at best, incomplete during the 1994–2005 sample period. Of the four banks, only CCB evinced declining sensitivity to the SOE variable over time.[17] The empirical results also suggested that higher levels of funds on deposit were associated with higher loan-to-deposit ratios and that the importance of deposits increased over time for two of the four SOCBs. The apparent absence of more broad-based changes in SOCB behavior is itself qualified by the fact that the sample period largely predated the transition of three of the four SOCBs to joint-stock companies.

Meanwhile, another unfortunate area of constancy after the 1998 reforms has been an ongoing, near-total exclusion of private sector borrowers from SOCB loans. Although private sector firms' share of China's gross domestic product had been above 30% since 2002, less than 2% of total short-term bank credits were allocated to private Chinese firms as recently as 2003 (Huang, 2006). At the same time, state-owned banks were still allocating 75% of their short-term loans to SOEs (Chiu and Lewis, 2006, p. 208). This unbalanced loan allocation had SOEs and collective enterprises still receiving nearly half of total corporate loans despite contributing little more than a quarter of GDP (Barth and Caprio, 2007). The benefits of such SOE funding are doubtful in light of the SOEs' lower-than-average productivity (Dobson and Kashyap, 2006), in turn making it unsurprising that provinces with greater SOE shares in industrial production have, on average, consistently experienced lower growth rates in the past (Phillips and Kunrong, 2005). Meanwhile, private companies, especially those of small to medium size, often seem to have been shut out of the formal lending market altogether (Zhu, 2002) – forcing them to rely disproportionately on other financial channels such as trade credits (Ge and Qiu, 2007).

Besides trade credits, private entrepreneurs in China have utilized a wide variety of informal financing practices including "rotating credit associations, grassroots credit cooperatives, and even full-service yet unsanctioned private banks" (Tsai, 2002, p. 3). Although the costs of such informal finance methods undoubtedly vary widely, curb market rates at triple the prevailing standard bank lending rate have been observed (Huang, 2006). In practice, self-financing and retained profits appear to have remained the chief source of finance for Chinese private enterprises, however (see Chiu and Lewis,

---

[17] Factional ties almost certainly complicate the relationship between SOE concentration and bank lending. Shih (2004) draws attention, for example, to the consistently lower loan-to-deposit ratios for the province of Liaoning relative to the neighboring province of Jilin during 1978–1998. Even though Liaoning had a high concentration of SOEs, the greater availability of funds to Jilin may be explained by its leaders' much closer ties to the central government elite. Ties to the ruling party likely remained an important influence on bank lending even after the 1998 reforms (cf. Dobson and Kashyap, 2006, pp. 126–127).

2006, pp. 213–214). Besides SOCB discrimination against private borrowers, another factor in the near-zero reliance on traditional bank loans could be a simple inability to meet the banks' collateral and credit standards. Given the abysmally poor repayment record of many SOE borrowers, however, this latter explanation would, at best, smack of a double standard. On the other hand, it is possible that private entrepreneurs are reluctant to expose their businesses to official scrutiny owing to concerns about revealing information on the nature of the enterprise or its true level of earnings (Chiu and Lewis, 2006, pp. 216–218) – as well as possible exposure to informal levies, or even outright demands for bribes, by local government officials (Bai, Lu, and Tao, 2006, p. 617).

Protection of private property was not even formally included in China's constitution until 2004. Bai, Lu, and Tao (2006) conclude that, based on the results of a survey conducted in 2000, lack of formal protection of private property played a key role in limiting access to bank loans. Access to bank loans appeared to be significantly boosted by political participation and philanthropic activities, however, suggesting that political connections may well remain as important as ever in China. Another drawback for private borrowers has been the fact that banks had only very limited scope for charging higher interest rates to less established borrowers, giving them little incentive to give smaller enterprises, whether private or public, a chance to borrow funds. In this respect, the greater freedoms offered to banks under the 2004 interest rate liberalization measures seem to have had some initial positive effects, giving rise to "a new and growing 'fat tail' of smaller corporate customers" (Anderson, 2006a, p. 245). Lending to small companies by China's top ten listed banks reportedly expanded by 15% in 2006, and even larger increases of 26% and 72% were seen for CCB and ICBC, respectively.[18] Still, rightly or wrongly, the perception that the SOCBs are simply not interested in private borrowers may be hard to shake off. Consider, for example, the views rather forcefully expressed by a Chinese business owner surveyed by Tsai (2002, p. 2):

A state bank wouldn't give me a loan if Chairman Mao himself rose from the dead and told them to give me one!

Foreign Competition, Public Listing, and WTO Entry

Although banking inefficiencies and distortions appear to have diminished under the reforms of the 1990s and after, it is clear that China's banking

---

[18] Comtex News Network, May 14, 2007.

and financial institutions still have a long way to go to match the more-established systems in place in much of the West. Guariglia and Poncet (2006) suggest, however, that China's large levels of foreign direct investment (FDI) have played a significant role in helping insulate the economy's growth rates from financial distortions. Guariglia and Poncet (2006, p. 20) conclude that

> private firms, which are generally discriminated against by the local financial system, might be able to use foreign joint-ventures as sources of finance, and might consequently achieve higher productivity and growth rates. FDI could therefore provide an explanation for why ... China is a counter-example to the findings of the finance-growth literature, being characterized by malfunctioning financial institutions and phenomenal growth rates.

Since China's 2001 WTO entry, increasing amounts of this FDI have actually been channeled into the banking system itself. The sheer size of China's deposit market acts as a magnet in this regard. Despite declines in early 2007 that appeared to reflect the attractiveness of China's stock markets (see Chapter 8), December 2007 household deposits stood at just under RMB 18 trillion – or approximately $US 2.5 trillion. The first case of partial foreign ownership predated WTO membership, with the Asian Development Bank's purchase of a stake in China's Everbright Bank in 1997. In December 2001, HSBC bought a piece of the Bank of Shanghai quickly followed in 2002 by Citigroup, who bought a 5% stake in Shanghai Pudong Development Bank. Pudong and Shenzhen offered test cases in which foreign banks were granted access to domestic markets, while by no means dominating them. More complete nationwide access to Chinese markets was provided, in theory, with legislation that allowed foreign banks to offer a full range of services to local customers as of December 2006. The burdensome requirements imposed by this legislation, which forced such foreign banks to incorporate locally and barred them from accepting deposits under RMB 1 million in the absence of a local subsidiary, however, suggests that the authorities still felt the need to buffer the domestic banks against foreign competition (Dickie and Tucker, 2006, p. 1).[19]

China's 2001 WTO membership did seem to be associated with a welcome shift in central government rhetoric toward outwardly encouraging bank profitability. More importantly, the authorities set out specific guidelines for future progress, stating that the SOCBs should lower their NPL levels by at least 2% to 3% a year so that NPLs would be down to 15% by the end of 2005.

---

[19] As of year-end 2005, although 70 foreign banks were operating 238 branches in China, they still accounted for just 0.55% of total renminbi loans (Dickie and Tucker, 2006).

Table 7.4. *Bank of China and China Construction Bank after the 2003 Recapitalization*

	BOC	CCB	2004 Target	2005 Target	2007 Target
Return on assets	0.6	0.9	–	0.6	≈ 1.0
Return on equity	10.0	17.3	–	11.0	≥ 13.0
Cost/income ratio	40.0	39.2	–	35–45	35–45
NPL/loan ratio	5.1	3.9	3–5	3–5	3–5
Capital adequacy	10.0	11.3	≥ 8.0	≥ 8.0	≥ 8.0
NPL coverage	68.0	70.0	–	60–80	> 60–80

Source: Podpiera (2006, p. 5).

Table 7.2 shows the overall progress achieved in NPL levels between 1999 and 2005. Meanwhile, the 2003 recapitalization of BOC and CCB was accompanied by strengthened corporate governance and provisions for qualified external auditing and oversight. The targeted NPL to total loan ratio of 3% to 5% for 2004 was met by CCB and essentially achieved by BOC – while both banks achieved a capital-asset ratio above 8% (see Table 7.4).[20] Both banks also became joint-stock companies with independent directors. On May 16, 2006, the CBRC served notice that it expected the SOCBs to maintain NPL levels below 5% going forward. NPL ratios below this threshold have been realized recently but only in the immediate aftermath of the 2003 and 2005 recapitalizations of BOC, CCB, and ICBC.[21]

CCB achieved an NPL level of just 3.9% in 2004 – and 3.8% in 2005 – thanks to its major 2003 recapitalization, compared to the 15% that the government had itself projected in 2002. CCB also drastically increased its NPL write-offs and was particularly aggressive in disposing of bad debts through Cinda and diversifying its loan base, actually achieving control of a majority of the mortgage market in Shanghai. The newfound strength of CCB's balance sheet made possible its successful IPO on the Hong Kong market in October 2005. Earlier in 2005, Bank of America acquired an 8.67% ownership share (Ernst & Young, 2006, p. 11).

---

[20] There was also improved return on equity, especially for CCB – previously none of the SOCBs had managed to record a return on equity of even 5% over the 2001–2003 period (Thomas and Ji, 2006).

[21] There is also the question of just how many additional dubious "special mention" loans may turn into future NPLs. For example, 12.7% of BOC's loans were classified as special mention in 2005 – more than double the level of acknowledged NPLs (*Financial Times*, May 12, 2006b).

Meanwhile, BOC prepared for its eventual full Hong Kong listing (garnering $US 9.73 billion in May 2006) by first raising $US 2.8 billion in selling a 25% stake in its Hong Kong operations in the first IPO of a major state-owned bank on July 26, 2002. BOC hired Goldman Sachs to manage the process, and the 2002 partial IPO was pushed through quickly – only one year after BOC's ten subsidiaries in Hong Kong were merged together and even amid a banking scandal and a sagging market.[22] In August–September 2005 an investor group including Royal Bank of Scotland and Merrill Lynch invested $US 3.1 billion for a 10% stake in BOC – and additional holdings were acquired by Singapore's Temasek Holdings (one of the sovereign wealth funds discussed in Chapter 2) at 10%, UBS at 1.8%, and the Asian Development Bank at 0.24% (Ernst & Young, 2006, p. 11). Interest in the 2006 IPO was spurred by the earlier share price gains of 50% and 100% enjoyed through mid-May 2006 by CCB and Bank of Communications shareholders, respectively, since those banks' own 2005 Hong Kong share flotations.

ICBC actually hired Solomon Smith Barney as early as 2001 in order to begin merging its branches and preparing its own Hong Kong listings for an IPO (Clifford, Balfour, and Webb, 2001, p. 50). Its 4.7% NPL level in 2005 can be compared to an historical NPL level that had gradually declined from 34.4% in 2000 to 19% in 2004 (see Table 7.2). The gradual decline in ICBC's NPL ratio was accompanied by a fivefold profit increase over 2000–2004, combined with a halving in the number of branches and an employee head count reduction of around one-third. Public listing required a more dramatic drop in ICBC's NPL ratio, however, which was achieved during 2005 thanks to a government support package estimated at $US 80 billion in the first half of that year. ICBC achieved a capital adequacy ratio of over 10% at year-end 2005 and realized over RMB 90 billion in profits (*People's Daily Online*, January 20, 2006a). With ICBC's transformation into a shareholding company, Goldman Sachs, Allianz, and American Express subscribed to $US 3.78 billion in ICBC shares in 2006 to attain a 10% stake (Ernst & Young, 2006, p. 11).[23] However, neither ICBC's foreign investors

---

[22] While the privatization of BOC Hong Kong appeared to have beneficial effects on the share prices of financial institutions in mainland China, Chen, Li, and Moshirian (2005) find that there tended to be a negative reaction among banks and other financial institutions in Hong Kong. Similar negative reactions followed the successful culmination of China's efforts to enter the WTO.

[23] Its October 2006 IPO brought in $US 16.1 billion in Hong Kong plus another $US 5.1 billion in Shanghai, producing a new world record total of $US 21.2 billion. ICBC's

nor those of BOC and CCB have demonstrated any real involvement with the bank's core operations. This limits the likelihood that such foreign participation will produce meaningful changes in bank behavior. Indeed, the foreign investments in noncore areas could remain profitable even if the banks' overall performance failed to improve (see Leigh and Podpiera, 2006).

Repeated corruption scandals themselves hardly seem consistent with an improved corporate culture in the SOCBs. CCB and BOC were both embroiled in scandals in 2001–2002 that pointed to a severe lack of oversight. In the first case, the former president of BOC and CCB Wang Xuebing allegedly made improper loans to his wife. Second, on a smaller provincial level, three BOC bank branch managers in Guangdong laundered $US 480 million over nine years. With top officials at the four major banks only making between $US 3,600 and $US 4,350 annually at the time, while exercising control over huge stocks of funds, the temptation to steal was obvious (Clifford and Fong, 2002, p. 48).[24] Although the authorities dealt harshly with the guilty bank officials and pushed through the 2002 partial IPO of BOC, these episodes served as a reminder of underlying problems. Indeed, there were further fraud cases in 2003, including fraudulent home loans by officials at eight CCB branches in Guangdong province (Leggett, 2003). A new embezzlement scandal emerged at BOC in June 2006, right on the heels of its full Hong Kong IPO (Dickie, 2006). Although such developments surely continue to raise questions about the soundness of the banks' internal controls, public interest in the newly available BOC, CCB, and ICBC shares seemingly remained unabated.

ABC was left as the only SOCB without foreign ownership in 2007 and without any specific timetable for going public. Although Premier Wen Jiabao stated in January 2007 that ABC would be put on a path to its own IPO, the potentially long road ahead is highlighted by the fact that, at the end of September 2006, ABC's bad loans of $US 95.5 billion accounted for over half the bad loans in the entire Chinese banking system.[25] It has obviously

rising share price subsequently made it the world's biggest lender by market capitalization as of July 23, 2007 (Ren, 2007).

[24] The government-controlled oversight procedures were also at fault. As a general rule, Barth, Caprio, and Levine (2006, p. 256) have found that "official supervisory power is associated with greater corruption in lending." In this regard, the 2003 establishment of the CBRC did at least lead to some separation in authority by establishing a nominally independent regulatory body.

[25] Assuming its balance sheet could be cleared up in time, ABC's potential 2008 IPO was estimated to be about $US 10 billion (see Carew, 2007).

continued to lag well behind the other SOCBs and its 2005 cost-to-income ratio was more than twenty percentage points above those of BOC, CCB, and ICBC (see Podpiera, 2006, p. 8). In mid-2007, estimated restructuring costs for ABC exceeded $US 100 billion, comprising approximately $US 76 billion to reduce the bank's NPL ratio to 5% (from a 2006 ratio of 23.4%), plus another $40 billion or so to boost ABC's capital adequacy ratio to the international standard of 8% (McGregor, 2007, p. 18). Fraud has been an issue at ABC as well. A June 2006 audit conducted by China's National Audit Office suggested that ABC had irregular deposits of RMB 14.27 billion, problem loans of RMB 27.62 billion, and fraudulently issued debt securities totaling RMB 9.72 billion in 2004 (Areddy, 2006).

Remaining Problems and Future Prospects

The SOCBs were basically held hostage for much of the post-reform era by the demands of the credit plan. This credit plan dictated the banks' distribution of loans according to preset quotas, and government initiatives often ran counter to commercial forces. As a result, the banks each year issued billions of dollars worth of policy loans to the SOEs, fueling a rapid buildup of NPLs on their balance sheets. The banks were not permitted to write off these NPLs because the government depended upon bank profit for tax purposes. Even after the 1998 reforms, the government continued to exert considerable influence on SOCB lending patterns, and interest rates remained largely administratively determined. Although increased interest rate liberalization in 2004 and after may help, continued concentration on SOE lending, coupled with extremely low levels of lending to China's smaller private firms, did not yet suggest a very market-based allocation of credit.

Reform measures have attempted to correct some of the problems through policy and bank structure changes. Many early policy changes had only limited effects, however, reflecting little initial provision for enforcing such innovations as the new bankruptcy law. More meaningful structural changes have been seen recently, prompted in significant part by the opening up to foreign competition required under the terms of China's WTO entry. Public listings of CCB, BOC, and ICBC in Hong Kong during 2005–2006 were preceded by substantial balance sheet improvements. Reduced loan-to-deposit ratios and a downward trend in SOE lending after 2000 also suggest progress toward more commercially oriented bank policies. However, the repeated need for government bailouts raises the question of whether the commercialization of the banks is, in fact, going fast enough.

Foreign ownership appears to have delivered at least some visible benefits to other Chinese banks, however, and may help the SOCBs as well going forward. It is important that foreign investors have a stake in the SOCBs core business, though, rather than limiting their involvement to noncore areas.

Looking ahead, the authorities must not only pursue further liberalization of interest rates and other aspects of bank lending practices but also find a way to finally lay to rest lingering concerns about the NPL problem. There is a stark contrast between the relatively benign official estimates and the much higher outside estimates (cf. Ernst & Young, 2006; Setser, 2006). There may well be substantial additional bad loans on the banks' balance sheets that have not yet been formally acknowledged – as well as the risk that renewed increased lending rates could generate new NPL problems in the future. The lending increase itself is connected to the exchange rate dilemma discussed in Chapter 1 – with the role of foreign capital inflows in adding to the run-up in real estate prices, for example, drawing the attention of China's National Statistical Bureau in April 2006 (see also Chapter 8).[26] The AMCs are another potential source of concern. Although they provided a much needed vehicle for removing NPLs from SOCB balance sheets, the built-in loss associated with purchasing the debt at between 50% and 100% of its nominal value suggests that the AMCs may eventually need a substantial bailout themselves.

Although the popularity of the recent major Chinese bank IPOs suggests that investors believe these banks have evolved away from their old habit of extending loans to bad-risk borrowers, the rapid growth in fixed asset investment in 2006–2007 did not exactly seem consistent with conservative lending practices. Future progress may depend just as much upon the stability of China's macroeconomy as upon the banks' own efforts to measure up to the standards expected by their new foreign investors. Progress toward more market-driven lending practices will also require a willingness on the part of the Chinese government to cede meaningful market share to foreign entrants. Even the legislation implemented at the end of the five-year "buffer period" in December 2006 seemed to embody excessive amounts of protection for domestic banks. It is to be hoped that predictions of intensified competition between domestic and foreign banks (cf. Qian, 2006) come to pass and that a better allocation of credit to China's rapidly growing private sector can be achieved in the future. On a positive note, some foreign banks, such as Standard Chartered Bank and Citibank, had already launched

[26] "Foreign Capital Add to China's Real Estate Bubble" (April 25, 2006).

special services for small and medium-sized companies by 2007. Foreign banks also began providing meaningful competition in the home loan market in Shanghai, offering rates as low as 5.5 to 5.75% compared to 7.85% from Chinese lenders.[27]

---

[27] Comtex News Network, March 7, 2007; and May 14, 2007.

PART III

THE PEOPLE'S REPUBLIC'S ROLE WITHIN GREATER CHINA AND ASIA

EIGHT

Asset Market Expansion and Shanghai vs. Hong Kong Listings of Chinese Firms

with Gregory C. Arquette and William O. Brown, Jr.[1]

[U]nlike pawnshops in most countries, the real business [in China] is a steady stream of people putting their houses in hock . . . Beijing residents [in 2006] pawned houses valued at Rmb 1.5bn, much of it in order to buy shares.

(Dyer, 2007, p. 3)

Introduction

China's asset market development has lagged well behind the extraordinary growth in the real economy during the post-1978 period. Secondary markets for government bonds did not even exist until the latter half of the 1980s and the interbank market was established only in 1997. Although stock exchanges were opened in the early 1990s, market capitalizations remained quite low relative to the size of China's economy and, on average, market performance was rather poor relative to the robust growth registered elsewhere. Finally, bond and equity prices, as well as real estate prices, have been vulnerable to the effects of abrupt regulatory policy shifts by the government. All this helps explain why asset markets have historically played only a small role in the funds raised by China's nonfinancial institutions. Indeed, even in 2006, bank financing still accounted for over 85% of total finance raised within China (Table 8.1). A positive element, though – as discussed in the following section – was the increase in the importance of corporate bonds from a minimal 1% share of total financing in 2004 to above 5% in 2005 and 2006.

---

[1] Gregory C. Arquette is Vice President of Performance Systems at Pendo Systems in Seattle, Washington (garquette@gmail.com), and William O. Brown is Associate Professor in the Bryan School of Business and Economics at the University of North Carolina-Greensboro (wobrown@uncg.edu). The authors are grateful to Nancy Tao for her research support.

Table 8.1. *Financing Sources for China's Domestic Non-Financial Sector, 2000–2006*

	2006	2005	2004	2003	2002	2001	2000
Total	4,385.9	3,150.7	2,902.3	3,515.4	2,397.6	1,655.5	1,716.3
	(100)	(100)	(100)	(100)	(100)	(100)	(100)
Bank Loans	3,764.5	2,461.7	2,406.6	2,993.6	1,922.8	1,255.8	1,249.9
	(85.8)	(78.1)	(82.9)	(85.1)	(80.2)	(75.9)	(72.8)
Government Securities	251.1	299.6	312.6	352.5	346.1	259.8	247.8
	(5.7)	(9.5)	(10.8)	(10.0)	(14.4)	(15.7)	(14.4)
Corporate Bonds	241.1	201.0	32.7	33.6	32.5	14.7	8.3
	(5.5)	(6.4)	(1.1)	(1.0)	(1.4)	(0.9)	(0.5)
Equities	129.2	188.4	150.4	135.7	96.2	125.2	210.3
	(2.9)	(6.0)	(5.2)	(3.9)	(4.0)	(7.6)	(12.2)

Notes: Amount of financing is in billions of renminbi; percentages are given in parentheses; and 2006 figures have been annualized based on data from the first three quarters of the year.
Source: People's Bank of China, *Monetary Policy Report*, various issues; author's calculations.

Chinese authorities are well aware of the importance of establishing a more advanced system of asset markets and reducing the dependence upon a banking system that, despite great strides triggered by China's entry into the World Trade Organization, still falls short of being an adequate supplier of funds to China's rapidly growing private sector (Chapter 7). A much richer array of securities has emerged in China in recent years, with subordinated debt, asset-backed securities, and short-term corporate paper all entering the interbank market since 2004. The nation's stock markets, meanwhile, dramatically exploded onto the world stage when a near 9% drop in the Shanghai stock market on February 27, 2007 – which a year or two before would have, at best, merited a few lines at the back of the financial papers – was seen as a trigger for major market declines in the United States and around the world the next day. The strong rise in the Chinese markets during most of 2006–2007 itself followed a much longer, but also much less widely noted, period of moribund performance that left average stock prices in early 2005 no higher than in 1993. Comparisons with the neighboring Hong Kong stock exchange reveal that the valuations attached to Chinese stocks were, for the most part, rising less quickly in Shanghai than in Hong Kong as this advance got underway. Whereas Shanghai prices did accelerate ahead of Chinese stock prices in Hong Kong after April 2006, the relative price level in Shanghai at the end of June 2007 was still cheaper than any time from September 1997 to January 2005. This performance rather calls into question the extent to which the initial large advances in the Shanghai market were necessarily as "excessive" as some have claimed.

Bond Market Development

The People's Republic of China issued two series of bonds in 1950 and 1954–1958. As discussed in Chapter 3 (see also Burdekin and Wang, 1999), however, the government's new "Victory bonds" were sold with the help of coercive methods. No further bond issues were made until after economic reforms began in 1978. When government bond issuance did resume in 1981, these bonds were initially paid for by payroll deduction and represented little more than another form of taxation. In an attempt to elicit voluntary purchases, the coupon payments were gradually raised and maturities shortened from ten years down to two- or three-year terms during the 1980s. With no secondary market in place, the only way to trade government bonds was with black marketers, who apparently did not pay very good prices. Bei, Koontz, and Lu (1992, p. 158) point to sales "for much lower than par value, sometimes for as little as fifty percent of par."

In a path-breaking step, the Shenyang Trust and Investment Company launched over-the-counter security trading on August 5, 1986. By June 1988, trading had expanded to sixty-three cities and security trading volume in that year was RMB 2.62 billion, with government bonds accounting for over 92% of this total (Burdekin and Hu, 1999, p. 68). Meanwhile, reliance on enforced bond purchases declined until, in 1993, all government bond issues were underwritten by financial institutions. The first underwriting syndicate was formed in 1991 (Bei, Koontz, and Lu, 1992, p. 161). Another key step was the October 1990 establishment of a nationwide information and exchange network that achieved more uniform pricing. The Wuhan Securities Exchange Center, established in 1992, briefly served as the main bond trading hub until it was superseded by the new national stock exchanges (Bottelier, 2007).

When the Shanghai Stock Exchange opened on December 19, 1990, followed by the Shenzhen Stock Exchange on April 11, 1991, government bonds dominated the floor trading. Over 83% of the RMB 37 billion total trading volume in 1991 was accounted for by government bonds (Burdekin and Hu, 1999). Their share of total trading volume subsequently dropped to 39% in 1992, and 10% in 1993, after stock trading got fully underway in China in 1992 (Burdekin and Hu, 1999, p. 68). However, there was a fresh surge of interest in government debt after a new series of indexed bonds was issued in June 1993 in the face of spiraling inflation in 1993–1994 (Chapter 3).[2]

---

[2] An earlier issue of indexed bonds was implemented during the 1988–1989 inflation spike and accounted for over two-thirds of total bond issuance in 1989. Inflation, however, was brought down by the time the bonds matured (see Chapter 3).

Table 8.2. *China's Public and Corporate Bond Issuance, 1986–2005*

	Issues of Public Bonds	Outstanding Public Bonds	Issues of Corporate Bonds	Outstanding Corporate Bonds
Dec-86	6.25	29.34	10.00	8.38
Dec-87	11.79	39.73	3.00	8.64
Dec-88	18.89	56.42	7.54	11.50
Dec-89	18.73	73.83	7.53	14.64
Dec-90	23.42	87.89	12.64	19.54
Dec-91	28.00	97.27	25.00	33.11
Dec-92	45.59	127.45	60.96	80.20
Dec-93	38.48	157.25	2.01	76.80
Dec-94	113.76	228.64	16.18	67.99
Dec-95	151.09	330.03	21.61	33.27
Dec-96	184.78	436.14	26.89	59.77
Dec-97	241.18	550.89	25.52	52.10
Dec-98	380.88	776.57	14.79	67.69
Dec-99	401.50	1,054.20	15.80	77.86
Dec-00	465.70	1,367.40	8.30	86.16
Dec-01	488.40	1,561.80	14.70	100.86
Dec-02	593.43	1,933.61	32.50	–
Dec-03	628.01	2,260.36	35.80	–
Dec-04	692.39	2,577.76	32.70	–
Dec-05	704.20	2,877.40	204.65	–

Note: All data are in billions of renminbi.
Source: Great China Database.

The government actually announced that all bonds with maturities over three years would be indexed retroactively as of July 11, 1993. Treasury bond futures were introduced on the Shanghai and Shenzhen Stock Exchanges in October 1993. Total public bond issuance more than tripled from RMB 38.48 billion in 1993 to RMB 113.76 billion in 1994, by far the biggest percentage increase recorded (see Table 8.2).

Bond trading volumes rocketed upward in 1995 as investors reacted to the fact that the first set of indexed bonds, maturing in July 1995, were set to pay out more than 25% – based on the official inflation adjustment of 13.01% plus a base interest rate of 12.2%.[3] The largest trading volumes were seen in the futures market, apparently fueled by widespread short-selling by brokers who had been caught on the wrong side of the market and were suffering severe losses from the ongoing advance in indexed bond prices.

---

[3] The inflation expectations implied by the trading prices of these indexed bond issues, as well as the earlier indexed bonds of 1989, are assessed in Burdekin and Hu (1999).

One particularly vigorous attempt to drive down prices is described by Poon, Firth, and Fung (1998, p. 208):

On February 23, 1995, an attempt by a Shanghai broker, Shanghai International Securities, to drive the futures market down by enormous short-selling closed the futures market amid chaos. Trading on this contract surged more than tenfold to nearly 100 billion yuan.

The authorities terminated all futures trading in government securities on the Shanghai Stock Exchange in May 1995. Following this step, total futures market turnover steadily declined from RMB 10,057 billion in 1995 to just RMB 1,608 billion in 2000 (Organisation for Economic Co-operation and Development, 2003).

Concerns about short-selling by securities firms also led the government to ban all commercial bank lending to such companies in August 1997, while further outlawing any participation in stock market trading by the commercial banks themselves.[4] Since that time, although the government has sold about 25% of its new bond issues via the stock exchanges (Bottelier, 2007), the larger portion has been sold through the interbank market. After its establishment in 1997, China's interbank market was expanded to include both financial and nonfinancial institutions. The role played by nonfinancial institutions has remained small, however, accounting for only about 6% of total bond issues going into 2006 (Hale, 2007). The Governor of the People's Bank, Zhou Xiaochuan (2006a, p. 7), characterizes the interbank market as having "little regulation, and institutions are free to participate and strike deals at the prevailing market prices." The growing liquidity of the interbank bond market, and the increasing stress on the trading of central bank bills, was discussed in Chapter 4. The expanding range of debt instruments also includes subordinated debt issued by commercial banks, asset-backed securities, and short-term corporate bonds (see Bottelier, 2007).

Although government bond issuance has steadily expanded since the early 1990s, reaching RMB 704.2 billion at the end of 2005, the RMB 2,877.40 billion stock of outstanding public debt shown in Table 8.2 was still relatively modest – representing only approximately 18% of China's overall 2005 gross domestic product (GDP). Corporate bond issuance, meanwhile, was still below 1992 levels as recently as 2004. One barrier to further development of this market has been the limited access to bank credit hitherto enjoyed by China's private sector (see also Chapter 7). This restriction has left most private firms with "no means of developing a reputation for repayment that

---

[4] Short-selling on the nation's stock exchanges has been prohibited since June 1997.

is essential for borrowing from the bond market" (Hale, 2007). Moreover, tight regulation by China's National Development and Reform Commission (NDRC) kept most firms from entering the market at all. The NDRC set the price and issue date of each issue using a quota system and required that all bond issues be underwritten by the state-owned commercial banks. Other problems included a lack of information disclosure to potential investors and inadequate protection for creditors under existing bankruptcy laws (Zhou, 2006a, p. 8).

Corporate bond issuance accelerated rapidly in 2005, however, rising from RMB 32.7 billion in 2004 to RMB 204.65 billion in 2005. This rise occurred as the People's Bank established a new market for short-term corporate paper, with maturities limited to no more than one year, which began interbank trading in 2005. In the first six months, RMB 160 billion of these new instruments were issued and the total reached RMB 300 billion in 2006 (Anderlini, 2007b). Draft rules published in June 2007 potentially laid the foundation for still more rapid expansion in China's nascent corporate debt market. A transfer of regulatory control from the NDRC to the China Securities Regulation Commission was to "do away with any kind of quota, allow bond prices to be set by the market, lay out clear criteria for issuance and require bonds to be backed by assets of the issuing company" (Anderlini, 2007b, p. 21). These new rules could well lead to a dramatic expansion in China's corporate debt market in the future.

Equity Markets

The growth in China's stock markets is evident in Table 8.3, which reveals the expansion in the number of listed companies, total market capitalization, and trading volume over the 1992–2006 period. Relative to the size of China's economy, however, as reflected in GDP data, the upward trend is seen to temporarily break down after 2000. Despite a big increase from 2005 to 2006, total market capitalization remained, at just over 42% of GDP, still lower than in 2000 – when it exceeded 48%. In percentage terms the biggest advances, in both market capitalization and trading volume, occurred in 1993 and 1996. The 1993 gains, of course, occurred as the stock exchanges were just getting going and so built upon only a very small base. Meanwhile, the 1996 advance saw market capitalization nearly triple from RMB 347 billion to RMB 984 billion, while annual trading volume – for the Shanghai and Shenzhen markets combined – rose from 70 billion shares in 1995 to 253 billion shares in 1996. In retrospect, this was a major volume jump, with trading volumes subsequently increasing much more

Table 8.3. *The Growth of China's Stock Markets, 1992–2006*

Year	Number of Listed Companies	Total Market Capitalization (billions of renminbi)	Total Market Capitalization as Percentage of GDP	Total Trading Volume (millions of shares)
1992	53	104.81	3.89%	3,795
1993	183	353.10	9.99%	23,422
1994	291	369.06	7.66%	201,334
1995	324	347.43	5.71%	70,547
1996	530	984.24	13.83%	253,314
1997	745	1,752.92	22.20%	256,079
1998	851	1,950.56	23.11%	215,411
1999	949	2,647.12	29.52%	293,239
2000	1,088	4,809.09	48.47%	475,840
2001	1,160	4,352.22	39.69%	315,229
2002	1,200	3,832.91	31.85%	301,618
2003	1,263	4,245.77	31.26%	415,808
2004	1,353	3,705.56	23.18%	582,773
2005	1,357	3,243.03	17.71%	662,373
2006	1,411	8,940.39	42.69%[a]	1,614,523

Note: Data include Shanghai "A" and "B" shares and Shenzhen "A" and "B" shares.
[a] Based on preliminary data from China's National Bureau of Statistics.
Sources: Great China Database; National Bureau of Statistics of China (http://www.stats.gov.cn/ english); People's Bank of China (http://www.pbc.gov.cn); Organisation for Economic Cooperation and Development (2003); and author's calculations.

gradually and remaining below 500 billion shares until 2004. Ironically, the 1996 advance may well have been tied to the aforementioned bond futures trading suspension in May 1995. Poon, Firth, and Fung (1998) identify an improvement in equity market liquidity following the May 1995 intervention – with the gains derived from a forced shift of investors away from the closed bond futures market seemingly offsetting any loss of investor confidence owing to the suspension.

The short history of China's stock exchanges is, in fact, dominated by the effects of government administrative measures that have produced sudden – actual or anticipated – jumps in the supply and demand for shares. Almost from the outset, both the Shanghai and Shenzhen stock markets had two initially quite separate classes of shares: "A" shares for domestic residents and "B" shares for foreigners. Trading of "B" shares commenced on February 21, 1992 in Shanghai – quoted and settled in US dollars – and February 28, 1992 in Shenzhen – in this case quoted and settled in Hong Kong dollars. Companies wishing to issue "B" shares had to meet stricter requirements, including having an audit performed by an international accounting group

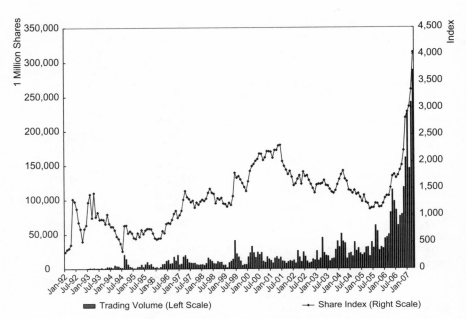

Figure 8.1. Shanghai "A" Share Index Values and Trading Volume. *Source:* Great China Database.

as well as demonstrating a proven record of profitability or minimum return on capital (see Ma, 1996). Substantially lower "B" share prices, relative to "A" shares of the same company, raised the possibility of more speculative, less risk-averse market sentiment among local investors.

Ma (1996) finds a significant role for this sentiment effect in accounting for some of the "B" share discount but also points to stronger reactions to regulatory changes on the part of local investors. For example, an austerity plan adopted to rein in inflation in 1993, which had the effect of restricting the flow of funds into the nation's stock markets, produced much larger declines in "A" shares than in "B" shares, narrowing the discount. Meanwhile, the market rescue plan adopted on July 30, 1994, which temporarily froze new equity issues as well as allowing more money into the market, produced a much larger advance in the "A" shares than in the "B" shares. Indeed, as Ma (1996, p. 237) points out, the Shanghai "A" share index rose by over 100% in a single week after this plan was announced. This advance at the end of July 1994, as well as the preceding sharp decline in the "A" share index, can also be seen in Figure 8.1, which plots the movements in the Shanghai "A" share index, and corresponding trading volumes, over the January 1992–April 2007 period. Wang, Burton, and Power (2004, p. 439) find that greater volatility in "A" shares relative to "B" shares persisted over the August 1994–July 2000 period – with "A" shares revealing a consistently stronger tendency to overreact to both good and bad news.

Later policy changes have removed the strict separation between the "A" and "B" share markets. The purchase of "B" shares by domestic individuals was legalized in February 2001, whereas limited foreign investor entry into the "A" share market was approved in December 2002. Correlations between "A" and "B" shares increased sharply after the February 2001 opening up of the "B" share market, rising above 65% for both Shanghai and Shenzhen over the 2001–2003 period compared to a less than 30% correlation earlier on (Chiu, Lee, and Chen, 2005, p. 278).[5] Another major regulatory change was the relaxation of restrictions, starting from September 1999, on the purchase of equities by state-owned enterprises (SOEs) and other institutional investors (Wong, 2006, pp. 398–399). The sharp stock market advance during 1999–2001 was likely significantly influenced by these developments. As shown in Figure 8.1, the Shanghai "A" share market rose from around 1,200 in early 1999 to nearly 2,500 in the summer of 2001. However, after rising in the face of a new source of government-led demand for equities, the markets then declined substantially on fears of a government-led influx of new supply. This involved the June 2001 announcement of China's State Council's plans to sell off substantial portions of the government's remaining ownership stake in listed SOEs.

The government had previously kept share supply under tight control, using an explicit quota on total IPO issuance from 1993–1998 – a self-imposed restriction that began to be relaxed in 1999 but was not formally abolished until 2001 (see Wong, 2006). The market continued to fall even after the sell-off plan was officially scrapped in June 2002, with the Shanghai "A" share index dropping back to 1990s levels by early 2005. This drop likely reflected fresh worries about increased government-led share supply in 2003–2005. The government's new push to privatize some of its SOEs – which were typically more than 95% government-owned – threatened to unleash large amounts of additional traded shares onto the market. Chow (2007, p. 250) states that the "government had to stop such selling several times and design schemes to prevent its significant depressing effect on the prices of traded shares."

---

[5] The December 2002 partial opening of the "A" share market to foreign investors hurt the "B" shares, though, and "B" shares were left trading at an approximate 30% discount by September 2006 – before enjoying a sudden 9.7% jump in one day, on September 18, 2006, based on rumors that they would be merged with the "A" shares (Mitchell, 2006).

A major rule change in January 2006 sought to finally resolve the market overhang represented by the large set of nontradable shares that, unlike the "A" and "B" shares, cannot be transferred without special administrative approval. Such shares still accounted for approximately two-thirds of total Shanghai and Shenzhen stock market capitalization in 2005. During 2005, the government began implementing a plan to convert such shares into tradable "A" shares (*Shenzhen Daily*, November 7, 2005). Econometric evidence of favorable investor reaction to the earlier stages of the nontradable share reform process arises from Feng and Xu (2007) – who identify significant abnormal returns for a small set of "pilot" companies that began the process of releasing nontradable shares onto the market on April 29, 2005.[6] The government took further steps to deepen the market on January 31, 2006 by allowing "strategic" foreign investors to purchase "A" shares rather than being restricted to nontradable shares. Such foreign investors, who had typically remained shut out of the "A" share market before, were not only allowed entry but permitted to purchase stakes of more than 10% – albeit subject to a three-year "lockup" period. Dyer (2006, p. 17) points to this pending rule change as a "factor behind [the] . . . rebound in China's stock market, which [rose] . . . 13 per cent in . . . two months [during November 2005–January 2006] after a four-year slump."

Needless to say, the advance that began in late 2005 subsequently accelerated in 2006–2007. It is important to note, however, that this rally came after an extended period of nonperformance. As shown in Figure 8.2, the Shanghai "A" share index in June 2006, even after more than six months of gains off the 2005 lows, was still almost unchanged from its January 2000 value. Even in mid-2006, the Shanghai index still marginally lagged the performance of Hong Kong's Hang Seng index since January 2000, while only slightly bettering the performance of the US S&P 500 index. The near 130% advance from June 2006–June 2007 seems less remarkable when one considers that this figure also represents almost all the total gains realized over the preceding seven and a half years – for an overall impressive but far from unprecedented average of around 20% per year.

Speculative Pressures in the Equity and Real Estate Markets

Notwithstanding China's continued modest rates of consumer price inflation going into 2007, some economists have pointed to financial imbalances

---

[6] Each of these companies had to publicize a plan for compensating holders of its preexisting tradable shares, usually via bonus shares and/or convertible bonds, warrants, dividends, etc. Approval by two-thirds of the owners of the firm's tradable shares was required in order to proceed.

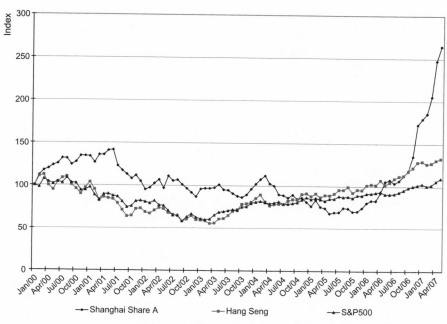

Figure 8.2. Shanghai vs. Hong Kong and New York Share Price Movements, 2000–2007.

being channeled into credit and asset price advances. In such a case, the central bank might consider acting preemptively to contain swings in asset prices and limit the risk of extreme boom-bust cycles (cf. Borio, 2005). According to Wu (2003), asset prices were an important conduit for excess money growth in China even over the pre-2001 period. Turning to the more recent 2006–2007 advance in Chinese share prices, former Federal Reserve Chairman Alan Greenspan – who famously raised the question of "irrational exuberance" in US financial markets in 1996 – issued a warning on May 23, 2007 that the gains were "unsustainable" and that a "dramatic correction" was inevitable (see Lima and Kennedy, 2007). Even more dramatic than the share price advance was the volume increase in the Shanghai market going into 2007 (shown in Figure 8.1). On May 9, 2007, the combined trading volume in Shanghai and Shenzhen, for the first time, exceeded that of all other Asian bourses combined. An aggregate RMB 376.9 billion worth of shares changed hands that day, up from levels typically below RMB 40 billion just six months earlier (Anderlini, 2007a).

The stock market rally was accompanied by record numbers of Chinese companies issuing shares after the government lifted its temporary ban on domestic IPOs in May 2006. Substantial flows of funds into the nation's stock markets out of individual savings accounts were seen in 2007. In Shanghai alone, over RMB 70 billion was transferred from savings accounts into stock trading accounts during the first four months of 2007 – and 421,831 new stock accounts were opened in a single day on May 8, following a weeklong holiday (*China Securities Journal*, 2007a). Meanwhile, national household bank deposits dropped by RMB 167.4 billion in April 2007 compared to a RMB 60.6 billion increase in April 2006 (*China Securities Journal*, 2007b). Fluctuations in household deposits appeared to be correlated with the ups and downs in the stock market, with a further RMB 278.4 billion decline in household deposits in May 2007 being followed by an RMB 167.8 billion increase the next month when the stock market corrected in June 2007 (*People's Daily Online*, August 11, 2007c).

April 2007 saw the combined market capitalization of the Shanghai and Shenzhen stock exchanges exceed the total value of savings deposits for the first time ever. One factor in the increased flow of funds into the stock market, aside from the self-fulfilling draw of the recent strong gains enjoyed there, was likely government intervention aimed at cooling off China's strong property markets.[7] In March 2005, the regulated interest rate on home loans was raised, higher down payments were required, and the Shanghai authorities imposed a 5.5% capital gains tax on home sellers' profits (Bradsher, 2005). There was also a special 5% tax on the total sales price for any property sold within two years of the original date of purchase. The Shanghai property market tailed off after these government measures, ending a run-up that saw average home sale prices double since 1997, including a 26% gain in 2004 alone. As shown in Figure 8.3, the flow of funds into the nation's property markets was already turning down sharply in 2004. Given that price movements appear to have typically lagged behind innovations in property-related development by one or two years in China (Liang and Cao, 2007), it is actually not so obvious that the government initiatives were the decisive factor in the housing market downturn on this occasion.[8]

---

[7] A negative relationship between stock prices and housing prices over the 1997–2005 period in China is identified by Zhang and Fung (2006, pp. 31–32), offering support for the "hypothesis that stocks and real estate are competing investment channels."

[8] The largest run-ups in China's real estate market actually occurred well before 2000, with a first cycle that peaked in 1988 and a second, most extreme one that topped out in 1992–1993. The first cycle followed the initial building up of the property sector after private home ownership was permitted, for the first time, in June 1980 (Liang and Cao, 2007, p. 66). The second cycle was linked to development in the coastal cities and "Special Economic Zones" and occurred in the midst of rising consumer price inflation (Chapter 3). Government initiatives seem to have been responsible for abruptly reversing this expansion in 1993, imposing a set of measures that choked off funding for the real estate sector – giving

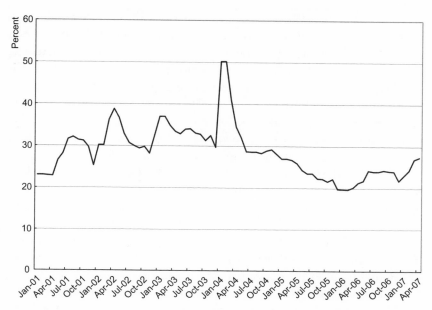

Figure 8.3. Annualized Growth Rate of Real Estate Investment in China. *Source:* Great China Database.

Some picking up in the rate of real estate investment was evident through 2006 and early 2007, potentially foreshadowing renewed strength in housing prices. High lending rates by Chinese banks seem to point in this direction given the historical link between bank lending rates and property prices (Liang and Cao, 2007). Nationwide year-on-year housing price increases averaged 7.1% through June 2007, led by an overall 15.9% advance in Shenzhen (Sito, 2007). Prior to the currency policy change on July 21, 2005 (Chapter 1), there were concerns that foreign investors seeking to profit both from a hot housing market and from renminbi revaluation were driving the market up excessively. This perspective receives support from the fact that hot money inflows do indeed seem to have exerted systematic, positive effects on Chinese housing prices during 1997–2005 (Zhang and Fung, 2006). In addition, even though hot money inflows appeared to diminish after the break from the fixed exchange rate policy, China's National Bureau of Statistics continued to express concerns about the level of foreign direct investment in China's real estate industry ("Foreign Capital Add to China's Real Estate Bubble," April 25, 2006).

rise to substantial defaults on loans as well as a plunging real estate market (see Zhang and Sun, 2006).

As noted earlier, China's stock market gains through 2007, although seeming outlandish to many based upon comparisons with the much lower levels of 2005, should properly be assessed relative to the longer-run record. Indeed, not only was the market essentially flat during 2000–2006 but the lows of early 2005 matched levels seen as long ago as 1993 (see Figure 8.1)! The concern should not be the size of the share price increase itself but its source. If share price gains are an indication of excess liquidity, rather than improving fundamentals, then this would indeed suggest potentially worrisome parallels with the boom-bust cycles in Japanese and Taiwanese asset prices during the 1980s (Chapter 2). The Japanese experience of sudden tightening at the end of the 1980s, as well as the aftermath of the Chinese government's own past heavy-handed interventions, argues against drastic action, however. Whereas the authorities did increase the stamp duty payable on stock transactions in May 2007, fears of a capital gains tax on stock gains were initially left unrealized.[9] The ongoing program of steadily placing previously nontradable shares onto the market may actually offer a more gradualist approach to soaking up some of the fervent demand for stocks. In the meantime, the authorities began a crackdown against banks whose loans had been illegally channeled into the stock market, announcing an initial series of penalties in June 2007.[10]

Shanghai vs. Hong Kong

One way to address the difficult question of whether China's recently buoyant stock markets became "overexuberant" is to compare local investors' own valuations of Chinese equities to those of foreign investors. This analysis involves setting the local prices for Chinese share issues against the prices at which they trade in offshore markets like Hong Kong and New York.[11] Hong Kong has consistently been the most popular choice of Chinese firms seeking an offshore listing, accounting for about two-thirds of all Chinese listings outside the mainland. This apparent preference for Hong Kong over

---

[9] With no capital gains tax in place, stock market profits have remained tax-free in China.

[10] Penalties were announced against eight different banks, including the Beijing branch of the Bank of Communications, China's fifth largest bank (see China Banking Regulatory Commission, June 19, 2007). Meanwhile, ten foreign banks and nineteen domestic banks were punished by China's State Administration of Foreign Exchange for "assisting speculative foreign capital to enter the country disguised as trade or investment" (Anderlini, 2007c, p. 13).

[11] Although this chapter focuses on comparisons with Hong Kong, analysis of the American Depository Receipt market in Arquette, Brown, and Burdekin (2008) reveals a similar pattern of relative valuations.

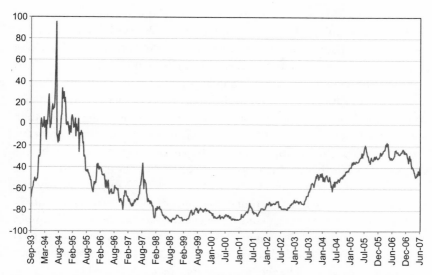

Figure 8.4. Discount Attached to Hong Kong Listings Relative to Shanghai Listings of Chinese Firms.

New York, the second most popular destination, may reflect greater access to external financing in Hong Kong. Yang and Lau (2006), for example, find that firms with New York listings were more likely to be capital-constrained than their Hong Kong counterparts. Meanwhile, Girardin and Liu (2007) identify a long-run relationship between the Shanghai "A" share index and Hong Kong's Hang Seng stock index that appears to begin around the time of Hong Kong's return to Chinese rule after June 30, 1997.[12] After some wild gyrations between 1993 and 1997 (Figure 8.4), however, a steep discount persisted in the Hong Kong price relative to the Shanghai price after 1997.

Over the 1997–2001 period, Chinese companies on average had a Hong Kong share ("H-share") price that was 80% to 90% lower than the trading price in Shanghai, after correcting for the different currencies involved. A gradual shrinkage in the Hong Kong discount occurred during 2001–2006, however, with the average discount falling to as low as 17% for the week ending April 21, 2006. This decline suggests that, relative to the more established market in Hong Kong, any overvaluation of Shanghai shares was, for the most part, greater before the rally period that began in late 2005. Whereas "A" share prices in Shanghai did accelerate faster than

---

[12] Meanwhile, a prior long-term relationship between the Shanghai "A" share index and the New York S&P 500 index seems to have broken down just before the apparent link with Hong Kong emerged.

H-share prices after April 2006, the 38% Hong Kong discount at the end of June 2007 was still lower than any of the values observed from August 29, 1997, through January 14, 2005. Through June 2007, therefore, the Hong Kong discount remained quite low relative to its own past history.

At the individual firm level, Wang and Jiang (2004, p. 1295) point to significant commonality between individual firms' "A" shares and H-shares, concluding that the H-shares "behave more like Hong Kong stocks than mainland Chinese stocks" but "retain significant exposure to their domestic market."[13] The general importance of the Hong Kong market to Chinese shares receives further confirmation from Kutan and Zhou's (2006) analysis of Chinese shares traded on the New York Stock Exchange. In theory, the H-share price should be a function of the value of the underlying security in its home market of Shanghai and the exchange rate between the renminbi and the Hong Kong dollar – with arbitrage conditions implying that H-share and "A" share prices diverge solely due to exchange rate expectations and transaction costs. The relationships may be complicated by variations in market sentiment, however – a factor that seems to have played a role in the persistent discount of foreign-held "B" shares relative to locally held "A" shares that was discussed earlier.[14] Both Wei (2000) and Wang and Jiang (2004) suggest that market sentiment may be an important factor explaining the differences in the prices of cross-listed Chinese shares as well. Higher "A" share volatility relative to the firm's corresponding H-share listing, for example, could indicate "more mood swings or noises in the Chinese market" (Wei, 2000, p. 238).

There is also the issue of capital controls, with Chinese restrictions on capital outflows potentially pushing up the relative price of domestic listings insofar as domestic investors are prevented from placing funds abroad.[15]

---

[13] Less consistent evidence of co-movement emerges from Chong and Su's (2006) analysis of intraday data, with evidence of a cointegrating relationship seemingly limited to firms with the most liquid H-shares.

[14] There have been numerous studies documenting that, when the same or equivalent securities trade in multiple markets, the law of one price is often violated. The price deviations, however, have generally been insufficient to create profitable arbitrage opportunities (see, for example, Rosenthal and Young, 1990; Froot and Dabora, 1999; Kim, Szakmary, and Mathur, 2000; and Chan, Hameed, and Lau, 2003). One possible explanation for these varying share price influences concerns the impact of market sentiment in the different markets, with variations in sentiment accounting for at least some of the price differentials.

[15] On August 20, 2007, the Chinese government announced plans for a pilot program that would, for the first time, allow individual mainland investors to directly trade Hong Kong stocks by opening accounts at the Bank of China's Tianjin branch. Although this news was initially accompanied by a strong rally in the Hong Kong market and downward pressure on the Hong Kong discount (Batson, 2007), government restrictions would likely still limit the potential outflow of funds to Hong Kong under this program.

Girardin and Liu (2007, p. 368) suggest that capital controls have not precluded an "internationalization" of the strategy adopted by Chinese investors, however, and suggest that "[c]apital flight is already used by Chinese residents to buy shares in Hong Kong, including IPOs of Mainland firms listed in Hong Kong."[16] In the empirical work following we show that both expected exchange rate changes and different market sentiment levels play a significant role in accounting for the changing size of the Hong Kong discount over time. Our empirical analysis focuses on comparisons with the Shanghai market, which accounted for approximately 80% of total mainland China stock market capitalization in 2006. We use a "panel" approach that looks at variations both across the two markets and over time – and control not only for overall market sentiment but also for company-specific measures of market sentiment.

Assessing the Determinants of the Hong Kong Discount

Our sample comprises thirty Chinese firms, with both "A" share and H-share listings, for which we obtained data from Bloomberg. Our maximum sample period runs from December 1998 through September 2006. Table 8.4 lists the individual companies along with the relevant period for which the company's data is included in our sample. We calculate the H-share discount as:

$$\text{H-share discount} = [(\text{H-share Price} - \text{Implied H-share Price})/$$
$$\text{Implied H-share Price}] \quad\quad (1)$$

where the Implied H-share Price = [Price in renminbi/(RMB/\$HK)] * H-share Conversion ratio.

Table 8.5 presents summary statistics on the H-share discount as well as the additional variables used in the regression model. The expected exchange rate change versus the Hong Kong dollar is derived from the twelve-month renminbi nondeliverable forward contract rate.[17] As shown in Figure 8.5, the implied expected appreciation of the renminbi against the Hong Kong

---

[16] Although more widespread purchases would, of course, be expected if existing impediments were alleviated or removed. At the same time, Auguste et al.'s (2006) analysis of the very large premiums attached to local Argentinean share listings in 2001–2002 suggests that these premiums derived primarily from exchange rate expectations – and not the draconian capital controls imposed by the Argentinean authorities at this time.

[17] This rate actually utilizes the trading prices of the same renminbi nondeliverable forward contracts discussed in Chapter 1. Given the fixed exchange rate between the Hong Kong dollar and the US dollar that was maintained throughout our sample period, the expected move of the renminbi against the US dollar implies an identical expected move against the Hong Kong dollar.

Table 8.4. *Chinese Firms Included in the Empirical Work*

Company Name	H-Share Data Begins	H-Share Data Ends
Angang New Steel Co.	Dec. 11, 1998	Sept. 29, 2006
Anhui Conch Cement Co. Ltd.	Feb. 8, 2002	Sept. 29, 2006
Anhui Expressway	Jan. 10, 2003	Sept. 29, 2006
Beiren Printing Machinery	Dec. 11, 1998	Sept. 29, 2006
China Eastern Airlines Co.	Dec. 11, 1998	Sept. 29, 2006
China Petroleum & Chemical	Aug. 10, 2001	Sept. 29, 2006
China Shipping Development	May 24, 2002	Sept. 29, 2006
China Southern Airlines Co.	July 25, 2003	Sept. 29, 2006
Dongfang Electrical Machin.	Dec. 11, 1998	Sept. 29, 2006
Guangdong Kelon Elec. Hld.	July 16, 1999	Sept. 29, 2006
Guangzhou Pharmaceuticals	Feb. 9, 2001	Sept. 29, 2006
Guangzhou Shipyard Intl. Co.	Dec. 11, 1998	Sept. 29, 2006
Huadian Power Intl. Corp.	Feb. 4, 2005	Sept. 29, 2006
Huaneng Power Intr.	Dec. 7, 2001	Sept. 29, 2006
Jiangsu Expressway Co. Ltd.	Jan. 19, 2001	Sept. 29, 2006
Jiangxi Copper Co. Ltd.	Jan. 11, 2002	Sept. 29, 2006
Jiaoda Kunji High-Tech Co.	Dec. 11, 1998	Sept. 29, 2006
Jilin Chemical Indus. Co.	Dec. 11, 1998	Sept. 30, 2005
Jingwei Textile Machinery	Dec. 11, 1998	Sept. 29, 2006
Luoyang Glass Company Ltd.	Dec. 11, 1998	Sept. 29, 2006
Maanshan Iron & Steel	Dec. 11, 1998	Sept. 29, 2006
Nanjing Panda Elec. Co. Ltd.	Dec. 11, 1998	Sept. 29, 2006
Shandong Xinhua Pharm. Co.	Dec. 11, 1998	Sept. 29, 2006
Shenzhen Expressway Co. Ltd.	Dec. 28, 2001	Sept. 29, 2006
Sinopec Shanghai Petrochem	Dec. 11, 1998	Sept. 29, 2006
Sinopec Yizheng Chemical Fib.	Dec. 11, 1998	Sept. 29, 2006
Tianjin Capital Environ.	Dec. 11, 1998	Sept. 29, 2006
Tsingtao Brewery Co. Ltd.	Dec. 11, 1998	Sept. 29, 2006
Yanzhou Coal Mining Co.	Dec. 11, 1998	Sept. 29, 2006
ZTE Corp.	Dec. 10, 2004	Sept. 29, 2006

dollar peaks at just over 5% in mid-2005 before falling back after the actual 2.1% appreciation imposed by the Chinese authorities on July 21, 2005 (Chapter 1). Furthermore, the spikes in revaluation pressure in September–December 2003, as well as the later mid-2005 spike, appear to coincide with drawdowns in the H-share discount as shown in Figure 8.4.[18] The

---

[18] Although occurring outside the sample period covered in our econometric analysis, a third spike in revaluation expectations in March–April 2007 also appears to coincide with a shrinking of the H-share discount.

Table 8.5. *Summary Statistics for Chinese Firms Traded in Hong Kong (Weekly Values)*

	Observations	Mean	Std. Dev.	Minimum	Maximum
	Panel A: China–Hong Kong H-Share Sample				
H-Share Discount	9,886	−0.5961	0.2823	−0.9765	0.3761
Expected Exchange Rate Change	408	0.0010	0.0396	−0.0512	0.1113
Relative Market P/E Ratios	261	3.0034	1.4093	1.5353	6.3344
Relative Company P/E Ratios	8,734	2.0446	2.9582	0.2067	52.845
Market Capitalization (in millions of renminbi)	6,997	25.187	63.041	0.5977	584.95
	Panel B: Values at End of Sample on September 29, 2006				
H-Share Discount	29	−0.2788	0.2706	−0.7235	0.15

suggested association between rising exchange rate expectations and a shrinking H-share discount is consistent with increased demand for renminbi-based Chinese stocks at times when investors expect exchange rate gains that would translate these renminbi values into larger Hong Kong dollar amounts.

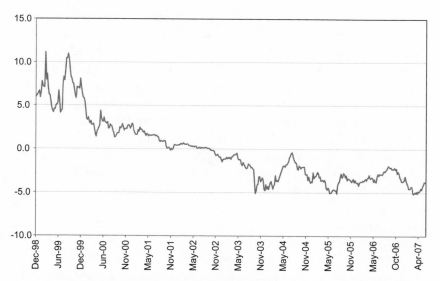

Figure 8.5. Implied Expected Change in the RMB/$HK Exchange Rate (One-Year Non-deliverable Forward Contract).

Figure 8.6. Average Price/Earnings Ratios for the Shanghai and Hong Kong Stock Exchanges.

The "relative market P/E ratio" reflects the price earnings ratio of the Shanghai "A" share Total Stock Index divided by the Hang Seng China Enterprises Index, whereas the "relative company P/E ratio" is the company's price-earnings ratio divided by the price-earnings ratio of the Shanghai "A" share Total Stock Index. Figure 8.6 depicts the relative differences in price-earnings ratios between our Hong Kong and Shanghai market indices over the 2001–2006 period. We use the ratio of the price-earnings ratios as a proxy for differences in investor sentiment across countries. The average price-earning ratio attached to "A" shares steadily declines over 2001–2005, dropping from more than forty to below twenty in 2005 before rising again in 2006–2007. From mid-2005 through the end of our sample, the price-earnings ratios in both Shanghai and Hong Kong trend upward. The price-earnings ratios for the Hong Kong and Shanghai indices converge to a spread of ten points or less during most of 2005–2006. The gap between the respective price-earnings ratios then widens to around twenty points in mid-2007, still below the greater than thirty point gap seen in the past.[19]

---

[19] The relatively low price-earnings ratio seen for the Hong Kong index reflect the fact that the data are for only the Chinese Enterprise Sub-Index and not for the Hang Seng as a whole.

In order to pin down the relative importance of exchange rate expectations and sentiment effects on the H-share discount, we estimate the following model:

$$\text{ADR\_discount}_{it} = \alpha_0 + \beta_1 \text{Expected\_Exchange\_Rate\_Change}_t$$
$$+ \beta_2 \text{Market\_Sentiment}_t + \beta_3 \text{Company\_Sentiment}_{it}$$
$$+ \epsilon_{it} \tag{2}$$

In this equation, the *Expected_Exchange_Rate_Change* is the predicted change in exchange rates implied by the twelve-month renminbi nondeliverable forward contract rate,[20] our *Market_Sentiment* measure is proxied by the price-earnings ratio on the Shanghai "A" share Total Stock Index divided by the price-earnings ratio on the Hang Seng China Enterprises Index, and the *Company_Sentiment* variable is measured by the individual company's price-earnings ratio relative to the overall marketwide price-earnings ratio in Shanghai.[21] If the company's price-earnings ratio is high relative to the overall Shanghai market, then it may suggest local Chinese sentiment toward this security is high – and, should Hong Kong investors not share such strong sentiment toward the security, the H-share will sell at a steeper discount.[22]

Our estimation results are presented in Table 8.6. The negative coefficients indicate that the variables have the effect of making the H-share discount bigger, i.e., more negative. Each of the explanatory variables is significant at better than the 99% confidence level.[23] Column (1) indicates that the expected change in the renminbi exchange rate accounts for more than 40% of the total variation in the H-share discount on its own. The impact of expected exchange rate movements remains both statistically and economically significant as we add additional explanatory variables. Column (2) through Column (5) reveal that the market sentiment and company sentiment measures are also significantly related to the H-share discount,

---

[20] Employing the current exchange rate, the weekly change in exchange rates, or expected changes using shorter duration futures contracts, had no substantive effect on the results.

[21] Experimentation with various other measures of market sentiment, including price-to-book ratios, price-to-sales ratios, and dividend yields, produced results similar to those obtained using the price-earnings ratio.

[22] We also include the market capitalization of the firm. We expect that on average larger companies will have lower trading costs, more cross-country information, and fewer barriers to arbitrage resulting in the H-share discount shrinking as the company becomes larger. The predicted positive coefficient is found in the empirical estimation below.

[23] As described in Arquette, Brown, and Burdekin (2008), these results remain most robust if we control for different firm-level reactions to the right-hand-side variables by reestimating the panel regressions allowing for firm-specific "fixed effects."

Table 8.6. *Relationship Among the Hong Kong Discount, Exchange Rates,*
and Market Sentiment

We estimate the following model:

H-Share discount$_{it}$ = α_0 + β_1 Expected_Exchange_Rate_Change$_t$ + β_2 Market_ Sentiment$_t$
   + β_3 Company_Sentiment$_{it}$ + Market_Capitalization$_{it}$ + ϵ_{it}

where the *Expected_Exchange_Rate_Change* is measured as the predicted change in exchange
rates over the next twelve months as measured by the 12-month futures rate. The *Market_*
Sentiment measure is the ratio of the Shanghai "A"-Share Index P/E ratio to the Hang Seng
P/E ratio at time t. The *Company_Sentiment* measure is the ratio of company i's P/E ratio to
the Shanghai "A"-Share Index P/E ratio at time t. *Market_Capitalization* is measured in
local currency at time t. All models are estimated using weekly data.

	Dependent Variable = Hong Kong Discount				
	(1)	(2)	(3)	(4)	(5)
Expected Exchange	−5.327*	−2.344*	−5.531*	−1.834*	−1.901*
Rate Change	(0.074)	(0.277)	(0.088)	(0.261)	(0.256)
Relative Market		−0.108*		−0.110*	−0.109*
P/E Ratio		(0.003)		(0.003)	(0.003)
Relative Company			−0.021*	−0.023*	−0.022*
P/E Ratio			(0.001)	(0.001)	(0.001)
Market Cap					0.586*
(in billions)					(0.026)
Constant	−0.625*	−0.243*	−0.579*	−0.177*	−0.201*
	(0.002)	(0.016)	(0.003)	(0.015)	(0.015)
Observations	9,8876	7,192	8,734	7,001	6,997
R-squared	0.402	0.432	0.434	0.491	0.511

Note: Robust standard errors are in parentheses; *denotes significance at the 99% confidence level or
better.

whether included alone or together. On average, the higher the relative
market sentiment in Shanghai is, the lower the relative price in Hong Kong
is and, hence, the larger the H-share discount. Similarly, when local Chinese investors drive up the market price of an individual company relative
to other companies listed in Shanghai, that company's H-share price lags
behind. Either way, if the sentiment change is local in origin, the effect
evidently does not spill over to Hong Kong holders of the same security.
These findings suggest that differences in investor sentiment across the two
markets help explain the price differentials across the two markets, consistent with past studies. Our results imply that, should rising local sentiment,
or "overexuberance," make investors in Shanghai willing to pay more for

the same predicted earnings, we should see the H-share discount reaching higher than normal levels.

Conclusions

The expanding role for China's asset markets, which has been accompanied by ongoing interest rate liberalization, is a most welcome development. Given that these markets are still at a relatively early stage of development, however, risks of excesses remain high. It is to be hoped that the government will maintain its recent cautious approach to dealing with these issues – and avoid the kinds of drastic interventions that were associated with such large fluctuations in the nation's bond and real estate markets, as well as stock markets, in the past. With regard to the share price advance that began at the end of 2005, the relatively low levels of the H-share discount relative to its own past history did not seem to offer any initial proof of overly bullish sentiment on the part of local Chinese investors. As shown in Arquette, Brown, and Burdekin (2008), comparison with New York trading prices of Chinese firms yields similar conclusions. Whereas it is still quite possible that overexuberance began to emerge in the midst of the huge increases in trading volumes seen in 2007, this certainly does not seem to have been true during the large gains enjoyed on the Shanghai Stock Exchange in 2005–2006.

NINE

Economic Interdependence with Taiwan

with Hsin-hui I. H. Whited[1]

"Made by Taiwan but made in China" would be a new expression to describe the global division of labor across the Taiwan Strait driven by Taiwanese business-people's direct investment in China.

(Tung, 2004, p. 6)

Introduction

This chapter examines the relationship between mainland China and Taiwan both in terms of trade integration and flows of foreign direct investment and in terms of overall macroeconomic interdependence as represented by output, money, inflation, and financial market interrelationships. There has been striking ongoing growth in trade linkages and investments flows in the years since Taiwan's government eased its blanket restrictions on interactions with mainland China in 1985. These trade flows also accelerated sharply after mainland China and Taiwan each joined the World Trade Organization (WTO) around the end of 2001. The importance of Taiwanese foreign direct investment, however, clearly remains understated in official data. Limits imposed by Taiwan's government on allowed investments in the mainland have sparked considerable Taiwan-led investments entering the mainland via third areas like Hong Kong, the British Virgin Islands, and the Cayman Islands. This trend is reflected in the fact that official figures of foreign direct investment inflows to mainland China (otherwise inexplicably) rank the British Virgin Islands second in importance only to

[1] Hsin-hui I. H. Whited is Associate Professor of Economics at Colorado State University-Pueblo (ida.whited@colostate-pueblo.edu). The authors thank Kishen Rajan and Tom Willett for their helpful comments and are grateful to Nancy Tao for her valuable research assistance.

Hong Kong. The cumulative total of Taiwanese foreign direct investment in mainland China through 2007 may actually have reached $US 150 billion.

The growing economic integration between mainland China and Taiwan is also reflected in substantial interdependence between output, price, money, and stock price variables in the two economies. Whereas stronger influences generally extend out from mainland China to Taiwan, evidence of at least some degree of mutual interdependence arises in most cases. Although it is possible that some of the indicated effects of mainland China on Taiwan reflect China's influence on world markets as a whole in addition to direct transmission effects, the empirical results generally seem consistent with the quite close ties between the two economies suggested in trade and capital flow data. Consistent responses of each M2 money supply measure to developments in the other economy are particularly noteworthy as M2 was the main target variable for both central banks over our sample period. These implied monetary interactions are very much in keeping with the overall importance of external influences on Chinese monetary policy emphasized in Part I of this volume.

The Growing Importance of Cross-Strait Linkages

Mainland China's high degree of openness, especially in comparison to Japan, was discussed in Chapter 2. As with the rapid growth spurts enjoyed by other Asian economies, including Hong Kong and Taiwan in the 1970s and 1980s, openness has allowed mainland China to capitalize on high-quality human capital while acquiring advanced technology from abroad.[2] China is, in fact, already ranked among the top twenty-five countries in the world in terms both of its overall globalization level and its level of "economic globalization" – as reflected in the importance of trade, foreign direct investment, portfolio investment, and income flows (see Lockwood and Redoano, 2005).[3] An important element of mainland China's increased globalization has been growing economic ties with Taiwan, helped, of course, by geographical proximity as well as common heritage and language. A newfound common emphasis on export promotion (cf. Chow, 2007, pp. 58–59), coupled with the gradual easing of government restrictions on

---

[2] See Chow (2006, 2007) for comparative analysis and detailed discussion of the overall importance of globalization to mainland China's economy.

[3] One concern with mainland China's rapidly increased globalization is that it has been accompanied by increased inequality, however, as manifested not only across individual income levels but also rural-urban income differentials and regional income differentials (cf. Siddique, 2006).

cross-strait trade, has set the stage for a considerable degree of economic interdependence despite continuing political ambiguity (and animosity).

The separate political systems of mainland China and Taiwan date, of course, from the exodus of the defeated Nationalists to Taiwan at the end of the 1940s (Chapter 6). After the Nationalists established themselves on the island, Taiwan and mainland China followed entirely separate paths. Taiwan adopted an export promotion strategy amid close ties with the West while mainland China largely withdrew from world markets as discussed in Chapter 1. Even after US President Richard Nixon's visit to China in 1972 marked the beginning of a thawing in US–mainland China relations, there was, at first, still no *rapprochement* between the People's Republic and Taiwan. Indeed, Taiwanese firms were expressly forbidden any involvement on the mainland under Taiwan President Chiang Ching-kuo's 1979 policy of "no contact, no negotiation, no compromise."[4] Even so, mainland China began officially encouraging links with Taiwan, including the adoption of a zero-tariff policy on imports from Taiwan in 1980 (Tung, 2004, p. 1) – which was subsequently abandoned after one year for want of interest on the other side of the Taiwan Strait. A major shift in Taiwanese policy occurred in 1985, however, with the announcement by Taiwan's government of a "Noninterference Principle of Indirect Exports to the Mainland." In turn, mainland China offered special incentives for Taiwanese investment. Two investment zones, with special tax privileges for Taiwan-invested enterprises, were established in Fujian province in May 1989, for example, and new legislation was passed in 1994 protecting investment from Taiwan (Sutter, 2002, p. 524; Tung, 2004, p. 4).

Estimated total trade between mainland China and Taiwan rose from just $US 1.1 billion in 1985 to $US 88.1 billion in 2006 – with the 2006 figures comprising $US 63.3 billion flowing from Taiwan to mainland China and $US 24.8 billion in exports from mainland China to Taiwan (see Table 9.1). Trade flows accelerated considerably after Taiwan, like mainland China, joined the WTO around the end of 2001 – with Taiwan's entry date of January 1, 2002 close on the heels of mainland China's own December 11, 2001 entry. Indeed, during the five-year period from 2001–2006, cross-strait trade volumes increased by over 194%. In 2006, cross-strait trade accounted for just over 20.65% of Taiwan's total foreign trade and for 5% of mainland China's total foreign trade (Table 9.2). Taiwan's overall positive

---

[4] Chiang Ching-kuo was the son of former leader Chiang Kai-shek. They both left mainland China for the last time on December 10, 1949, after directing the last-ditch defense of Chengdu (by then the only remaining Nationalist-controlled city on the mainland).

Table 9.1. *The Level of Cross-Strait Trade Between Taiwan and Mainland China*

	Taiwan Exports to Mainland China	Mainland China Exports to Taiwan	Total Bilateral Trade
1985	$986.8	$115.9	$1,102.7
1986	811.3	144.2	955.5
1987	1,226.5	288.9	1,515.4
1988	2,242.2	478.7	2,720.9
1989	3,331.9	586.9	3,918.8
1990	4,394.6	765.4	5,160.0
1991	7,493.5	1,125.9	8,619.4
1992	10,547.6	1,119.0	11,666.6
1993	13,993.1	1,103.6	15,096.7
1994	16,022.5	1,858.7	17,881.2
1995	19,433.8	3,091.4	22,525.2
1996	20,727.3	3,059.8	23,787.1
1997	22,455.2	3,915.4	26,370.6
1998	19,840.9	4,110.5	23,951.4
1999	21,312.5	4,522.2	25,834.7
2000	25,009.9	6,223.3	31,233.1
2001	24,061.3	5,902.0	29,963.3
2002	31,528.8	7,968.6	39,497.4
2003	38,292.7	11,017.9	49,310.6
2004	48,930.4	16,792.3	65,722.7
2005	56,271.5	20,093.7	76,365.2
2006	63,332.4	24,783.1	88,115.5

Notes: Figures are in $US millions and are based on estimates by Taiwan's Mainland Affairs Council that include transit trade between Taiwan and Mainland China via Hong Kong.
Source: Mainland Affairs Council.

trade balance in recent years has, in fact, been very much dependent upon its surpluses with mainland China. In 2006, for example, Table 9.2 shows that Taiwan's estimated trade surplus with mainland China via Hong Kong was $US 38.5 billion while its overall surplus was just $US 21.3 billion – implying a deficit of $17.2 billion with the rest of the world. Indeed, despite ongoing governmental limitations, and continued disallowance of direct trade links, mainland China became Taiwan's second largest export market by 1993 and has been its top export market since 2002 (Tung, 2004). The importance of this relationship to mainland China is reflected in the fact that Taiwan became China's fourth largest trading partner over the 1990s.

Table 9.2. *Cross-Strait Trade Relative to Taiwan and Mainland China's Overall World Trade*

	Taiwan's Trade Balance with Mainland China	Taiwan's Trade Balance with the Rest of the World	Cross-Strait Trade as Share of Total Taiwan Trade	Cross-Strait Trade as Share of Total Mainland China Trade
1985	$870.9	$10,623.7	2.17%	1.58%
1986	667.1	15,680.0	1.49	1.29
1987	937.6	18,695.3	1.71	2.06
1988	1,763.5	10,994.6	2.47	2.65
1989	2,745.0	14.038.6	3.31	3.51
1990	3,629.2	12,498.4	4.23	4.47
1991	6,367.6	13,420.7	6.17	6.35
1992	9,428.6	9,769.7	7.55	7.05
1993	12,889.5	8,564.0	9.24	7.71
1994	14,163.8	8,602.5	9.93	7.55
1995	16,342.4	9,330.5	10.36	8.02
1996	17,667.5	14,658.6	10.79	8.21
1997	18,539.8	9,214.8	11.03	8.11
1998	15,730.4	7,365.6	11.00	7.39
1999	16,790.3	12.537.3	11.00	7.16
2000	18,786.6	11,217.8	10.67	6.60
2001	18,159.3	18,343.7	12.79	5.88
2002	23,560.2	22,071.6	15.89	6.36
2003	27,274.8	22,590.4	17.70	5.79
2004	32,138.1	13,612.8	18.72	5.69
2005	36,177.8	15,817.3	20.04	5.37
2006	38,549.3	21,296.2	20.65	5.00

Notes: Figures in the first two columns are in $US millions and the third and fourth columns are in percentages.
Source: Mainland Affairs Council.

WTO membership has been accompanied by increased liberalization of mainland China–Taiwan trade.[5] Should this eventually allow direct trade and transport ties to replace indirect shipping via Hong Kong or, to some extent, Japan, the reduction in shipping costs would significantly add to the attractiveness of cross-strait trade. Transshipping goods via a third area may have added as much as $US 1.51 billion to annual cross-strait transportation costs in 2001, or just over 5% of the total trade value (Lardy, 2002, p. 166).

[5] The trend toward shrinking interest rate differentials between the Greater China economies of mainland China, Hong Kong, and Taiwan during 1996–2003 was already "suggestive of increasing integration between these economies" (Cheung, Chinn, and Fujii, 2007a, p. 63).

Table 9.3. *Taiwan Remittances to and from Mainland China, 2002–2006*

	Taiwan Remittances to Mainland China	Growth Rate	Mainland China Remittances to Taiwan	Growth Rate
2002	$13,596	–	$4,846	–
2003	39,596	191.23%	19,268	297.61%
2004	65,680	65.88	33,644	74.61
2005	98,200	49.51	46,781	39.05
2006	128,942	31.31	72,571	55.13

Notes: Figures in the first and third columns are in $US millions and the second and fourth columns are in percentages. Remittance data were expanded in September 2006 to include the Offshore Banking Unit as well as the Designated Foreign Exchange Bank of Taiwan. Complete series are available only from June 2001.
Source: Mainland Affairs Council.

In 2006, 28.27% of Taiwan's total exports and 12.23% of Taiwan's total imports were attributed to mainland China. If trade with Hong Kong is added to these figures, we then have 38.87% of Taiwan's total exports and 13.55% of Taiwan's total imports.[6] Mainland China itself accounted for over 80% of Taiwan's total foreign investment in 2006, with a cumulative total of $US 56.98 billion in approved investments in mainland China from 1991 through March 2007. During the first three months of 2007 alone, 258 cases totaling $US 2.08 billion were approved, representing an 8.4% increase year-on-year. The dramatic rise in the flows of funds between mainland China and Taiwan in recent years is shown in Table 9.3. Remittances from Taiwan to mainland China exceeded $US 128 billion in 2006, up 31% from 2005 and up almost tenfold since 2002. Remittances from mainland China to Taiwan have also soared, reaching over $US 72 billion in 2006, up 55% from 2004 and up nearly fifteenfold since 2002.

Official Chinese statistics show Taiwan accounting for 12.74% of all foreign direct investment (FDI) projects in mainland China over the 1979–1999 period, second only to Hong Kong. Meanwhile Taiwan's 7.76% share in the realized value of mainland China FDI ranked fourth, just behind the United States and Japan (Zhang, 2005).[7] Taiwan's official share of realized FDI was 6.25% over the January 1979–March 2007 period as a whole but

[6] The cross-strait totals discussed in this section are all drawn from issues of the *Cross-Strait Economic Statistics Monthly* – available from Taiwan's Mainland Affairs Council (http://www.mac.gov.tw/english/index1-e.htm).

[7] Taiwan also has been the fourth largest contributor of intraregional FDI in the East Asian and South-East Asian regions as a whole in recent years (United Nations Conference on Trade and Development, 2006, pp. 54–57).

Table 9.4. *Mainland China FDI Contributions from Greater China Compared,*
2002–2007

	Realized Foreign Direct Investment				
	Hong Kong and Macau	British Virgin Islands	Japan	United States	Taiwan
2002	$ 18,329.31	$ 6,117.39	$ 4,190.09	$ 5,423.92	$ 3,970.64
	(34.75%)	(11.60%)	(7.94%)	(10.28%)	(7.53%)
2003	18,116.70	5,776.96	5,054.19	4,198.51	3,377.24
	(33.86%)	(10.80%)	(9.45%)	(7.85%)	(6.31%)
2004	19,546.60	6,730.30	5,451.57	3,940.95	3,117.49
	(32.24%)	(11.10%)	(8.99%)	(6.50%)	(5.14%)
2005	18,549.25	9,021.67	6,529.77	3,061.23	2,151.71
	(30.75%)	(14.96%)	(10.82%)	(5.07%)	(3.57%)
2006	20,835.82	11,247.58	4,598.06	2,865.09	2,135.83
	(29.99%)	(16.19%)	(6.62%)	(4.12%)	(3.07%)
Cumulative:	284,713.00	60,749.00	59,089.00	54,647.00	44,245.00
Jan. 1979–	(40.23%)	(8.58%)	(8.35%)	(7.72%)	(6.25%)
March 2007					

Notes: Figures are in $US millions with the corresponding percentage shares given in parentheses.
Source: Mainland Affairs Council.

has evidenced a declining trend since 2002 – steadily falling from 7.53% in 2002 to 3.07% in 2006 (Table 9.4). However, these figures fail to fully account for reexporting from Taiwan to mainland China via Hong Kong. They also ignore substantial Taiwanese investment via holding companies in tax-exempt countries like the British Virgin Islands and the Cayman Islands (Tung, 2004). It is not known precisely how much Taiwanese FDI enters mainland China via these "third areas." However, Taiwan's Central Bank Governor Perng Fai-nan concluded that, by the end of 2002, cumulative FDI from Taiwan into mainland China had already reached $US 66.8 billion – after incorporating "tallies on investments made by Taiwan business people via third countries or areas" (*Taipei Times*, January 17, 2003, p. 11). Meanwhile, Sutter (2002, p. 528) estimates that total FDI from Taiwan to mainland China reached $US 70–100 billion over the 1989–2000 period alone – after taking account of the role played by Taiwanese offshore companies in Hong Kong as well as the British Virgin Islands and the Cayman Islands. A 2007 estimate put the cumulative total as high as $US 150 billion (see Hille, 2007, p. 22). This figure compares with cumulative direct investment from Taiwan since 1979, as officially reported by the Mainland Affairs Council, of just $US 44.25 billion through March 2007!

The British Virgin Islands became mainland China's second most important reported source of realized FDI over the January 1979–March 2007 period (after Hong Kong and Macau). Its share of total realized FDI reached 16.19% in 2006, with total realized investment up 67% in just two years – rising from $US 6.73 billion in 2004 to $US 11.25 billion in 2006 (see Table 9.4). Although we cannot be sure just how much of this accelerating British Virgin Islands activity reflects funds channeled from Taiwan, the overall increases in the British Virgin Islands' share of realized FDI certainly far outweigh the declines observed in the official figures for direct FDI into mainland China from Taiwan since the early 2000s. Moreover, the decline in Taiwan's reported share of total mainland China FDI to below 5% after 2004 can be compared with estimates of a "true share" in the 20.0 to 22.5% range (see Cooke, 2006, p. 5).

Taiwan's FDI in China, like that of the largest contributor, Hong Kong, remains heavily export-orientated. Mainland China's pool of cheap labor, coupled with the incentives offered to FDI by the People's Republic, have been key factors fueling the inflow of funds from Taiwan.[8] Taiwanese FDI has been further boosted by the common heritage of mainland China and Taiwan and the short distance between them (cf. Gao, 2005). The risk of political factors disrupting economic ties has remained an omnipresent concern, however, with Taiwanese investors almost certainly having more to fear than other foreign investors in mainland China. This fact may help explain why the average size of Taiwanese investments in mainland China has tended to be much smaller than average, typically only half the size of the average Japanese investment, for example (Hsiao and Hsiao, 2004). Another factor in these smaller-sized investments is almost certainly the past Taiwan government policy of prohibiting mainland China investments over $US 50 million, however, while allowing investments under $US 30 million to proceed subject only to mainland government approval (Sutter, 2002, pp. 525–526). The blanket $50 million cap on individual investments was lifted in August 2001, at which time the cap on total investment in China by Taiwan-listed firms was also raised (*Asia Pacific Bulletin*, 2001).

In spite of the gradually eased restrictions over the years, in 2007 Taiwan's government still imposed an overall cap of 20% – for Taiwanese companies with total capitalization of $US 300 million or more – on the share of the firm's total business that could be conducted on the mainland. Democratic Progressive Party Legislator Hong Chi-chang urged that the cap be raised to

---

[8] China's possible displacement of FDI that would otherwise have gone elsewhere remains a controversial issue (see, for example, Fung, Iizaka, and Siu, 2005).

40%,[9] arguing that, with Taiwanese firms already circumventing the current rules by investing via third areas (as discussed earlier), a higher cap would at least allow them to legally reinvest some of their profits in Taiwan (see Huang, 2007, p. 8). One way to skirt the government-imposed cap has been to list separately in Hong Kong and thereby raise capital to support separate business operations there. As Cooke (2006, p. 6) puts it:

> Taiwanese companies are essentially voting with their feet in favor of the long-term prospects of the mainland economy and against the economic policies of the Taiwanese government.

Such a strategy could involve listing in mainland China as well as Hong Kong. Whereas approximately forty Taiwanese companies were listed on Hong Kong stock exchange in early 2007, the strength of mainland China's stock markets (Chapter 8) appeared to be fueling interest in bypassing Hong Kong to list directly on the mainland. Although only five Taiwanese companies had issued Shanghai or Shenzhen "A" shares at the beginning of 2007, this number was expected to double by the end of the year – and perhaps even double again in 2008 (Hille, 2007, p. 22).

In the following sections, we turn to the question of whether the growing trade and FDI links between mainland China and Taiwan may be reflected in overall co-movement between the two economies. If the mainland China and Taiwan economies have become more closely linked, as the preceding discussion would suggest, we would expect this to be associated with co-movement of such key variables as output, money growth, inflation, and share price indices. In examining the possible linking of these broader macroeconomic variables over the post-1994 period, we hope to shed some light on whether the idea of a unified "Greater China" region – including Taiwan as well as mainland China and Hong Kong – indeed seems to be emerging economically in spite of continued political impediments.[10]

Comparative Trends in Taiwan's Macroeconomy

As discussed in Chapter 3, after an inflation spike in 1993–1994, mainland China went into deflation when it was hit by the 1997–1998 Asian financial

---

[9] A higher 40% cap already applied to smaller companies with net values below $US 150 million – whereas companies lying between $US 150 million and $US 300 million faced a 30% cap.

[10] The 1994 start date allows us to obtain consistent money supply series from the two economies. We cannot examine the still more recent post-WTO period in isolation because we would be left with insufficient observations to perform empirical tests.

crisis. Taiwan did not initially slide into deflation at that time, but deflation did emerge in the island's economy during the later 2000–2001 global slowdown. Unlike mainland China, and most other East Asian countries, Taiwan moved away from a fixed exchange rate regime well prior to the Asian financial crisis. After switching to its current "managed float" exchange rate regime in 1978, Taiwan enjoyed both low levels of inflation and low variability of inflation, with inflation generally kept below 5% since the end of the 1979–1980 oil price shock. Central bank policy responsiveness to inflation is implied by such recent reaction function studies as Chang (2005) and Huang and Lin (2006). Chang (2005) also identifies a significant response to stock prices. Although neither study finds a significant response to output fluctuations, Cover, Hueng, and Yau (2002) argue that actual performance of the Taiwanese economy in terms of both output and price variability compares favorably to simulated performance under a variety of hypothetical central bank policy rules over the 1978–1999 period. None of these studies, however, considers central bank responses to mainland Chinese variables. Given the high level of openness of Taiwan's economy (the share of exports and imports being close to 100% of GDP) and dependence on China, both direct policy responses to Chinese variables, as well as indirect responses via the effects of mainland China variables on domestic economic indicators, seem plausible. Indeed, the relationship between Taiwan and its much larger main trading partner and neighbor bears some basic similarity with that between Canada and the United States – a case where such direct and indirect responses to developments in the larger partner are known to have been of considerable importance (cf. Burdekin and Burkett, 1992).

As discussed in Chapter 4, the People's Bank has adopted a money supply targeting strategy, with a particular emphasis on broad money (M2). Taiwan's central bank also emphasized M2 growth during the 1990s. Whereas the link between M2 growth and consumer price inflation in Taiwan has not always been consistent over the post-1961 period (Shen, 2002), both M2 and the consumer price index (CPI) trend downward over the 1990s. As with mainland China, these declines accelerated with the coming of the Asian financial crisis and (eventually) culminated in outright deflation. Nevertheless, mainland China and Taiwan both weathered the Asian financial crisis much better than almost all other East Asian economies, which typically experienced both massive currency depreciation and severe recession.[11] Although not sharing mainland China's rigid capital

---

[11] Taiwan's relatively robust weathering of the Asian financial crisis actually seemed to have the additional effect of breaking the high degree of commonality previously observed between Taiwan and Korea (Hsiao and Hsiao, 2001).

controls – that still leave the renminbi convertible only on the current account today (Chapter 1) – Taiwan shared China's strong foreign reserve position and low level of external debt. Taiwan's economy subsequently turned downward in 2001, however, as reflected in both negative economic growth and a sharp increase in unemployment. The unemployment rate actually jumped from just under 3% in 2000 to 4.57% in 2001, while the New Taiwan dollar depreciated by over 6% against the US dollar in that year. Although this depreciation was considerably smaller than the 18.7% depreciation experienced in 1997 during the Asian financial crisis, Taiwan's economy was quite severely impacted – much more so than mainland China's – by the bursting of the Nasdaq bubble in 2000 and the terrorist attacks of September 11, 2001. Political frictions likely also acted to exacerbate the 2001 economic weakness in Taiwan (see Yang and Shea, 2005).

An ongoing concern is that excessive flows of Taiwanese investment capital to the mainland may have left domestic producers starved of capital – leading Lin (2005), for example, to strongly argue against any creation of a "cross-strait common market" that would further integrate Taiwan into mainland China's economy. Meanwhile, Huang (2007) argues that capital outflows to mainland China, recently running at 4% to 6% of Taiwan's overall GDP, have been a major factor depressing Taiwan's domestic investment rates. On the other hand, Chen (2006) believes that Taiwan is in a transition phase from a traditional export-orientated economy to a more advanced intensive economy – and sees the capital outflow as a positive factor allowing Taiwanese firms to benefit from a cheaper manufacturing base and an expanded market.[12] In any event, declines in Taiwan's GDP deflator and CPI ended in 2004. Wholesale prices recovered earlier, generally trending upward from 2000. Yang and Shea (2005) attribute this divergence between wholesale and consumer price performance in Taiwan to the influence of mainland China's demand for raw materials and capital goods in boosting global prices of such goods and thereby boosting Taiwan's import prices as well. Expansionary policy by Taiwan's central bank was reflected in successive reductions of the discount rate from 4.75% in June 2000 to 1.375% in June 2003 (Yang and Shea, 2005).

Meanwhile, the seeming undervaluation of Taiwan's currency was accompanied by foreign reserve accumulation that, in percentage terms at least, rivaled that enjoyed by mainland China. Mainland China's ongoing reserve

---

[12] The situation varies by industry, however, and Chen (2006) offers some specific suggestions as to how Taiwanese industries may seek to maintain competitive advantage and long-term operations.

buildup, as well as the hefty Taiwanese reserve accumulation over the 1980s and 1990s, was discussed in Chapter 2. Central bank foreign exchange reserves in Taiwan actually increased by nearly 100% from 2000–2003, rising from $US 106.7 billion at the end of 2000 to $US 206.6 billion at the end of 2003 (Yang and Shea, 2005). The rate of increase of Taiwan's foreign exchange reserves slowed after 2003, however, increasing by only a total 28.8% over the next three years to $US 266.1 billion at the end of 2006 (Central Bank of China [Taiwan]). In order to see how Taiwan has fared overall in recent years, and the extent to which its performance may have become linked to mainland China, we consider data on a key set of macroeconomic variables collected over a 1994–2005 sample period.[13]

Although the economies of mainland China and Taiwan can certainly not be said to always move in lockstep, both economies do appear to have enjoyed a similarly strong pickup in industrial production after 2001 (Figure 9.1).[14] In Taiwan's case, the return to positive real growth in 2002 was reflected in gains in industrial production that then accelerated after 2002. The question of whether any of this recovery is linked to the turnaround in mainland China's economic position is addressed empirically in the next section. Meanwhile, the upward trend in both consumer price indices prior to the Asian financial crisis is evident in Figure 9.2 – followed by a leveling off in both series prior to renewed increases in 2003–2004. As noted earlier, the exact timing of the deflation differs somewhat, though, with mainland China both entering and exiting deflation earlier than Taiwan. Comparison between mainland China's producer price index (PPI) and Taiwan's wholesale price index (WPI) in Figure 9.3 suggests divergent trends over the earlier part of the sample followed by common upward movements after 1998. However, Taiwan's WPI enjoys a noticeably bigger increase from 2001 onward.

We also consider possible commonalities between money growth rates in mainland China and Taiwan, considering year-to-year growth rates in both M2 and M1 money supply measures – and in Taiwan's case an

---

[13] In order to make econometric analysis feasible, from this point on we must limit our attention to series that are available on a monthly basis. The trade and FDI data discussed earlier, although playing a critical role in explaining the interdependence of the two economies, are available only on an annual basis and so would not leave us with enough observations for sensible econometric analysis. All mainland China data assessed here are drawn from the Great China Database and the Taiwan data are from the Republic of China Statistical Database and the Central Bank of China (Taiwan).

[14] We use industrial production as our output series because, unlike GDP data, it is available on a monthly basis.

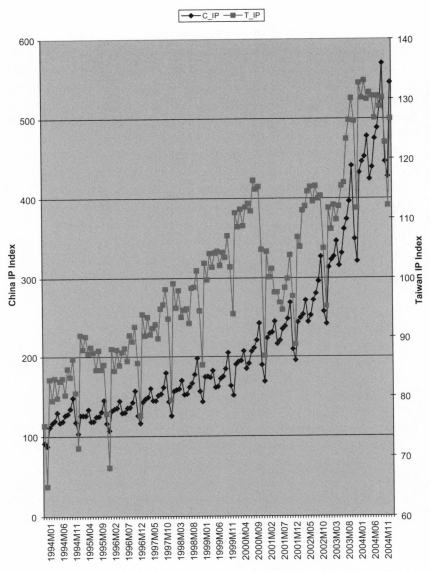

Figure 9.1. Mainland China Industrial Production (C_IP) vs. Taiwan Industrial Production (T_IP), 1994–2005.

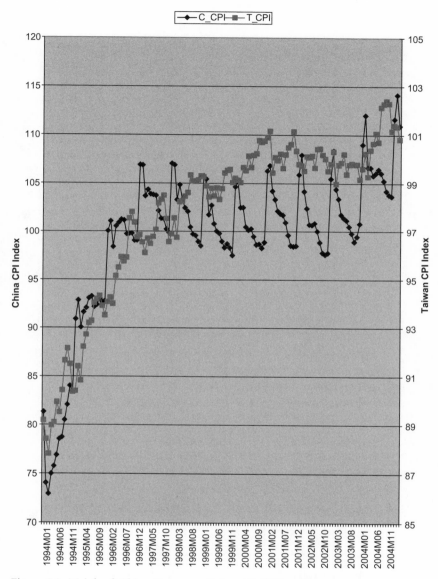

Figure 9.2. Mainland China Consumer Prices (C_CPI) vs. Taiwan Consumer Prices (T_CPI), 1994–2005.

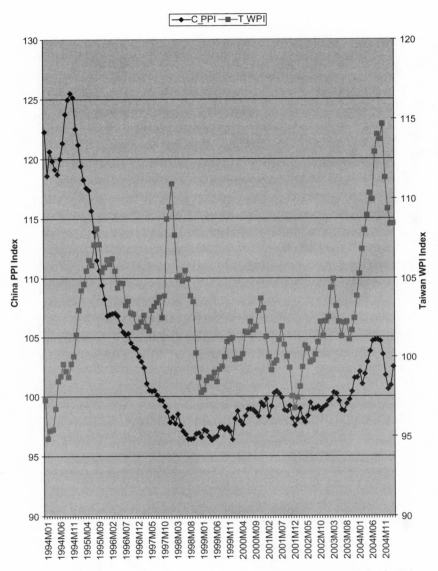

Figure 9.3. Mainland China Producer Prices (C_PPI) vs. Taiwan Wholesale Prices (T_WPI), 1994–2005.

extended M1 money supply definition (M1B) that includes passbook savings deposits (Figures 9.4–9.6).[15] The different pairs of money growth rates generally appear to match each other's ups and downs quite closely over 1994–2005, with mainland China's M1 and Taiwan's M1A growth especially moving almost in tandem save for an extra surge in Taiwanese M1A in 2004. Finally, we consider respective stock market performances based on the value of the Taipei stock market and the Shanghai "A" Share index (Figure 9.7). The linkages between mainland China and Hong Kong financial markets, and possible long-run, cointegrating relationship between the Shanghai and Hong Kong stock markets, was discussed in the preceding chapter. The data displayed in Figure 9.7 suggest that the Shanghai and Taipei stock markets may also feature a certain degree of commonality, insofar as both markets appear to follow a similar trajectory over the 1994–2000 period. After that point, the Taipei index breaks down sharply before recovering in 2002, however, whereas the Shanghai index peaks in early 2001 and then enters an extended downturn through 2005.[16]

Empirical Evidence on the Relationship Between the Mainland China and Taiwan Macro Variables

Strong output correlations between mainland China and Taiwan have been identified by Cheung, Chinn, and Fujii (2007a, p. 39), who point to the degree of output co-movement rising above 0.5 during 1991–2002 – higher, in fact, than the implied output co-movement between mainland China and Hong Kong.[17] While Cheung, Chinn, and Fujii (2007a, chapter 4) suggest that overall integration between mainland China and Taiwan outweighed financial market linkages, they do not explicitly consider possible monetary policy responsiveness to developments in the other economy. Otherwise, most prior studies of interactions between mainland China and Taiwan

[15] Taiwan's M1A contains currency held by the public plus checking accounts and passbook deposits of enterprises and individuals (includes nonprofit organizations) in monetary institutions. M1B is defined as M1A plus passbook savings deposits of individuals (includes nonprofit organizations) in monetary institutions.

[16] The Shanghai market's subsequent moves to record highs in 2006–2007, which were discussed in Chapter 8, lie outside the present sample period – which is limited by the availability of other variables.

[17] Cheung and Yuen (2005) also identify commonality in long-run and short-run output fluctuations based on their cointegration analysis. Overall integration between mainland China and Hong Kong, however, seems to have remained higher than between mainland China and Taiwan (Cheung, Chinn, and Fujii, 2007a).

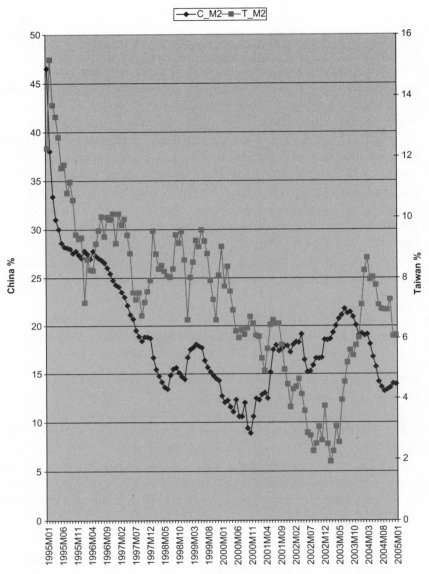

Figure 9.4. Mainland China M2 Growth (C_M2) vs. Taiwan M2 Growth (T_M2), 1994–2005.

have tended to be more narrowly focused on either trade relationships or stock market interdependence. Significant linkages between mainland China and Taiwan stock markets, as well as with Hong Kong, have been consistently identified in such studies as Bahng and Shin (2004), Cheng and Glascock (2005, 2006), and Chi, Li, and Young (2006). Notwithstanding

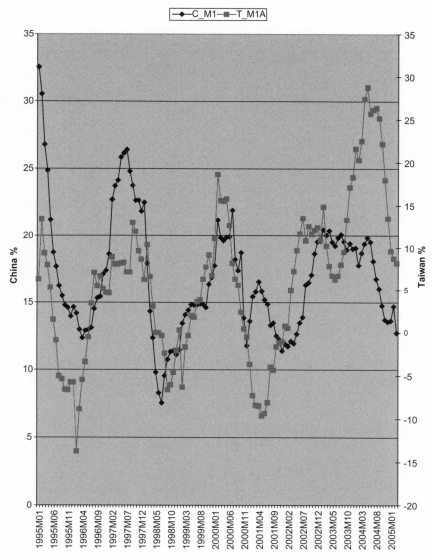

Figure 9.5. Mainland China M1 Growth (C_M1) vs. Taiwan M1A Growth (T_M1A), 1994–2005.

significant short-run effects of US markets on the Greater China group (Wang and Firth, 2004), there is more mixed evidence concerning longer-run integration, or cointegration, with the US market (Cheng and Glascock, 2005, 2006; Chi, Li, and Young, 2006).

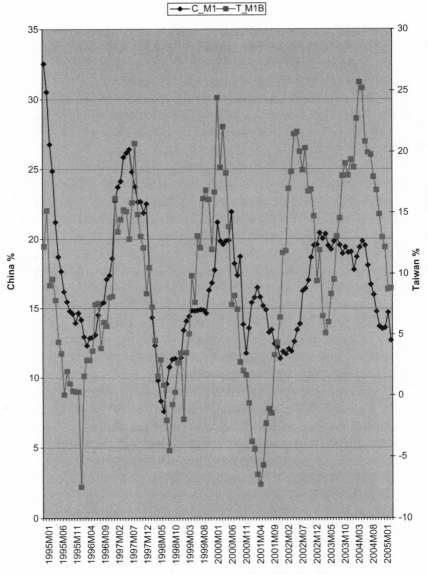

Figure 9.6. Mainland China M1 Growth (C_M1) vs. Taiwan M1B Growth (T_M1B), 1994–2005.

It seems important to allow for a broader range of potential interactions and interdependence between mainland China and Taiwan that goes beyond stock market indices alone and considers possible monetary interdependence as well as price and output relationships. We begin by examining the

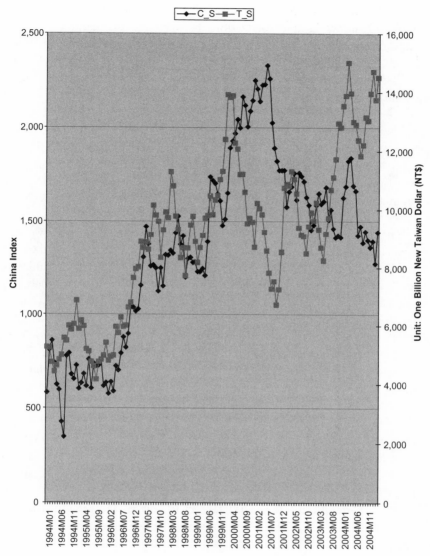

Figure 9.7. Shanghai "A" Shares (C_S) vs. Taipei Market Value (T_S), 1994–2005.

simple correlation coefficients between our mainland China and Taiwan variables. These data are all monthly series from January 1994 through March 2005.[18] These correlations generally reflect the correspondence

---

[18] Seasonality has been removed from the data via the Holt-Winters exponential smoothing method.

suggested in the preceding figures. With the series specified in levels, Table 9.5 shows sample correlations between the mainland China and Taiwan series pairs to be 0.89 for industrial production, 0.82 for consumer prices, 0.9 or higher for the three money supply pairs, and 0.67 for the stock market series. Only the mainland China PPI and Taiwan WPI fail to exhibit such conformity with a correlation of −0.05. When the series are converted to growth rates, the correlation values naturally decline but still remain substantial. Table 9.6 shows sample correlations of 0.24 for industrial production growth, 0.73 for consumer price inflation, 0.54 for M2 growth, 0.44 and 0.43 for mainland China M1 growth versus Taiwan M1A and M1B growth, respectively, and 0.42 for the stock market series. The mainland China PPI versus Taiwan WPI correlation becomes 0.10 with the series in growth rate form.

The Table 9.6 correlations also suggest high degrees of co-movement between M2 growth and consumer price inflation in both mainland China and Taiwan, with M2-CPI correlations of 0.79 for mainland China and 0.71 for Taiwan. Furthermore, there is a correlation coefficient of 0.49 between mainland China M2 growth and Taiwanese consumer inflation and a correlation of 0.65 between Taiwan's M2 growth and mainland China's consumer inflation. These results suggest possible mutual sensitivity of inflation performance to monetary policy on the other side of the Taiwan Strait. There are also some high correlations between money growth and industrial production growth and share price movements. Chinese industrial production growth exhibits a 0.25 correlation with own M1 growth and a 0.62 correlation with Taiwan M1A growth but no positive correlation with either M2 measure. Taiwanese industrial production growth has a 0.36 correlation with mainland China M1 growth and a correlation of 0.68 with Taiwan M1A growth but only minimal positive correlations with the M2 measures. Finally, Shanghai share price growth has a 0.37 correlation with mainland China M1 growth and 0.36 with respect to Taiwan M2 growth, whereas Taiwanese share growth has a correlation of 0.52 with mainland China M1 growth and even higher correlations with Taiwan M1A and M1B growth.

Causal relationships between the mainland China and Taiwan variables are examined by Granger-causality testing (a technique previously illustrated in Chapter 5). It is possible for both variables to exert causal effects on each other, a situation described as "bidirectional" causality. The data series are all specified in growth rate form in this case in order to assure stationarity. The results reported in Table 9.7 generally suggest that significant, bidirectional relationships underlie the sizeable correlations displayed in Table 9.6

Table 9.5. *Means, Standard Deviations, and Correlations with Data in Levels*

Chinese Variables	C_IP	C_CPI	C_PPI	C_M2	C_M1	C_S
Mean	216.84	99.33	103.32	12,564.98	4,708.03	1,357.74
Standard Deviation	109.19	7.84	7.83	6,249.90	2,277.16	482.18

Taiwanese Variables	T_IP	T_CPI	T_WPI	T_M2	T_M1A	T_M1B	T_S
Mean	100.25	97.72	102.74	168,970.31	18,220.16	43,922.48	90,734.71
Standard Deviation	15.35	3.46	3.92	36,452.48	3,427.91	12,920.12	27,536.49

Correlation Table

	C_IP	C_CPI	C_PPI	C_M2	C_M1	C_S	T_IP	T_CPI	T_WPI	T_M2	T_M1A	T_M1B	T_S
C_IP	1												
C_CPI	0.47	1											
C_PPI	-0.31	-0.79	1										
C_M2	0.94	0.62	-0.52	1									
C_M1	0.95	0.59	-0.49	1.00	1								
C_S	0.44	0.56	-0.73	0.62	0.61	1							
T_IP	0.89	0.51	-0.50	0.89	0.90	0.62	1						
T_CPI	0.64	0.82	-0.87	0.79	0.78	0.81	0.75	1					
T_WPI	0.46	0.42	-0.05	0.34	0.34	-0.10	0.34	0.24	1				
T_M2	0.86	0.69	-0.66	0.97	0.96	0.77	0.88	0.89	0.24	1			
T_M1A	0.94	0.53	-0.31	0.92	0.93	0.42	0.85	0.62	0.49	0.84	1		
T_M1B	0.95	0.59	-0.44	0.98	0.99	0.56	0.89	0.73	0.39	0.94	0.97	1	
T_S	0.71	0.68	-0.63	0.79	0.78	0.67	0.81	0.76	0.25	0.83	0.80	0.83	1

Notes: C_Y and T_Y refer to mainland China and Taiwan industrial production; C_IP and T_IP refer to mainland China and Taiwan industrial production; C_CPI and T_CPI refer to mainland China and Taiwan consumer price indices; C_PPI and T_WPI refer to mainland China and Taiwan producer price and wholesale price indices; C_M1, T_M1A, and T_M1B refer to mainland China and Taiwan narrow money supplies; C_M2 and T_M2 refer to mainland China and Taiwan broad money supplies; and C_S and T_S refer to mainland China and Taiwan stock market indices.

Sources: Data sources are noted in the body of the chapter.

Table 9.6. *Means, Standard Deviations, and Correlations with Data in Growth Rate Form*

Chinese Variables.	C_IP	C_CPI	C_PPI	C_M2	C_M1	C_S
Mean	14.99	3.22	−1.52	18.95	16.88	11.91
Standard Deviation	10.38	5.80	4.05	6.15	4.48	29.82

Taiwanese Variables	T_IP	T_CPI	T_WPI	T_M2	T_M1A	T_M1B	T_S
Mean	4.92	1.19	1.34	7.36	5.98	9.44	12.88
Standard Deviation	7.63	1.37	4.80	2.58	9.02	7.96	27.69

Correlation Table

	C_IP	C_CPI	C_PPI	C_M2	C_M1	C_S	T_IP	T_CPI	T_WPI	T_M2	T_M1A	T_M1B	T_S
C_IP	1												
C_CPI	−0.19	1											
C_PPI	0.66	−0.34	1										
C_M2	−0.20	0.79	−0.52	1									
C_M1	0.25	0.33	0.12	0.40	1								
C_S	−0.27	0.06	−0.16	0.01	0.37	1							
T_IP	0.24	0.02	0.24	0.01	0.36	0.12	1						
T_CPI	−0.39	0.73	−0.47	0.49	0.00	0.24	−0.07	1					
T_WPI	0.27	0.46	0.10	0.14	0.26	−0.13	0.19	0.23	1				
T_M2	−0.46	0.65	−0.39	0.54	0.19	0.36	0.06	0.71	0.11	1			
T_M1A	0.62	−0.07	0.51	−0.10	0.44	0.00	0.68	−0.23	0.35	−0.13	1		
T_M1B	0.40	−0.13	0.36	−0.04	0.43	0.04	0.67	−0.33	0.14	−0.14	0.90	1	
T_S	0.11	0.02	0.01	0.15	0.52	0.42	0.59	−0.02	−0.06	0.22	0.66	0.75	1

Notes: All series are expressed as year-to-year growth rates.

Table 9.7. *Granger-Causality Between Taiwan and Mainland Variables*

Null Hypothesis	F-Statistic	Probability
T_Y does not Granger-cause C_Y	5.43293	0.00545
C_Y does not Granger-cause T_Y	28.76580	5.00E–11
T_CPI does not Granger-cause C_CPI	12.56710	10.00E–05
C_CPI does not Granger-cause T_CPI	5.60818	0.00463
T_WPI does not Granger-cause C_PPI	0.01298	0.98710
C_PPI does not Granger-cause T_WPI	1.09567	0.33745
T_M1A does not Granger-cause C_M1	17.02400	2.80E–07
C_M1 does not Granger-cause T_M1A	9.11325	0.0002
T_M1B does not Granger-cause C_M1	15.20790	1.20E–06
C_M1 does not Granger-cause T_M1B	5.58614	0.00473
T_M2 does not Granger-cause C_M2	7.35183	0.00095
C_M2 does not Granger-cause T_M2	6.65427	0.00179
T_S does not Granger-cause C_S	0.98484	0.37622
C_S does not Granger-cause T_S	0.77853	0.46126
T_M2 does not Granger-cause C_M1	8.41077	0.00037
C_M1 does not Granger-cause T_M2	10.58760	5.60E–05
T_M1A does not Granger-cause C_M2	15.06900	1.30E–06
C_M2 does not Granger-cause T_M1A	7.25695	0.00104
T_M1B does not Granger-cause C_M2	10.07000	8.70E–05
C_M2 does not Granger-cause T_M1B	4.91217	0.00881
T_CPI does not Granger-cause C_M2	18.77680	7.20E–08
C_M2 does not Granger-cause T_CPI	1.77745	0.17325
T_Y does not Granger-cause C_M2	10.95710	4.10E–05
C_M2 does not Granger-cause T_Y	5.40058	0.00561
T_M1A does not Granger-cause C_CPI	2.98119	0.05429
C_CPI does not Granger-cause T_M1A	0.96619	0.38331
T_S does not Granger-cause C_PPI	2.55097	0.082
C_PPI does not Granger-cause T_S	0.49896	0.60834
T_Y does not Granger-cause C_PPI	0.13960	0.86984
C_PPI does not Granger-cause T_Y	7.67532	0.00071
T_CPI does not Granger-cause C_Y	6.17693	0.00275
C_Y does not Granger-cause T_CPI	2.64906	0.07462
T_M1A does not Granger-cause C_Y	88.9482	7.00E–25
C_Y does not Granger-cause T_M1A	0.5796	0.5616
T_M1B does not Granger-cause C_Y	40.95010	1.90E–14
C_Y does not Granger-cause T_M1B	0.12004	0.88698
T_M2 does not Granger-cause C_Y	33.06100	2.80E–12
C_Y does not Granger-cause T_M2	0.44482	0.64194

Notes: All data series are in percentage change form to assure stationarity.

Table 9.8. *Significant Granger-Causality Pairs for the Mainland China*
Variables

Null Hypothesis	F-Statistics	Probability
C_M1 does not Granger-cause C_CPI	18.3550	9.9E–08
C_CPI does not Granger-cause C_M1	15.5739	8.9E–07
C_M2 does not Granger-cause C_CPI	4.84528	0.00938
C_CPI does not Granger-cause C_M2	14.6167	1.9E–06
C_M2 does not Granger-cause C_M1	6.28912	0.00249
C_M1 does not Granger-cause C_M2	12.0929	1.6E–05
C_PPI does not Granger-cause C_M1	0.88423	0.41556
C_M1 does not Granger-cause C_PPI	2.89761	0.05881
C_Y does not Granger-cause C_M1	6.07875	0.00301
C_M1 does not Granger-cause C_Y	3.14545	0.04642
C_Y does not Granger-cause C_M2	25.5511	4.7E–10
C_M2 does not Granger-cause C_Y	10.3926	6.6E–05
C_PPI does not Granger-cause C_CPI	0.43435	0.64864
C_CPI does not Granger-cause C_PPI	3.30406	0.03992
C_S does not Granger-cause C_CPI	0.11304	0.89320
C_CPI does not Granger-cause C_S	2.07110	0.13028
C_Y does not Granger-cause C_CPI	17.8074	1.5E–07
C_CPI does not Granger-cause C_Y	17.7977	1.5E–07
C_Y does not Granger-cause C_PPI	1.64847	0.19643
C_PPI does not Granger-cause C_Y	2.81699	0.06353

Notes: All data series are in percentage changes to assure stationarity.

earlier.[19] Table 9.7 shows significant bidirectional causality between main-land China and Taiwan industrial production, mainland China and Taiwan consumer prices, and each pair of narrow and broad money supply measures. However, the producer price/wholesale price indices and share price measures do not significantly Granger-cause each other. Results for other significant combinations of mainland China and Taiwan variables are also reported in Table 9.7 and these findings suggest that increased money growth in one economy tends to be followed by increased industrial production in the other economy. Additional significant causal effects are seen running from the mainland China PPI to Taiwanese industrial production and from the Taiwanese CPI to mainland China industrial production.

Table 9.8 reports significant Granger-causality pairs among different combinations of mainland China variables, and Table 9.9 provides analogous results for the set of Taiwanese variables. Table 9.8 suggests strongly

[19] A lag length of two is imposed throughout based on the Schwartz criterion. (Additional allowance for an extended lag length of three was seen to have little impact on the results.)

Table 9.9. *Significant Granger-Causality Pairs for the Taiwan Variables*

Null Hypothesis	F-Statistics	Probability
T_M1A does not Granger-cause T_CPI	0.92733	0.39827
T_CPI does not Granger-cause T_M1A	7.75071	0.00067
T_M1B does not Granger-cause T_CPI	2.62747	0.07619
T_CPI does not Granger-cause T_M1B	9.40311	0.00016
T_M2 does not Granger-cause T_CPI	5.24209	0.00649
T_CPI does not Granger-cause T_M2	5.20690	0.00671
T_Y does not Granger-cause T_M1A	0.24094	0.78624
T_M1A does not Granger-cause T_Y	34.2098	1.3E–12
T_Y does not Granger-cause T_M1B	0.31650	0.72927
T_M1B does not Granger-cause T_Y	15.7812	7.6E–07
T_S does not Granger-cause T_M1B	2.62454	0.07640
T_M1B does not Granger-cause T_S	2.14804	0.12093
T_Y does not Granger-cause T_M2	0.08839	0.91546
T_M2 does not Granger-cause T_Y	7.91591	0.00058
T_WPI does not Granger-cause T_CPI	2.04127	0.13410
T_CPI does not Granger-cause T_WPI	0.83703	0.43537
T_Y does not Granger-cause T_CPI	24.2309	1.2E–09
T_CPI does not Granger-cause T_Y	3.39176	0.03673
T_WPI does not Granger-cause T_S	0.10023	0.90470
T_S does not Granger-cause T_WPI	2.62001	0.07673

Notes: All data series are in percentage changes to assure stationarity.

significant causal effects of M1 and M2 growth on CPI inflation in mainland China as well as significant bidirectional causality between the two different money supply measures. Money supply effects on the PPI are less consistent, however, with only M1 growth having any significant effects, and even here the significance level drops to around the 94% level. There are strongly significant bidirectional relationships between money growth and industrial production growth and between CPI inflation and industrial production growth. There is weaker evidence of an effect of PPI inflation on industrial production and an effect of CPI inflation on share prices that is significant at around the 87% confidence level. In the case of Taiwan, Table 9.9 reveals significant effects of money growth on CPI inflation and industrial production for M2 but generally not for M1A or M1B. Although there is significant bidirectional causality between CPI inflation and industrial production growth in Taiwan, no such relationship holds for the WPI.

A more general assessment of the importance of macroeconomic interactions between mainland China and Taiwan is provided by "decomposing" the variance of each of the mainland China and Taiwan variables.[20] This variance decomposition assesses the relative importance of fluctuations in domestic variables relative to the effects of their counterpart variables in the other economy. The total effect of the other-economy variables provides a potentially valuable yardstick as to the overall sensitivity of each economy to the other. Given that the application of this procedure is based on examining the full set of variables together as part of a single system, we had to make a choice between the alternative price measures. In light of the findings reported earlier, we employ consumer prices as the price measure for both mainland China and Taiwan. We also use M2 as the money supply measure for both economies – although very similar results were found if the narrow money supply measures are used instead. We look at effects extending over a twelve-period window, which boils down to one year given that all the data are monthly.

The results reported in Table 9.10 show that the average sensitivity to Taiwanese variables ranges from 21.38% to 12.41% across the four mainland China series. Mainland China CPI appears to feature the greatest sensitivity to developments in Taiwan, while share prices feature the lowest sensitivity. As would be expected, the Taiwanese variables almost always reveal stronger responsiveness to economic fluctuations on the other side of the Taiwan Strait. The only exception to this is the Taiwanese CPI, for which the average contribution to total variance arising from mainland China variables is almost the same as mainland China CPI's overall sensitivity to the effects of Taiwanese variables. Mainland China variables account for as much as 52.18% of the overall variation in Taiwanese industrial production; 29.35% of the variation in Taiwanese M2; 20.91% for Taiwanese CPI; and 13.97% for Taiwanese share values. These results offer additional confirmation of the high degree of overall interdependence suggested by the preceding correlations and causality-test results, while also revealing that – as would have been expected – Taiwan's smaller economy is more sensitive to these effects than mainland China's.

---

[20] Prior testing using the MacKinnon-Haug-Michelis (1999) critical values revealed the presence of four cointegrating equations for the equation system. All variables are specified in levels for the purposes of this last empirical exercise so as to utilize the properties of the cointegration relationship – with each series featuring the same I(1) order of integration. Burdekin and Whited (2007) provide further details on this point, together with the results of applying impulse response analysis to the mainland China and Taiwan variable set. This impulse response procedure examines how shocks in one variable produce ongoing movements in another. The results reported in Burdekin and Whited (2007) appear to confirm the importance of cross-strait effects on M2 money growth rates, in particular.

Table 9.10. *Variance Decompositions of the Mainland China and Taiwan Variables*

Period	C_CPI	C_Y	C_M2	C_S	T_CPI	T_Y	T_M2	T_S	Total % from Taiwanese Variables
Variance Decomposition of C_CPI									
1	100	0	0	0	0	0	0	0	0
2	81.45	6.03	1.25	0.01	1.94	2.26	6.50	0.56	11.26
3	63.44	19.04	0.96	0.18	4.71	2.66	7.34	1.68	16.38
4	56.94	22.94	0.98	1.99	3.89	4.86	6.15	2.25	17.15
5	52.87	22.59	1.58	2.57	5.89	6.67	5.66	2.17	20.38
6	50.00	21.97	1.53	2.87	9.44	6.78	5.32	2.08	23.63
7	47.58	20.98	1.87	2.86	12.86	6.68	5.19	1.98	26.71
8	46.39	20.75	1.87	2.79	14.41	6.73	5.12	1.93	28.19
9	45.72	21.25	1.89	2.75	14.60	6.80	5.06	1.91	28.37
10	45.21	21.76	1.87	2.76	14.43	7.02	5.06	1.89	28.40
11	44.68	22.42	1.90	2.78	14.07	7.32	4.99	1.85	28.23
12	43.99	23.36	1.90	2.87	13.70	7.52	4.87	1.80	27.88
Average					9.16	5.44	5.10	1.68	21.38
Variance Decomposition of C_Y									
1	36.82	63.18	0	0	0	0	0	0	0
2	43.33	43.92	1.74	0.60	1.33	0.00	8.99	0.09	10.41
3	36.68	37.62	3.87	1.21	6.57	0.05	13.85	0.15	20.63
4	35.64	36.52	4.61	1.17	6.62	0.95	14.20	0.29	22.06
5	33.83	37.27	5.26	1.15	6.37	2.47	13.33	0.33	22.50
6	31.76	38.42	5.65	1.25	6.21	2.48	13.69	0.54	22.92
7	29.29	39.43	8.25	1.33	6.10	2.43	12.67	0.50	21.71
8	27.84	39.82	8.32	2.67	5.82	2.66	12.36	0.50	21.35
9	26.74	38.68	8.90	3.73	5.74	2.74	12.93	0.54	21.95
10	25.53	38.39	9.84	4.10	5.56	3.01	12.86	0.73	22.15
11	24.40	37.86	9.90	4.84	5.35	3.44	13.13	1.09	23.00
12	23.17	36.36	10.49	5.61	5.10	3.55	14.02	1.70	24.37
Average					5.06	1.98	11.84	0.54	19.42
Variance Decomposition of C_M2									
1	3.43	4.23	92.34	0	0	0	0	0	0
2	3.05	2.00	89.54	0.65	1.03	0.10	2.06	1.57	4.75
3	6.30	2.06	81.99	4.16	0.74	0.10	1.49	3.17	5.49
4	10.45	3.13	74.52	4.83	0.63	0.07	1.90	4.48	7.07
5	10.38	2.98	72.48	5.09	0.47	0.12	1.45	7.04	9.07
6	11.44	3.14	66.62	6.61	0.43	0.14	1.76	9.86	12.19
7	13.04	3.21	61.60	7.16	0.42	0.10	2.47	12.00	14.99
8	13.40	2.83	58.30	7.63	0.77	0.08	2.61	14.39	17.84
9	14.13	2.52	54.06	8.65	1.17	0.06	3.06	16.35	20.65
10	15.22	2.26	50.47	9.29	1.49	0.08	3.59	17.60	22.76
11	15.77	1.95	47.87	9.81	1.95	0.10	3.76	18.79	24.60
12	16.37	1.70	45.17	10.51	2.35	0.13	4.04	19.74	26.25
Average					0.95	0.09	2.35	10.41	13.81

(*continued*)

Table 9.10 (continued)

Period	C_CPI	C_Y	C_M2	C_S	T_CPI	T_Y	T_M2	T_S	Total % from Taiwanese Variables
Variance Decomposition of C_S									
1	2.98	0.18	0.00	96.85	0	0	0	0	0
2	2.02	0.23	0.38	95.87	0.04	1.15	0.25	0.06	1.51
3	2.89	0.39	0.78	92.08	0.03	1.68	1.27	0.88	3.86
4	3.29	0.96	0.98	88.07	0.14	2.19	2.78	1.59	6.70
5	3.20	1.56	1.19	84.25	0.19	2.48	4.37	2.76	9.79
6	3.14	1.97	1.33	81.48	0.16	2.72	5.22	3.98	12.07
7	2.88	2.20	1.50	79.12	0.22	2.86	6.04	5.18	14.30
8	2.55	2.21	1.89	77.00	0.48	2.84	6.69	6.32	16.34
9	2.27	2.11	2.36	74.92	0.94	2.77	7.24	7.40	18.35
10	2.06	2.00	2.87	72.79	1.41	2.66	7.83	8.39	20.29
11	1.91	1.91	3.43	70.69	1.80	2.54	8.40	9.32	22.06
12	1.80	1.84	3.95	68.75	2.10	2.45	8.91	10.21	23.67
Average					0.63	2.19	4.92	4.67	12.41

Period	C_CPI	C_Y	C_M2	C_S	T_CPI	T_Y	T_M2	T_S	Total % from Chinese Variables
Variance Decomposition of T_CPI									
1	9.95	2.33	1.76	0.01	85.96	0	0	0	14.04
2	6.16	5.35	2.86	0.65	78.65	5.40	0.60	0.31	15.02
3	8.76	5.78	3.09	3.81	71.24	3.96	3.13	0.23	21.44
4	7.92	5.78	6.37	3.67	66.96	5.52	3.33	0.46	23.74
5	7.39	5.40	6.02	4.85	63.17	7.70	5.03	0.44	23.66
6	6.95	5.99	5.69	4.71	58.64	10.46	7.13	0.43	23.34
7	6.87	6.48	5.36	4.36	54.20	13.17	8.86	0.71	23.06
8	7.36	6.58	4.92	4.00	49.76	15.94	10.07	1.37	22.86
9	6.97	6.72	4.58	3.74	46.08	17.04	12.45	2.42	22.01
10	6.56	6.52	4.67	3.52	43.61	17.60	13.80	3.74	21.26
11	6.13	6.11	4.62	3.52	42.21	17.57	14.76	5.08	20.38
12	5.91	5.70	4.74	3.72	40.99	17.05	15.75	6.13	20.08
Average	7.24	5.73	4.56	3.38					20.91
Variance Decomposition of T_Y									
1	20.41	2.31	0.07	0.91	4.41	71.89	0	0	23.71
2	55.11	1.94	0.88	1.09	2.38	38.36	0.14	0.11	59.02
3	45.94	10.50	1.98	1.74	3.22	34.80	1.68	0.14	60.16
4	39.02	15.55	1.69	4.73	2.72	29.67	5.81	0.81	60.99
5	33.88	14.25	3.14	5.02	5.31	25.75	9.59	3.07	56.28
6	31.55	13.71	3.04	5.40	6.21	23.90	10.34	5.85	53.70
7	29.63	13.44	2.99	5.68	6.51	22.64	10.98	8.13	51.74
8	28.05	13.95	2.87	5.70	6.17	21.44	11.92	9.91	50.57

Period	C_CPI	C_Y	C_M2	C_S	T_CPI	T_Y	T_M2	T_S	Total % from Chinese Variables
9	26.42	16.02	2.94	5.61	6.22	20.12	11.60	11.08	50.99
10	24.60	18.19	2.82	6.13	6.47	18.74	11.39	11.66	51.74
11	23.22	20.05	3.00	6.62	6.46	17.64	11.22	11.79	52.88
12	21.95	22.33	3.07	7.02	6.40	16.70	10.81	11.71	54.38
Average	31.65	13.52	2.37	4.64					52.18
Variance Decomposition of T_M2									
1	1.45	3.01	11.78	0.45	0.99	0.12	82.21	0	16.68
2	0.74	10.11	6.48	1.94	0.62	0.84	78.93	0.35	19.26
3	1.44	15.95	7.30	2.39	2.11	1.63	67.28	1.89	27.08
4	4.31	16.98	7.34	3.20	5.63	3.11	57.70	1.74	31.82
5	7.85	13.89	6.26	3.62	13.03	2.94	50.94	1.47	31.62
6	9.53	11.58	5.40	3.58	19.30	2.75	46.63	1.22	30.09
7	12.77	9.96	4.64	3.08	21.72	2.41	44.39	1.03	30.46
8	15.41	9.16	4.15	2.83	22.15	2.24	43.14	0.92	31.56
9	16.82	8.72	4.10	2.70	21.93	2.25	42.62	0.86	32.34
10	17.63	8.64	4.19	2.67	21.03	2.34	42.66	0.82	33.14
11	18.01	8.75	4.25	2.80	20.16	2.45	42.79	0.78	33.82
12	18.04	8.89	4.43	2.99	19.47	2.62	42.83	0.73	34.36
Average	10.33	10.47	5.86	2.69					29.35
Variance Decomposition of T_S									
1	0.66	0.25	4.62	3.42	0.02	0.22	11.23	79.58	8.95
2	0.36	0.13	7.83	2.34	0.11	0.36	16.40	72.47	10.66
3	0.34	0.18	8.70	1.94	0.50	0.45	20.16	67.74	11.15
4	0.33	0.14	9.08	1.56	1.37	0.35	20.74	66.42	11.12
5	0.74	0.16	9.57	1.33	3.12	0.28	19.86	64.94	11.81
6	1.19	0.71	10.02	1.18	5.43	0.25	18.36	62.86	13.10
7	1.54	1.56	10.27	1.05	7.42	0.29	17.42	60.45	14.41
8	1.94	2.17	10.87	0.94	8.43	0.36	16.90	58.39	15.92
9	2.16	2.62	11.36	0.88	8.82	0.40	16.49	57.26	17.02
10	2.21	2.91	11.55	0.88	8.83	0.41	16.35	56.87	17.54
11	2.18	3.07	11.64	0.96	8.64	0.40	16.40	56.73	17.84
12	2.09	3.17	11.67	1.15	8.41	0.38	16.42	56.71	18.08
Average	1.31	1.42	9.77	1.47					13.97

Note: The analysis was performed with the variables ordered as follows: C_CPI, C_Y, C_M2, C_S, T_CPI, T_Y, T_M2, T_S.

Conclusions

The growing ties between mainland China and Taiwan are seen to be reflected in a substantial degree of macroeconomic interdependence between the two neighboring economies. These co-movements are quite in keeping with the strong trade linkages and flows of FDI from Taiwan to mainland China. Although Taiwan macroeconomic variables are generally more sensitive to cross-strait effects than mainland China's, significant bidirectional causality suggests a meaningful sensitivity to such effects on the mainland China side as well. Industrial production and money supply growth in the two economies seem to be particularly closely linked, and the results also suggest international transmission of money supply growth across the Taiwan Strait. Although this cannot be proven to represent deliberate policy responses, the monetary sensitivity identified for M2 captures reactions in the target variable pursued by both central banks over our sample period. The interpretation of any such reactions remains complicated, however, as they would necessarily combine direct responses to movements in the other economy with indirect reactions – whereby fluctuations abroad induce movements in domestic variables that the central bank is seeking to stabilize.

TEN

Conclusions and Future Prospects
for the Renminbi

On the condition that the [renminbi's] convertibility is realized, the Hong Kong dollar may be pegged to the [renminbi] instead of the dollar in the future.
(Donald Tsang, Chief Executive of the Hong Kong regional government, May 2006)[1]

Introduction

China's rise to prominence in the financial sphere – at last beginning to catch up with its long-standing powerful economic growth and growing importance in world trade – was symbolized in April 2007, when mainland China's stock exchanges in Shanghai and Shenzhen for the first time overtook Hong Kong in terms of total market capitalization. Although Hong Kong still had a substantial lead in initial public offerings (IPOs) in 2006 (Table 10.1), a majority of these funds were generated by the IPOs of two of mainland China's own state-owned banks (Chapter 7) – which on their own accounted for over $US 25 billion of the $US 41.22 billion total. Moreover, the Chinese authorities had kept the Shanghai and Shenzhen exchanges closed to new listings during the first half of 2006. Total mainland China IPOs were expected to exceed $US 52 billion during 2007. A senior Hong Kong banker was quoted as saying that "[a]uthorities in Hong Kong are going to have to work very hard to maintain the dominance and relevance of the bourse" (Kwong, Tucker, and Gangahar, 2007, p. 1).

There have been reports of the Shanghai Stock Exchange making new efforts to encourage listings by prominent foreign companies like HSBC (Dyer and Tucker, 2007). An HSBC listing would have special historic

---

[1] As quoted by Kwan (2006a).

The author is grateful to Tom Willett and Yanjie Feng Burdekin for their helpful comments.

Table 10.1 *Markets with Top Ten Initial Public Offering (IPO) Volumes in 2006*

Ranking	Stock Market	IPO Volume (in billions of US dollars)
No. 1	Hong Kong	$ 41.22
No. 2	London Main Market	39.31
No. 3	New York	29.22
No. 4	Nasdaq	17.47
No. 5	Euronext Amsterdam	12.52
No. 6	London AIM	11.92
No. 7	Moscow	11.76
No. 8	Frankfurt	9.74
No. 9	Shanghai	9.62
No. 10	Tokyo First Section	8.99

Source: Nie (2007)

significance, given the major role the bank has played in Shanghai, and mainland China generally (Chapter 5).[2] Despite the relatively undeveloped nature of China's financial markets overall, the increasing liquidity in the nation's debt markets, and broadening array of financial instruments, have been accompanied almost overnight by the emergence of the Shanghai Stock Exchange into the world spotlight. The market's rise has not only caught the world's attention but also led to a major influx of funds from China's vast horde of personal savings accounts. Although these new investors should not be counting on the kind of gains registered by the market in 2006–2007, such growing interest in the nation's financial markets offers some hope that China will be able to evolve away from its historically near-total reliance on bank credit as a form of finance (see Chapters 7 and 8).

It is certainly high time for China's financial system to start emulating the breathtaking growth registered in the real economy, not to mention the tremendous expansion in exports that has recently received so much attention, and ire, in the United States. As discussed in Chapter 2, China's import growth has actually been nearly as great as its export growth – seemingly belying any allegations that it has operated as a closed economy. Exchange rate policy, however, like financial market development, has admittedly lagged behind. The renminbi did not become fully convertible even for current account transactions until 1996. Nevertheless, the authorities have gradually moved to a somewhat more flexible exchange rate policy

---

[2] HSBC was listed in Shanghai before the old stock market was closed after the Communist takeover in 1949.

and the degree of renminbi overvaluation has by no means been sufficiently clear-cut as to justify recent US congressional demands for "mandatory" immediate further adjustment (Chapter 1). Nor is it obvious that any such adjustment would fundamentally change the US trade position, any more than the pressure for yen appreciation reversed ongoing Japanese surpluses in the 1970s and 1980s (Chapter 2). Directing efforts toward such legitimate concerns as China's insufficient protection of intellectual property rights, and widespread piracy, would surely be both more fruitful and more justifiable – and certainly better than the threat of punitive tariffs and the risk of a modern-day version of the old Smoot-Hawley tariff of June 1930.[3]

China's ongoing surpluses with the United States have already had the effect of making it a major player in the market for US Treasuries and other dollar assets. Thus far, most of the reserves accumulated by China have been kept in US dollar assets (Chapter 2). Should that change, any sudden sale of these holdings would likely exert significant new downward pressure on the dollar as well as on the price of US government bonds. Although such a move would cause China itself to incur losses on remaining dollar-based holdings, there remains some real vulnerability on the US side that is perhaps not sufficiently recognized. China's move to create a new sovereign wealth fund to invest some of its massive reserve holdings in higher-yielding assets has not so far been accompanied by any announced shift away from dollar assets – but rather from lower-risk, lower-return dollar holdings of Treasuries to higher-risk, potentially higher-return areas like China's 2007 investment in the Blackstone Group IPO (Chapter 2). Indeed, just as China's move toward higher-risk asset types seems to be part of a widespread trend, such changes in instrument composition appear to have dominated any more marginal adjustments in currency composition on the part of central banks around the world (Galati and Wooldridge, 2006, pp. 4–5).

It is hard to say how much, if any, currency diversification would be justified on purely economic terms (cf. Papaioannou, Portes, and Siourounis, 2006). The actual share of the US dollar in worldwide reserve holdings has, in fact, remained fairly stable – with the dollar's approximate two-thirds share in 2006 being essentially in line with the levels of the mid-1990s. The euro remained in distant second place in 2006, followed by the pound sterling, which – in a striking advance – has taken third place ahead of the Japanese yen (see Galati and Wooldridge, 2006). With the renminbi still not convertible for capital account purposes, the immediate prospects of

---

[3] This act has been seen by many as helping usher in the Great Depression.

China's currency emerging as another contending world reserve currency remain distant. According to Eichengreen (2007, p. 147):

> While the renminbi is many people's favorite candidate for the new reserve-currency champion four or five decades from now, such hopes, in my opinion, are highly premature.

Although Eichengreen could end up being proven correct, this volume's examination of monetary developments in China shows that dramatic, unexpected shifts are more the norm than the exception. As recently as 2005, for example, China's stock markets appeared totally moribund and a paucity of funds flowing into the market was the concern – in stark contrast to the later worries about having too much of a good thing. Meanwhile, in the late 1990s China faced deflation and devaluation seemed so inevitable that a survey was distributed in March 1998 to gauge the likely psychological impact of such a devaluation on financial market participants in Hong Kong (Wei et al., 2000)!

There are, in fact, already some early signs of an expanding role of the renminbi within Asia, especially in Hong Kong. While it is, indeed, much too early to say how far, or how fast, this process will go, the expanding use of the renminbi as a "vehicle" currency for making transactions has recently been accompanied by new renminbi-based bond issues in Hong Kong. On June 26, 2007, China Development Bank, the largest of the set of policy banks established in 1994 (Chapter 7), announced plans for a RMB 5 billion bond issue in Hong Kong (yielding 3% a year over a two-year term). This was the first such bond issue placed outside mainland China. The China Development Bank bond issue was almost three times oversubscribed and quickly followed by a RMB 2 billion bond sale by China Export-Import Bank (Chan and Nie, 2007). According to Henry Tang, financial secretary of the Hong Kong regional government:

> Although the total amount of renminbi in Hong Kong is not very large, about 25 billion HK dollars, I think that with further co-operation and integration between Hong Kong and the Mainland in terms of financial and monetary instruments, the pool can only grow.[4]

The People's Bank of China (2005b) reported that, as of November 1, 2005, there were already thirty-eight banks in Hong Kong – representing almost all banks offering retail services – providing personal renminbi business to their clients. One source of renminbi circulation outside the

---

[4] As quoted in the *People's Daily Online* (June 26, 2007b).

mainland has been through its use by the rising numbers of visitors traveling to Hong Kong from the mainland since individual visas, as well as group visas, were permitted in 2004.[5] The renminbi has also been used in border trade with neighboring economies like Taiwan, Malaysia, and Thailand. Renminbi circulation arising from this border trade was estimated at RMB 23.7 billion in 2002, and in 2003 such transactions were legitimized under a new Chinese government policy permitting the use of the renminbi as a settlement currency for border trade (Li, 2004). According to Zhang (2006, p. 34) this "carries the eventuality that the Chinese currency will become a vehicle currency for international trade and a currency for international settlement." It does appear that at least some meaningful internationalization of the renminbi has taken place in spite of the ongoing capital account restrictions. Indeed, Li (2004, p. 92) emphasizes the potential gains accruing from increased renminbi circulation in Macau and Taiwan, as well as Hong Kong, in helping to boost regional trade and foster the integration of "Greater China."

Until July 2005, the Hong Kong dollar and the renminbi were effectively linked via each currency's fixed exchange rate with the US dollar. The post-2005 appreciation of the renminbi against the dollar has led to accompanying appreciation against the Hong Kong dollar, however, as Hong Kong stuck to its "currency board" with the US dollar.[6] Von Furstenberg and Wei (2004, p. 39) argue that such a move is actually likely to end up hurting Hong Kong insofar as it "raises Hong Kong's cost of inputs used in its exports to the dollar zone more than the [Hong Kong dollar] value of the proceeds from Hong Kong's final sales to the mainland." At the very least, the de-linking of the Hong Kong dollar and the renminbi adds to the potential benefits of adopting a common currency by taking the exchange rate fluctuations of the post-2005 period out of the mix. Given the existing seemingly high degree of economic integration between the two economies, based on output and inflation co-movements, interest rate convergence, and trade linkages, the costs to Hong Kong of such an arrangement may well be

---

[5] The author's own experience during the summer of 2007 was that renminbi currency, at least in the larger RMB 50 and RMB 100 denominations, seemed commonly accepted for settling cash transactions in Hong Kong.

[6] Under a currency board with the US dollar, the monetary authorities commit to exchange local currency for US dollars at a fixed rate upon demand. This means that local currency issues are fully backed by US dollar holdings and holders can withdraw their funds as US dollars at any time. Hong Kong's present currency board arrangements date from 1983. It previously implemented a currency board with the pound sterling, starting from December 1935 (Chapter 5).

smaller than the benefits (cf. Cheung and Yuen, 2005; Cheung, Chinn, and Fujii, 2007a; Cavoli and Rajan, 2007).

Although Xu (2006) argues that lack of coordination of business cycles in mainland China and Hong Kong could be a potential pitfall, integration seems certain to only increase going forward and this is likely to increase synchronization. Additional impetus stems from the 2004 "Closer Economic Partnership Arrangement" between mainland China and Hong Kong, which offers zero tariffs on goods going in both directions as well as lower entry barriers for banking institutions and other service sectors. Indeed, the Chinese authorities appear to have already begun the process of expanding renminbi usage in Hong Kong and continued, albeit gradual, advancement seems inevitable. This could culminate in Hong Kong finding it "economically sensible to [if not] adopt the RMB ... at least peg to the RMB while maintaining some sort of convertibility agreement with the mainland similar to Singapore and Brunei, or ... Hong Kong and Macau ... " (Cavoli and Rajan, 2007, p. 32).

Although limitations on renminbi capital account convertibility make it implausible that the renminbi could completely supersede the Hong Kong dollar in the very near term, the barriers to renminbi circulation have already been significantly lessened in recent years. Zhang (2006, p. 29), lists a number of ways in which the renminbi was, *de facto,* at least partially convertible on the capital account by 2006:

There are no restrictions on foreign debts incurred by foreign invested enterprises. No approval is required for short-term and trade-related financing (three months or less). Non-residents can purchase both A shares and B shares, government bonds, commercial papers, H shares and [Non-tradable] shares. Foreign investors in China are allowed to repatriate to their home countries profits from direct investment and other investment. There are no restrictions on loans to foreign establishments by their parent or affiliated firms. And neither is international lending by foreign invested enterprises in China subject to restrictions.

Based on trade linkages and general economic interdependence between mainland China and Taiwan (Chapter 9), a case could be made on economic grounds for a currency union extending to Taiwan rather than just Hong Kong and mainland China (Cheung and Yuen, 2005). Cheung, Chinn, and Fujii (2007a) go further and consider an expanded currency union including other Asian economies such as Japan, Korea, and Singapore. Realistically, however, neither remaining limitations on renminbi convertibility nor political acceptability leave any prospect of the renminbi being adopted by these other states in the foreseeable future.

Monetary integration extending beyond just mainland China and Hong Kong would likely require a common currency basket as suggested, for example, by Williamson (2005). The practicability of such an arrangement, as well as how the system would be anchored, remains open to question, though. Mundell's (2003) suggestion that a fully dollarized Hong Kong might be the best anchor for such a system has surely been definitively ruled out by recent events, as has the idea of a generalized link to the US dollar among the different East Asian economies. Hefeker and Nabor (2005) suggest that the renminbi is the natural future anchor for such a system, but recognize that it is not yet ready to fulfill such a role. They propose setting up a currency basket system that allows the respective currency weights to change over time, suggesting that the weight attached to the Japanese yen should decline over time whereas the weight attached to the renminbi should increase. Indeed, Hefeker and Nabor (2005) draw parallels with the European experience whereby, starting from an initially more symmetric system, the Deutsche mark gradually emerged as the anchor currency.[7]

The proposed Asian Currency Unit (ACU) might conceivably serve as a first step in this direction. This concept derives from the earlier European Currency Unit, which came into being as an internal accounting unit in March 1979 and enjoyed some limited use in international financial transactions prior to the January 1999 introduction of the euro. Although the Asian Development Bank has been considering the launch of the ACU for some time, the proposed set of included currencies, and their respective weights, had still not been announced as of year end 2007. Meanwhile, Genberg (2006) argues that the East Asian economies should not, at least for now, adopt an exchange rate anchor of any kind owing to potential instability stemming from high degrees of financial market integration. Genberg argues in favor of a common pursuit of inflation targeting by separate independent central banks, which could help make full monetary integration feasible (much) further down the road.

Just how big a role the renminbi will play in Asia's future is, of course, unclear, as is the time frame. Yet it seems likely that we will see its role expand substantially within the forty- to fifty-year timeline referred to by Eichengreen (2007). Continued renminbi penetration in Hong Kong, and its eventual dominance there, seems assured within the next decade,

---

[7] Needless to say, the overall benefits of a broader Asian currency union are not so easily established as for mainland China and Hong Kong alone. Even assuming the nations concerned have any real interest in proceeding in this direction, Mushin (2006) correctly cautions against too readily drawing parallels from the European experience and assuming that what worked there would also work in Asia.

if not sooner. Although the renminbi is certainly not yet ready to be the centerpiece of any broader common currency arrangements in Asia, even assuming other economies were willing to accept it, the absence of any other obvious contender within the region suggests that it is the most viable long-term option there as well.[8] Meanwhile, rising renminbi usage as a vehicle currency outside mainland China–Hong Kong, as well as continued slow but steady capital account liberalization, should help pave the way for the much larger future role it seems destined to achieve. From Li's (2007, p. 42) perspective:

As the renminbi comes to serve as the vehicle currency in Asian trade and financial transactions, it will not only serve as a reserve asset for the public and for enterprises, but also as an intervention asset for the government, that is, as a part of reserve currency . . . The Chinese financial market will be more open and the renminbi will autonomously become the nominal anchor for some countries.

[8] The Japanese yen, while currently still the most widely held Asian currency, has been falling in importance worldwide due, in part, to the long-standing economic weakness in Japan.

References

Almanac of China's Finance and Banking, Beijing, various issues.

Anderlini, Jamil (2007a), "Chinese Bourses Eclipse All of Asia," *Financial Times*, May 10, p. 1.

Anderlini, Jamil (2007b), "China's Corporate Bonds Come of Age," *Financial Times*, June 15, p. 21.

Anderlini, Jamil (2007c), "China Hits Out over 'Hot Money,'" *Financial Times*, June 28, p. 13.

Anderson, Jonathan (2006a), "Five Persistent Myths about China's Banking System," *Cato Journal* 26 (Spring/Summer): 243–250.

Anderson, Jonathan (2006b), *The Complete RMB Handbook* (Fourth Edition), UBS Securities Asia Ltd, Hong Kong, September 18, 2006 (www.ubs.com/economics).

Areddy, James T. (2006), "China Turns Attention to Cleaning Up Rural Banks," *Wall Street Journal*, June 27 (http://online.wsj.com).

Ariff, Mohamed, and Can, Luc (2008), "Cost and Profit Efficiency of Chinese Banks: A Non-parametric Analysis," *China Economic Review* 19: forthcoming.

Arquette, Gregory C., Brown, William O., Jr., and Burdekin, Richard C. K. (2008), "US ADR and Hong Kong H-Share Discounts of Shanghai-Listed Firms," *Journal of Banking & Finance* 32: forthcoming.

Asia Pacific Bulletin (2001), "Taiwan Accepts the Need to Expand Economic Links with China," August 30 (http://www.asiapacificbusiness.ca/apbn/pdfs/bulletin22.pdf).

Asian Banker Journal (2001), "Bank of China Takes a Step Forward in Recognizing its Problem Loans," June 19.

Auguste, Sebastian, Dominguez, Kathryn M. E., Kamil, Herman, Tesar, Linda L. (2006), "Cross-Border Trading as a Mechanism for Implicit Capital Flight: ADRs and the Argentine Crisis," *Journal of Monetary Economics* 53 (October): 1259–1295.

Bahng, Seungwook, and Shin, Seung-Myo (2004), "Interactions of Stock Markets within the Greater China Economic Bloc," *Global Economic Review* 33: 43–60.

Bai, Chong-En, Lu, Jiangyong, and Tao, Zhigang (2006), "Property Rights Protection and Access to Bank Loans: Evidence from Private Enterprises in China," *Economics of Transition* 14 (October): 611–628.

Bailey, Warren, and Bhaopichitr, Kirida (2004), "How Important Was Silver? Some Evidence on Exchange Rate Fluctuations and Stock Returns in Colonial-Era Asia," *Journal of Business* 77 (January): 137–173.

227

Bajona, Claustre, and Chu, Tianshu (2004), "China's WTO Accession and Its Effect on State-Owned Enterprises," Working Paper No. 70, Economics Series, East-West Center, Honolulu, Hawaii, April.

Banaian, King, Burdekin, Richard C. K., and Willett, Thomas D. (1995), "On the Political Economy of Central Bank Independence," in Hoover, Kevin D., and Sheffrin, Steven M. (eds.), *Monetarism and the Methodology of Economics: Essays in Honour of Thomas Mayer*, Brookfield, VT: Edward Elgar, pp. 178–197.

Banerjee, Anindya, Lumsdaine, Robin L., and Stock, James H. (1992), "Recursive and Sequential Tests of the Unit-Root and Trend-Break Hypotheses: Theory and International Evidence," *Journal of Business and Economic Statistics* 10 (April): 271–287.

Bank for International Settlements (2005), *75th Annual Report*, Basel, Switzerland, June 27.

Barrell, Ray, Holland, Dawn, and Hurst, Ian (2007), "Sustainable Adjustment of Global Imbalances." Discussion Paper 290, National Institute of Economic and Social Research, London, England, March (http://www.niesr.ac.uk/pubs/DPS/dp290.pdf).

Barth, James R., and Caprio, Gerard, Jr. (2007), "China's Changing Financial System: Can It Catch Up With, or Even Drive Growth?" Networks Financial Institute at Indiana State University, Policy Brief 2007–PB-05, March (http://www. networksfinancialinstitute.org/pdfs/profiles/2007-PB-05_Barth-Caprio.pdf).

Barth, James R., Caprio, Gerard, Jr., and Levine, Ross (2006), *Rethinking Bank Regulation: Till Angels Govern*, New York: Cambridge University Press.

Barth, James R., Koepp, Rob, and Zhou, Zhongfei (2004), "Institute View: Disciplining China's Banks," *Milken Institute Review*, Second Quarter: 83–92.

Barth, James R., Zhou, Zhongfei, Arner, Douglas W., Hsu, Barry F. C., and Wang, Wei (eds.), (2007), *Financial Restructuring and Reform in Post-WTO China*, Alphen aan den Rijn, Netherlands: Kluwer Law International.

Batson, Andrew (2007), "Dilemma Made in China," *Wall Street Journal*, August 23, p. C2.

Bei, Duoguang, Koontz, Arden, and Lu, Lewis Xiangqian (1992), "The Emerging Securities Market in the PRC," *China Economic Review* 3: 149–172.

Berger, Allen N., Hasan, Iftekhar, and Zhou, Mingming (2008), "Bank Ownership and Efficiency in China: What Will Happen in the World's Largest Nation?" *Journal of Banking & Finance* 32: forthcoming.

Bergsten, C. Fred (2007), "The Dollar and the Renminbi," Statement before the Hearing on US Economic Relations with China, Subcommittee on Security and International Trade and Finance, United States Senate, May 23.

Bergsten, C. Fred, Gill, Bates, Lardy, Nicholas R., and Mitchell, Derek (2006), *China: The Balance Sheet*, New York: PublicAffairs.

Bernanke, Ben S. (2002), "Deflation: Making Sure 'It' Doesn't Happen Here," Remarks before the National Economists Club, Washington, DC, November 21.

Bernanke, Ben S. (2005), "The Global Savings Glut and the U.S. Current Account Deficit," Remarks at the Homer Jones Lecture, St. Louis, MO, April 14.

Bernanke, Ben S. (2007), "Global Imbalances: Recent Developments and Prospects," Remarks at the Bundesbank Lecture, Berlin, Germany, September 11.

Blanchard, Olivier, and Giavazzi, Francesco (2006), "Rebalancing Growth in China: A Three-Handed Approach," *China & World Economy* 14 (July–August): 1–20.

Blanchard, Olivier, Giavazzi, Francesco, and Sa, Filipa (2005), "International Investors, the U.S. Current Account, and the Dollar," *Brookings Papers on Economic Activity*, no. 1: 1–65.

Blum, John Morton (1959), *From the Morgenthau Diaries: Years of Crisis, 1928–1938*, Boston, MA: Houghton Mifflin.

Borio, Claudio (2005), "Monetary and Financial Stability: So Close and Yet So Far?" *National Institute Economic Review*, no. 192 (April): 84–101.

Bottelier, Pieter (2007), "China's Emerging Domestic Debt Markets," mimeo, School of Advanced International Studies, Johns Hopkins University, Washington, DC.

Bouvatier, Vincent (2007), "Hot Money Inflows and Monetary Stability in China: How the People's Bank of China Took up the Challenge," mimeo, Université de Rennes, France, January.

Bradsher, Keith (2005), "China Acts to Cool off Real Estate Market," *International Herald Tribune*, March 17 (http://www.iht.com).

Brandt, Loren, and Sargent, Thomas J. (1989), "Interpreting New Evidence about China and U.S. Silver Purchases," *Journal of Monetary Economics* 23 (January): 31–51.

Brown, William O., Jr., and Burdekin, Richard C. K. (2002), "German Debt Traded in London During the Second World War: A British Perspective on Hitler," *Economica* 69 (November): 655–669.

Browne, Andrew (2006), "Beijing Touts Flexibility after Yuan's Brief Rise," *Wall Street Journal*, May 16 (http://online.wsj.com).

Burdekin, Richard C. K. (2000), "Ending Inflation in China: From Mao to the 21st Century," *Cato Journal* 20 (Fall): 223–235.

Burdekin, Richard C. K. (2006), "China and the Depreciating US Dollar," *Asia Pacific Issues*, No. 79, January.

Burdekin, Richard C. K. (2007), "Nontraditional Monetary Policy Options and Commodity-Based Stabilization Policy," *International Economics and Finance Journal* 2 (January-December): 1–18.

Burdekin, Richard C. K. (2008), "US Pressure on China: Silver Flows, Deflation, and the 1934 Shanghai Credit Crunch," *China Economic Review* 19 (forthcoming).

Burdekin, Richard C. K., and Burkett, Paul (1990), "A Re-Examination of the Monetary Model of Exchange Market Pressure: Canada, 1963–1988," *Review of Economics and Statistics* 72 (November): 677–681.

Burdekin, Richard C. K., and Burkett, Paul (1992), "The Impact of U.S. Economic Variables on Bank of Canada Policy: Direct and Indirect Responses," *Journal of International Money and Finance* 11 (April): 162–187.

Burdekin, Richard C. K., and Hu, Xiaojin (1999), "China's Experience with Indexed Government Bonds, 1988–1996: How Credible Was the People's Republic's Anti-Inflationary Policy?" *Review of Development Economics* 3 (February): 66–85.

Burdekin, Richard C. K., and Siklos, Pierre L., Eds. (2004), *Deflation: Current and Historical Perspectives*. New York: Cambridge University Press.

Burdekin, Richard C. K., and Siklos, Pierre L. (2008), "What Has Driven Chinese Monetary Policy Since 1990? Investigating the People's Bank's Monetary Rule," *Journal of International Money and Finance* 27 (forthcoming).

Burdekin, Richard C. K., and Tao, Ran (2007), "China's State-Owned Banks' Lending Practices, 1994–2005: Empirical Tests and Policy Implications." Paper presented at the Asia-Pacific Economic Association Annual Conference in Kowloon, Hong Kong, July 25–26.

Burdekin, Richard C. K., and Wang, Fang (1999), "A Novel End to the Big Inflation in China in 1950," *Economics of Planning* 32 (October): 211–229.

Burdekin, Richard C. K., and Weidenmier, Marc D. (2001), "Inflation is Always and Everywhere a Monetary Phenomenon: Richmond vs. Houston in 1864," *American Economic Review* 91 (December): 1621–1630.

Burdekin, Richard C. K., and Weidenmier, Marc D. (2008), "The Development of 'Non-Traditional' Open Market Operations: Lessons from FDR's Silver Purchase Program," in Jeremy Atack and Larry Neal (eds), *The Evolution of Financial Markets and Institutions from the Seventeenth Century to the Present*, New York: Cambridge University Press.

Burdekin, Richard C. K., and Whited, Hsin-hui I. H. (2001), "Multiple Regime Shifts and Multiple Ends of the Taiwanese Hyperinflation, 1945–1953," *Southern Economic Journal* 68 (July): 77–91.

Burdekin, Richard C. K., and Whited, Hsin-hui I. H. (2005), "Exporting Hyperinflation: The Long Arm of Chiang Kai-shek," *China Economic Review* 16: 71–89.

Burdekin, Richard C. K., and Whited, Hsin-hui I. H. (2007), "Macroeconomic Interdependence between Mainland China and Taiwan: A Cross-Strait Perspective on Globalization." Paper presented at the Asia-Pacific Economic Association Annual Conference in Kowloon, Hong Kong, July 25–26.

Carew, Rick (2007), "Agricultural Bank of China May Chase IPO Wave," *Wall Street Journal*, March 12 (http://online.wsj.com).

Cargill, Thomas F., and Parker, Elliott (2004), "Price Deflation, Money Demand, and Monetary Policy Discontinuity: A Comparative View of Japan, China, and the United States," *North American Journal of Economics and Finance* 15 (March): 125–147.

Cavoli, Tony, and Rajan, Ramkishen S. (2006), "Capital Inflows Problem in Selected Asian Economies in the 1990s Revisited: The Role of Monetary Sterilization," *Asian Economic Journal* 20 (December): 409–423.

Cavoli, Tony, and Rajan, Ramkishen S. (2007), "Exploring the Case for Monetary Integration between the Chinese Mainland and Hong Kong," *China & World Economy* 15 (July–August): 17–34.

Central Bank of the Republic of China (Taiwan), Taipei (http://www.cbc.gov.tw).

Chan, Kalok, Hameed, Allaudeen, and Lau, Sieting (2003), "What if Trading Location is Different from Business Location? Evidence from the Jardine Group," *Journal of Finance* 58 (June): 1221–1246.

Chan, Maria and Nie, Nevin (2007), "Bank Eyes 2b Yuan Bond Sale in HK," *South China Morning Post*, July 27, p. B3.

Chang, George H. (1938), "A Brief Survey of Chinese Native Banks," *Central Bank of China Bulletin*, March, pp. 25–32.

Chang, Hui S. (2005), "Estimating the Monetary Policy Reaction Function for Taiwan: A VAR Model," *International Journal of Applied Economics* 2 (March): 50–61.

Chang, Kia-Ngau (1958), *The Inflationary Spiral: The Experience in China, 1939–1950*, Cambridge, MA: Technology Press of Massachusetts Institute of Technology.

Chen, Baizhu (1997), "Long-Run Money Demand and Inflation in China," *Journal of Macroeconomics* 19 (Summer): 609–617.

Chen, Huan-Chang (1911), *The Economic Principles of Confucius and His School*, Volume II, New York: Longmans, Green & Co.

Chen, Kathy (1997), "Newest Reforms in China May Be the Hardest Yet," *Wall Street Journal*, September 15, pp. A14, A16.

Chen, Nan-Kuang (2001), "Asset Price Fluctuations in Taiwan: Evidence from Stock and Real Estate Prices 1973 to 1992," *Journal of Asian Economics* 12 (Summer): 215–232.

Chen, Pochih, Schive, Chi, and Chu, Cheng Chung (1994), "Export Structure and Exchange Rate Variation in Taiwan: A Comparison with Japan and the United States," In Ito, Takatoshi, and Krueger, Anne O. Krueger (eds.), *Macroeconomic Linkage: Savings, Exchange Rates, and Capital Flows*, Chicago, IL: University of Chicago Press, pp. 227–243.

Chen, Yongjun (2006), "Taiwan Cross-Strait Economic Relations in the Era of Globalization," in Bao, Shuming, Lin, Shuanglin, and Zhao, Changwen (eds.), *The Chinese Economy after WTO Accession*. Burlington, VT: Ashgate, pp. 335–350.

Chen, Yun (1984), *Chen Yun wen xuan, 1949–1956 nian*, Beijing: Ren min chu ban she.

Chen, Zhian, Li, Donghui, and Moshirian, Fariborz (2005), "China's Financial Services Industry: The Intra-Industry Effects of Privatization of the Bank of China Hong Kong," *Journal of Banking & Finance* 29 (August–September): 2291–2324.

Cheng, Chu-yuan (1954), *Monetary Affairs of Communist China*. Kowloon, Hong Kong: Union Research Institute (Communist China Problem Research Series (EC5)).

Cheng, Hwahsin, and Glascock, John L. (2005), "Dynamic Linkages Between the Greater China Economic Area Stock Markets – Mainland China, Hong Kong, and Taiwan," *Review of Quantitative Finance and Accounting* 24 (June): 343–357.

Cheng, Hwahsin, and Glascock, John L. (2006), "Stock Market Linkage Before and After the Asian Financial Crisis: Evidence from the Three Great China Economic Area Stock Markets and the US," *Review of Pacific Basin Financial Markets and Policies* 9 (June): 297–315.

Cheng, Yu-Kwei (1956), *Foreign Trade and Industrial Development of China: An Historical and Integrated Analysis through 1948*, Washington, DC: University Press of Washington, DC.

Cheung, Yin-Wong, and Yuen, Jude (2005), "The Suitability of a Greater China Currency Union," *Pacific Economic Review* 10 (February): 83–103.

Cheung, Yin-Wong, Chinn, Menzie D., and Fujii, Eiji (2007a), *The Economic Integration of Greater China: Real and Financial Linkages and the Prospects for Currency Union*, Aberdeen, Hong Kong: Hong Kong University Press.

Cheung, Yin-Wong, Chinn, Menzie D., and Fujii, Eiji (2007b), "The Overvaluation of Renminbi Undervaluation," *Journal of International Money and Finance* 26 (September): 762–785.

Cheung, Yin-Wong, Chinn, Menzie D., and Fujii, Eiji (2008), "The Illusion of Precision and the Role of the Renminbi in Regional Integration," in Hamada, Koichi, Reszat, Beate, and Volz, Ulrich (eds.), *Prospects for Monetary Integration in East Asia: Dreams and Realities*, Cambridge, MA: MIT Press, forthcoming.

Chi, Jing, Li, Ke, and Young, Martin (2006), "Financial Integration in East Asian Equity Markets," *Pacific Economic Review* 11 (December): 513–526.

China Banking Regulatory Commission (2007), "The CBRC Punished Eight Banks whose Loans were Misappropriated by their Corporate Clients," June 19 (http://www.cbrc.gov.cn/english/home/jsp/docView.jsp?docID=200706191BE235028B7532D3FF4F92822E53F800).

China Daily (1999), "Completion of Banks' Reformation a Major Goal," January 21.

China Daily (2000), "Infrastructure Loans on the Up," February 11.

China Daily (2007), "US Economists Warn against Protectionist Measures," August 2 (http://www.chinadaily.com.cn/china/2007-08/02/content_5447614.htm).

China Securities Journal (2007a), "Chinese Pour Savings Deposits into Stock Market," May 14 (http://www.cs.com.cn/english/ei/200705/t20070514_1101649.htm).

China Securities Journal (2007b), "Deposits 'Diverted to Stocks,'" May 14 (http://www.cs.com.cn/english/ei/200705/t20070514_1101645.htm).

China Statistical Yearbook, Beijing: State Statistical Bureau, various issues.

"China Still Troubled by Deflation in October," (2002), November 13 (http://home.donews.com/donews/article/3/36342.html) (in Chinese).

Chiu, Becky, and Lewis, Mervyn K. (2006), *Reforming China's State-Owned Enterprises and Banks*, Northampton, MA; Edward Elgar.

Chiu, Chien-Liang, Lee, Mingchih, and Chen, Chun-Da (2005), "Removal of an Investment Restriction: The 'B' Share Experience from China's Stock Markets," *Applied Financial Economics* 15 (February): 273–285.

Chong, Terence Tai-Leung, and Su, Qian (2006), "On the Comovement of A and H Shares," *The Chinese Economy* 39 (September–October): 68–86.

Chou, Shun-Hsin (1963), *The Chinese Inflation: 1937–1949*, New York: Columbia University Press.

Chow, Gregory C. (2006), "Globalization and China's Economic Development," *Pacific Economic Review* 11 (October): 271–285.

Chow, Gregory C. (2007), *China's Economic Transformation*, Second Edition, Malden, MA: Blackwell Publishing.

Chow, Gregory C., and Shen, Yan (2005), "Money, Price Level and Output in the Chinese Macro Economy," *Asia-Pacific Journal of Accounting & Economics* 12 (December): 91–111.

Chung-kuo k'o-hsüeh yüan (1958), *Shang-hai chieh-fang ch'ien-hou wu-chia tzu-liao hui-pien (1921–1957)* [Collected Materials on Commodity Prices in Shanghai Before and After Liberation 1921–1957], Shanghai: Shang-hai ching-chi yen-chiu so.

Clifford, Mark L. (2002), "Caught in Quicksand," *Business Week*, November 25, p. 18.

Clifford, Mark L., and Fong, Petti (2002), "The Black Hole," *Business Week*, February 4, p. 48.

Clifford, Mark L., Balfour, Frederik, and Webb, Alysha (2001), "Money Mess," *Business Week*, March 12, p. 50.

Cohen, David (2007), "China Hints at Further Appreciation of Yuan," *Business Week*, May 22 (http://www.businessweek.com/investor/content/may2007/pi20070522_343319_page_2.htm).

Comtex News Network (accessible via LexisNexis), various dates.

Cooke, Terry (2006), "Taiwan's Economy: Missing a Needed 'Link' to China and the World," *China Brief* (Jamestown Foundation) 6 (October 4): 4–7.

Coudert, Virginie, and Couharde, Cécile (2007), "Real Equilibrium Exchange Rate in China: Is the Renminbi Undervalued?" *Journal of Asian Economics* 18 (August): 568–594.

Cover, James Peery, Hueng, C. James, and Yau, Ruey (2002), "Are Policy Rules Better than the Discretionary System in Taiwan?" *Contemporary Economic Policy* 20 (January): 60–71.

Dai, Genyou (2002), "China's Monetary Policy: Too Tight?" *China & World Economy* 10 (September–October): 16–20.

Dickie, Mure (2006), "Man to be Held over BoC Fraud," *Financial Times*, June 5, p. 21.

Dickie, Mure, and Tucker, Sundeep (2006), "China Paves Way for Foreign Banks to Offer More Services," *Financial Times*, November 16, p. 1.

Dobson, Wendy, and Kashyap, Anil K. (2006), "The Contradictions in China's Gradualist Banking Reforms," *Brookings Papers on Economic Activity*, no. 2: 103–162.

Dooley, Michael P., Folkerts-Landau, David, and Garber, Peter (2004), "The Revived Bretton Woods System," *International Journal of Finance & Economics* 9 (October): 307–313.

Dorn, James A. (1998), "China's Future: Market Socialism or Market Taoism?" *Cato Journal* 18 (Spring/Summer): 131–146.

Dorn, James A. (2006), "U.S.-China Relations: The Case for Economic Liberalism," *Cato Journal* 26 (Fall): 425–443.

Dunaway, Steven, Leigh, Lamin, and Li, Xiangming (2006), "How Robust are Estimates of Equilibrium Real Exchange Rates: The Case of China," Working Paper 06/220, International Monetary Fund, October.

Durdin, Tillman (1953), "China and the World," *Headline Series*, no. 99 (May 20): 3–49.

Dyer, Geoff (2006), "New Rules to Unlock Share-Buying in China," *Financial Times*, January 31, p. 17.

Dyer, Geoff (2007), "Chinese Bet the House on Shares Going through the Roof," *Financial Times*, February 3–4, p. 3.

Dyer, Geoff, and Tucker, Sundeep (2007), "Shanghai Moves to Woo HSBC and Others to List," *Financial Times*, May 1, p. 25.

Eckstein, Alexander (1977), *China's Economic Revolution*, New York: Cambridge University Press.

Edwards, Sebastian (1995), *Crisis and Reform in Latin America: From Despair to Hope*, New York: Oxford University Press.

Eichengreen, Barry (2005), "China's New Exchange Rate Regime," *Current History* 104 (September): 264–267.

Eichengreen, Barry (2007), *Global Imbalances and the Lessons of Bretton Woods*, Cambridge, MA: MIT Press.

Ernst & Young (2006), *Global Nonperforming Loan Report 2006*, May [subsequently withdrawn by Ernst & Young].

European Central Bank, International Relations Committee Task Force (2006), "The Accumulation of Foreign Reserves," Occasional Paper Series No. 43, February (http://www.ecb.int).

Feltenstein, Andrew, and Farhadian, Ziba (1987), "Fiscal Policy, Monetary Targets, and the Price Level in a Centrally Planned Economy: An Application to the Case of China," *Journal of Money, Credit, and Banking* 19 (May): 137–156.

Feltenstein, Andrew, and Ha, Jiming (1991), "Measurement of Repressed Inflation in China: The Lack of Coordination between Monetary Policy and Price Controls," *Journal of Development Economics* 36 (October): 279–294.

Fenby, Jonathon (2004), *Chiang Kai-Shek: China's Generalissimo and the Nation He Lost*, New York: Carroll & Graf.

Feng, Licheng, and Xu, Weihe (2007), "Has the Reform of Nontradable Shares Raised Prices? An Event-Study Analysis," *Emerging Markets Finance and Trade* 43 (March–April): 33–62.

Financial Times (2006a), "Chinese Monetary Policy," April 26, p. 16.

Financial Times (2006b), "Bank of China IPO," May 12, p. 12.

"Foreign Capital Add to China's Real Estate Bubble (2006)," *China Economic Net*, April 25 (http://en.ce.cn).

Frankel, Jeffrey (2006), "On the Yuan: The Choice between Adjustment under a Fixed Rate and Adjustment under a Flexible Rate," *CESifo Economic Studies* 52 (June): 246–275.

Frankel, Jeffrey A., and Wei, Shang-Jin (1994), "Yen Bloc or Dollar Bloc? Exchange Rate Policies of the East Asian Economies," in Ito, Takatoshi, and Krueger, Anne O. (eds.), *Macroeconomic Linkage: Savings, Exchange Rates, and Capital Flows*, Chicago, IL: University of Chicago Press, pp. 295–329.

Friedman, Irving S. (1940), *British Relations with China: 1931–1939*, New York: Institute of Pacific Relations.

Friedman, Milton (1992), "Franklin D. Roosevelt, Silver, and China," *Journal of Political Economy* 100 (February): 62–83.

Friedman, Milton, and Schwartz, Anna Jacobson (1963), *A Monetary History of the United States, 1867–1960*, Princeton, NJ: Princeton University Press.

Froot, Kenneth A., and Dabora, Emil M. (1999), "How Are Stock Prices Affected by the Location of Trade?" *Journal of Financial Economics* 53 (August): 189–216.

Fu, Xiaoqing (Maggie), and Heffernan, Shelagh (2007), "Cost X-Efficiency in China's Banking Sector," *China Economic Review* 18: 35–53.

Fung, Hung-Gay, Leung, Wai K., and Zhu, Jiang (2004), "Nondeliverable Forward Market for Chinese RMB: A First Look," *China Economic Review* 15: 348–352.

Fung, K. C., Iizaka, Hitomi, and Siu, Alan (2005), "The Giant Sucking Sound: Is China Diverting Foreign Direct Investment from East Asia and Latin America?" *HKCER Letters* (Hong Kong Centre for Economic Research), Vol. 81 (January–February) (http://www.hku.hk/hkcer/letters.htm).

Fung, K. C., Lau, Lawrence J., and Xiong, Yanyan (2006), "Adjusted Estimates of United States–China Bilateral Trade Balances: An Update," *Pacific Economic Review* 11 (October): 299–314.

Funke, Michael, and Rahn, Jörg (2005), "Just How Undervalued is the Chinese Renminbi?" *World Economy* 28 (April): 465–489.

Galati, Gabriele, and Wooldridge, Philip (2006), "The Euro as a Reserve Currency: A Challenge to the Pre-Eminence of the US Dollar?" Working Paper No. 218, Bank for International Settlements, Basle, Switzerland, October (http://www.bis.org/publ/work218.pdf).

Gao, Ting (2005), "Foreign Direct Investment in China: How Big Are the Roles of Culture and Geography?" *Pacific Economic Review* 10 (June): 153–166.

García-Herrero, Alicia, Gavilá, Sergio, and Santabárbara, Daniel (2006), "China's Banking Reform: An Assessment of its Evolution and Possible Impact," *CESifo Economic Studies* 52 (June): 304–363.

Garnham, Peter, Giles, Chris, and Brown-Humes, Christopher (2006), "The Buck Stops Where? How a Tattered Dollar Could Quickly Lose Further Allure," *Financial Times*, November 28, p. 11.

Ge, Ying, and Qiu, Jiaping (2007), "Financial Development, Bank Discrimination and Trade Credit," *Journal of Banking & Finance* 31 (February): 513–530.

Gee, San (1994), "The Effects of NT Dollar Variations on Taiwan's Trade Flows," in Ito, Takatoshi, and Krueger, Anne O. (eds.), *Macroeconomic Linkage: Savings, Exchange Rates, and Capital Flows*, Chicago, IL: University of Chicago Press, pp. 89–118.

Geiger, Michael (2006), "Monetary Policy in China (1994–2004): Targets, Instruments and their Effectiveness," mimeo, Universität Würzburg, Germany, April.

Genberg, Hans (2006), "Exchange-Rate Arrangements and Financial Integration in East Asia: On a Collision Course?" *International Economics and Economic Policy* 3 (December): 359–377.

Gerlach, Stefan, and Kong, Janet (2005), "Money and Inflation in China," Research Memorandum 04/2005, Hong Kong Monetary Authority, March.

Girardin, Eric, and Liu, Zhenya (2007), "The Financial Integration of China: New Evidence on Temporally Aggregated Data for the A-share Market," *China Economic Review* 18: 354–371.

Girton, Lance, and Roper, Don (1977), "A Monetary Model of Exchange Market Pressure Applied to the Postwar Canadian Experience," *American Economic Review* 67 (September): 537–548.

Global Financial Database, Los Angeles, CA (http://www.globalfindata.com).

Goh, Ming He, and Kim, Yoonbai (2006), "Is the Chinese Renminbi Undervalued?" *Contemporary Economic Policy* 24 (January): 116–126.

Goldstein, Morris (2006), "Renminbi Controversies," *Cato Journal* 26 (Spring/Summer): 251–266.

Goldstein, Morris, and Lardy, Nicholas (2006), "China's Exchange Rate Policy Dilemma," *American Economic Review* 96 (May): 422–426.

Goodfriend, Marvin, and Prasad, Eswar (2006), "A Framework for Independent Monetary Policy in China," Working Paper 06/111, International Monetary Fund, Washington, DC, May.

Goodman, Peter S. (2004), "China Regulator Warns of Investment Bubble," *Washington Post*, February 27.

Great China Database, Taipei, Taiwan (http://www.finasia.biz/tejonline/tejonline.htm).

Guariglia, Alessandra, and Poncet, Sandra (2006), "Could Financial Distortions Be No Impediment to Economic Growth After All? Evidence from China," Research Paper 2006/36, University of Nottingham, England.

Guerrera, Francesco, and McGregor, Richard (2005), "Huarong Seeks to Expand Beyond NPLs," *Financial Times*, November 7, p. 19.

Gujarati, Damodar N. (2003), *Basic Econometrics*, Fourth Edition, New York: McGraw-Hill/Irwin.

Guo, Yan (2004), "Bank Regulation in China: Property Rights, Incentives, and Accountability," in Wiemer, Calla, and Cao Heping (eds.), *Asian Economic Cooperation in the New Millennium: China's Economic Presence*, Hackensack, NJ: World Scientific Publishing, pp. 271–295.

Hale, Galina (2007), "Prospects for China's Corporate Bond Market," Federal Reserve Bank of San Francisco *Weekly Letter*, no. 2007–07, March 16.

He, Dong, Chu, Carmen, Shu, Chang, and Wong, Amy (2005), "Monetary Management in Mainland China in the Face of Large Capital Inflows," Research Memorandum 07/2005, Hong Kong Monetary Authority, April.

Hefeker, Carsten, and Nabor, Andreas (2005), "China's Role in East-Asian Monetary Integration," *International Journal of Finance & Economics* 10 (April): 157–166.

Higgins, Patrick, and Humpage, Owen F. (2005), "Nondeliverable Forwards: Can We Tell Where the Renminbi is Headed?" *Economic Commentary Series*, Federal Reserve Bank of Cleveland, September 1.

Hille, Kathrin (2007), "Tectonic Shift towards Shanghai Sees Taiwanese Groups Shun HK," *Financial Times*, April 27, p. 22.

Holden, Darryl, and Perman, Roger (1994), "Unit Roots and Cointegration for the Economist," in Rao, B. Bhaskara (ed.), *Cointegration for the Applied Economist*, New York: St. Martin's Press, pp. 47–112.

Hon, Chu Kam (2004), "Reflections on the New Taiwan Dollar Appreciation of the Mid-1980's," *HKCER Letters* (Hong Kong Centre for Economic Research) 79 (May–June) (http://www.hku.hk/hkcer/letters.htm).

Horesh, Niv (2008), "'Many a Long Day': HSBC and Its Note Issue in Republican China, 1912–1935," *Enterprise & Society* 9: forthcoming.

Hsia, Ronald (1953), *Price Control in Communist China*, New York: Institute of Pacific Relations.

Hsiao, Frank S. T., and Hsiao, Mei-Chu W. (2001), "Capital Flows and Exchange Rates: Recent Korean and Taiwanese Experience and Challenges," *Journal of Asian Economics* 12 (Autumn): 353–381.

Hsiao, Frank S. T., and Hsiao, Mei-Chu W. (2004), "The Chaotic Attractor of Foreign Direct Investment – Why China? A Panel Data Analysis," *Journal of Asian Economics* 15 (August): 641–670.

Hsiao, Katharine Huang (1971), *Money and Monetary Policy in Communist China*, New York: Columbia University Press.

Hsin, Ying (1954), *The Price Problems of Communist China*, Kowloon, Hong Kong: Union Research Institute (Communist China Problem Research Series (EC3)).

Hu, Fred (2005), "Capital Flows, Overheating, and the Nominal Exchange Rate Regime in China," *Cato Journal* 25 (Spring/Summer): 357–366.

Hua, Ping (2007), "Real Exchange Rate and Manufacturing Employment in China," *China Economic Review* 18: 335–353.

Huang, Ho-Chuan (River), and Lin, Shu-Chin (2006), "Time-Varying Discrete Monetary Policy Reaction Functions," *Applied Economics* 38 (March): 449–464.

Huang, Tien-lin (2007), "Why the Investment Cap Matters," *Taipei Times*, May 14, p. 8 (http://www.taipeitimes.com).

Huang, Yasheng (2006), "Do Financing Biases Matter for the Chinese Economy?" *Cato Journal* 26 (Spring/Summer): 287–306.

Hufbauer, Gary Clyde, Wong, Yee, and Sheth, Ketki (2006), *US–China Trade Disputes: Rising Tide, Rising Stakes*, Washington, DC: Institute for International Economics, August.

Imai, Hiroyuki (1994), "Inflationary Pressure in China's Consumption Goods Market: Estimation and Analysis," *The Developing Economies* 32 (June): 127–154.

International Center of Finance, *Shanghai Stock Exchange Research Project*, New Haven, CT: Yale University (http://icf.som.yale.edu/sse).

International Monetary Fund, *International Financial Statistics* database, Washington, DC.

International Monetary Fund (2007), *World Economic Outlook: Spillovers and Cycles in the Global Economy,* Washington, DC, April.

Ito, Takatoshi (2006), "Robust Monetary Framework for China," *China & World Economy,* 14 (September–October): 32–47.

Jao, Y. C. (1967–1968), "Some Notes on Repressed Inflation: A Suggested Interpretation of Money and Prices in Communist China, 1950–57," *United College Journal* (Chinese University of Hong Kong) 6: 99–114.

Jao, Y. C. (1991), "Financial Reform in China and Hong Kong 1978–89: A Comparative Overview," Pacific Economic Paper No. 193, Australia-Japan Research Centre, Canberra, Australia, March.

Jao, Y. C. (2001), *The Asian Financial Crisis and the Ordeal of Hong Kong.* Westport, CT: Quoram Books.

Jen, Stephen (2007), "How Big Could Sovereign Wealth Funds Be by 2015?" Morgan Stanley – Global Economic Forum, May 4 (http://www.morganstanley.com/views/gef/archive/2007/20070504-Fri.html).

Ji, Zhaojin (2003), *A History of Modern Shanghai Banking: The Rise and Decline of China's Financial Capitalism,* Armonk, NY: M.E. Sharpe.

Jia, Chunxin (2008), "The Effect of Ownership on the Prudential Behavior of Banks – The Case of China," *Journal of Banking & Finance* 32: forthcoming.

Jin, Li, and Li, Shan (2007), "The U.S.–China Trade Deficit, Debunked," *Wall Street Journal,* May 22 (http://online.wsj.com).

Johnson, Mark (2002), "China's Big Year," *Global Finance* 16 (March): 24–28.

Kahn, Joseph (1994), "Rebellion Grows in China's Cotton Fields," *Wall Street Journal,* November 15, p. A20.

Kerr, Simeon (2007), "Move by Kuwait Fuels Gulf Currency Debate," *Financial Times,* June 4, p. 13.

Kim, Minho, Szakmary, Andrew C., and Mathur, Ike (2000), "Price Transmission Dynamics between ADRs and their Underlying Foreign Securities," *Journal of Banking & Finance* 24 (August): 1359–1382.

King, Frank H. H. (1957), *Money in British East Asia,* London: Her Majesty's Stationery Office.

King, Frank H. H. (1988), *The Hongkong Bank Between the Wars and the Bank Interned, 1919–1945: Return from Grandeur,* Volume III of the History of the Hongkong and Shanghai Banking Corporation, New York: Cambridge University Press.

Krugman, Paul (1999), *The Return of Depression Economics,* New York: W.W. Norton.

Kutan, Ali M., and Zhou, Haigang (2006), "Determinants of Returns and Volatility of Chinese ADRs at NYSE," *Journal of Multinational Financial Management* 16 (February): 1–15.

Kuttner, Kenneth N., and Posen, Adam S. (2001), "The Great Recession: Lessons for Macroeconomic Policy from Japan," *Brookings Papers on Economic Activity,* no. 2: 93–185.

Kwan, Chi Hung (2006a), "The Hong Kong Dollar is not Following the Yuan's Rising Trend – It is too Early to Shift to a Yuan Peg," China in Transition column, Research Institute of Economy, Trade and Industry, Tokyo, Japan, June 28 (http://www.rieti.go.jp/en/china/06062803.html).

Kwan, Chi Hung (2006b), "China Faces a Tough Challenge in the Steering of Monetary Policy – The Room for Sterilization is Diminishing," China in Transition column,

Research Institute of Economy, Trade and Industry, Tokyo, Japan, August 23 (http://www.rieti.go.jp/en/china/06082302.html).

Kwong, Robin, Tucker, Sundeep, and Gangahar, Anuj (2007), "China on Course to Lead World IPO League," *Financial Times*, July 5, p. 1.

Lai, Cheng-chung, and Gau, Joshua Jr-Shiang (2003), "The Chinese Silver Standard Economy and the 1929 Great Depression," *Australian Economic History Review* 43 (July): 155–168.

Lardy, Nicholas R. (1992), *Foreign Trade and Economic Reform in China, 1978–1990*, New York: Cambridge University Press.

Lardy, Nicholas R. (1998), *China's Unfinished Economic Revolution*, Washington, DC: Brookings Institution Press.

Lardy, Nicholas R. (1999), "The Challenge of Bank Restructuring in China," in *Strengthening the Banking System in China: Issues and Experience*, Basle, Switzerland: Bank for International Settlements, Policy Paper No. 7, October.

Lardy, Nicholas R. (2002), *Integrating China into the World Economy*, Washington, DC: Brookings Institution.

Lardy, Nicholas R. (2005a), "Exchange Rate and Monetary Policy in China," *Cato Journal* 25 (Winter): 41–47.

Lardy, Nicholas R. (2005b), "China: The Great New Economic Challenge?" in Bergsten, C. Fred (ed.), *The United States and the World Economy*, Washington, DC: Institute for International Economics, pp. 121–141.

Larsen, Peter Thal (2008), "Resource-Rich and Sharing the Wealth," *Financial Times* Special Report (Davos edition), January 24, p. 2.

Lau, Lawrence J. (1999), "The Macroeconomy and Reform of the Banking Sector in China," in *Strengthening the Banking System in China: Issues and Experience*, Policy Paper No. 7, Bank for International Settlements, Basel, Switzerland, October, pp. 59–89.

Laurenceson, James, and Qin, Fengming (2006), "China's Exchange Rate Debate," in Wu, Yanrui (ed.), *Economic Growth, Transition and Globalization in China*, Northampton, MA: Edward Elgar, pp. 199–213.

Laurenceson, James, and Tang, Kam Ki (2006), "China's Equilibrium Exchange Rate and Trade Balance: A Tale of Apples and Pirates," East Asia Economic Research Group, Discussion Paper No. 8, University of Queensland, Australia, January.

Laurens, Bernard J., and Maino, Rodolfo (2007), "China: Strengthening Monetary Policy Implementation," Working Paper 07/14, International Monetary Fund, Washington, DC, January.

Leavens, Dickson H. (1939), *Silver Money*, Bloomington, IN: Principia Press.

Leggett, Karby (2003), "China's Shaky Banks Suffer a Blow," *Wall Street Journal*, June 27, p. A10.

Leigh, Lamin, and Podpiera, Richard (2006), "The Rise of Foreign Investment in China's Banks – Taking Stock," Working Paper 06/292, International Monetary Fund, Washington, DC, December.

Li, Gang, and Du, Xiongfei (2007), "Central Bank Bill," in Yin, Jianfeng (ed.), *Blue Book of Finance: China Financial Products and Service Report 2007*, Beijing: Social Sciences Academic Press, pp. 129–141 (in Chinese).

Li, Jing (2004), "Regionalization of the RMB and China's Capital Account Liberalization," *China & World Economy* 12 (March–April): 86–100.

Li, Jing (2007), "The Rise of the Renminbi in Asia: Cost-Benefit Analysis and Road Map," *The Chinese Economy* 40 (July–August): 29–43.

Li, Yitang, and Wu, Tsong-Min (1997), "U.S. Aid and the End of Taiwan's Big Inflation," mimeo, National Tsing Hua University, Hsin Chu, Taiwan, October 13.

Li, Yuefen (2006), "Trade Balance: Numbers Can be Deceiving," *China & World Economy* 14 (May): 54–70.

Liang, Qi, and Cao, Hua (2007), "Property Prices and Bank Lending in China," *Journal of Asian Economics* 18 (February): 63–75.

Lima, Joao, and Kennedy, Simon (2007), "Greenspan Says China Stocks may Post 'Dramatic' Drop," *Bloomberg.com*, May 23 (http://www.bloomberg.com).

Lin, Guijun, and Schramm, Ronald M. (2004), "China's Progression Toward Currency Convertibility: A Review and Assessment," *The Chinese Economy* 37 (July–August): 78–100.

Lin, Hwan C. (2005), "On Trade, Look East Instead of West," *Taipei Times*, June 30, p. 8 (http://www.taipeitimes.com).

Lin, Justin Yifu, Cai, Fang, and Li, Zhou (2003), *The China Miracle: Development Strategy and Economic Reform*, Revised Edition, Hong Kong: Chinese University Press.

Lin, Kenneth S., and Wu, Tsong-Min (1989), "Taiwan's Big Inflation: 1946–1949," in *The Second Conference on Modern Chinese Economic History (III)*, Taipei, Taiwan: The Institute of Economics, Academia Sinica, pp. 917–949.

Lin, W. Y. (1936), *The New Monetary System of China: A Personal Interpretation*, Shanghai: Kelly and Walsh.

Lipsky, John (2007), "Remarks at the Brussels Economic Forum," May 31 (http://www.imf.org/external/np/speeches/2007/053107.htm).

Liu, Fu-Chi (1970), *Studies in Monetary Development of Taiwan*, Taipei, Taiwan: Academia Sinica, October.

Ljung, G. M., and Box, G. E. P. (1978), "On a Measure of Lack of Fit in Time Series Models," *Biometrika* 65 (August): 297–303.

Lockwood, Ben, and Redoano, Michela (2005), "The CSGR Globalisation Index: An Introductory Guide," Coventry, England: University of Warwick, Centre for the Study of Globalisation and Regionalisation, Working Paper 155/04.

Lu, Maozu, and Zhang, Zhichao (2000), "Parallel Exchange Market as a Transition Mechanism for Foreign Exchange Reform: China's Experiment," *Applied Financial Economics* 10 (April): 123–135.

Ma, Guonan (1993), "Macroeconomic Disequilibrium, Structural Changes, and the Household Savings and Money Demand in China," *Journal of Development Economics* 41 (June): 115–136.

Ma, Guonan (2006), "Sharing China's Bank Restructuring Bill," *China & World Economy* 14 (May): 19–37.

Ma, Xianghai (1996), "Capital Controls, Market Segmentation and Stock Prices: Evidence from the Chinese Stock Market," *Pacific-Basin Finance Journal* 4 (July): 219–239.

MacKinnon, James G., Haug, Alfred A., and Michelis, Leo (1999), "Numerical Distribution Functions of Likelihood Ratio Tests for Cointegration," *Journal of Applied Econometrics* 14 (September–October): 563–577.

Mainland Affairs Council, Executive Yuan, *Cross-Strait Economic Statistics Monthly* (http://www.mac.gov.tw/english/index1-e.htm).

Makinen, Gail E., and Woodward, G. Thomas (1989), "The Taiwanese Hyperinflation and Stabilization of 1945–1952," *Journal of Money, Credit, and Banking* 21 (February): 90–105.

Max, Sarah (2004), "The Price of Latte in Lucerne," *CNNMoney.com*, January 30 (http://money.cnn.com/2004/01/16/news/funny/latteindex/).

McCallum, Bennett T. (1988), "Robustness Properties of a Rule for Monetary Policy," *Carnegie-Rochester Conference Series on Public Policy* 29 (Autumn): 173–203.

McCary, John, and Batson, Andrew (2007), "Punishing China: Will It Fly?" *Wall Street Journal*, June 23–24, p. A4.

McGregor, Richard (2006a), "China's Change of Tack Surprises Economists," *Financial Times*, April 28, p. 6.

McGregor, Richard (2006b), "Beijing Bank Chief Denies Bad Loan Problem," *Financial Times*, May 31, p. 4.

McGregor, Richard (2007), "Raid on a Piggy Bank," *Financial Times*, September 26, p. 11.

McGregor, Richard, Bream, Rebecca, and Morrison, Kevin (2005), "Copper Hits High after Chinese State Trader Disappears," *Financial Times*, November 15, p. 17.

McIver, Ron (2005), "Asset Management Companies, State-Owned Commercial Bank Debt Transfers and Contingent Claims: Issues in the Valuation of China's Non-Performing Loans," *Managerial Finance* 31 (12): 11–28.

McKinnon, Ronald I. (1994), "Financial Growth and Macroeconomic Stability in China, 1978–1992: Implications for Russia and Other Transitional Economies," *Journal of Comparative Economics* 18 (June): 438–469.

McKinnon, Ronald I. (2005), *Exchange Rates under the East Asian Dollar Standard: Living with Conflicted Virtue*, Cambridge, MA: MIT Press.

McKinnon, Ronald (2007), "Why China Should Keep Its Dollar Peg," *International Finance* 10 (Spring): 43–70.

McKinnon, Ronald I., and Schnabl, Gunther (2006), "China's Exchange Rate and International Adjustment in Wages, Prices and Interest Rates: Japan *Déjà Vu?*" *CESifo Economic Studies* 52 (June): 276–303.

Mitchell, Tom (2006), "B-Shares Shrug Off their Image as Relics and Spring to Life," *Financial Times*, September 21, p. 30.

Morrison, Wayne M., Labonte, Marc, and Sanford, Jonathan E. (2006), *China's Currency and Economic Issues*, New York: Novinka Books.

Mundell, Robert (2003), "Prospects for an Asian Currency Area," *Journal of Asian Economics* 14 (February): 1–10.

Mushin, Jerry (2006), "The Uncertain Prospect of Asian Monetary Integration," *International Economics and Finance Journal* 1 (June): 89–94.

Mussa, Michael (2005), "Sustaining Global Growth while Reducing External Imbalances," in Bergsten, C. Fred (ed.), *The United States and the World Economy*, Washington, DC: Institute for International Economics, pp. 175–207.

Nakamoto, Michiyo (2007), "China Overtakes US in Trade with Japan," *Financial Times*, April 26, p. 5.

Nanto, Dick K., and Sinha, Radha (2002), "China's Banking Reform," *Post-Communist Economies* 14 (December): 469–493.

National Bureau of Statistics of China, Beijing (http://www.stats.gov.cn/english).

Nie, Stella (2007), "Shanghai's Move towards a Competitive Financial Centre in the WTO Post-Accession Era," *Shanghai Flash* (Consulate General of Switzerland in Shanghai), no. 1, February (http://www.sinoptic.ch/shanghaiflash/2007/200701.htm).

Obstfeld, Maurice (2007), "The Renminbi Dollar Peg at the Crossroads," mimeo, University of California, Berkeley, CA, May 11.

Ogawa, Eiji, and Kudo, Takeshi (2007), "Asymmetric Responses of East Asian Currencies to the US Dollar Depreciation for Reducing the US Current Account Deficits," *Journal of Asian Economics* 18 (February): 175–194.

Ogawa, Eiji, and Sakane, Michiru (2006), "Chinese Yuan after Chinese Exchange Rate System Reform," *China & World Economy* 14 (November–December): 39–57.

Oppers, S. Erik (1997), "Macroeconomic Cycles in China," Working Paper No. 97/135, International Monetary Fund, Washington, DC, October.

Organisation for Economic Cooperation and Development (2003), "China's Securities Market" (www.oecd.org/dataoecd/5/32/18469881.pdf).

Ouyang, Alice Y., Rajan, Ramkishen S., and Willett, Thomas D. (2007), "China as a Reserve Sink: The Evidence from Offset and Stabilization Coefficients," Working Paper No. 10/2007, Hong Kong Institute for Monetary Research, May.

Papaioannou, Elias, Portes, Richard, and Siourounis, Gregorios (2006), "Optimal Currency Shares in International Reserves: The Impact of the Euro and the Prospects for the Dollar," Working Paper No. 12333, National Bureau of Economic Research, Cambridge, MA, June (http://www.nber.org/papers/w12333).

Park, Albert, and Sehrt, Kaja (2001), "Tests of Financial Intermediation and Banking Reform in China," *Journal of Comparative Economics* 29 (December): 608–644.

Peebles, Gavin (1991), *Money in the People's Republic of China: A Comparative Perspective,* Boston, MA: Allen & Unwin.

People's Bank of China (2004), "News Release," October 28 (in Chinese).

People's Bank of China (2005a), "Challenges to China's Monetary Policy," in *Globalisation and Monetary Policy in Emerging Markets,* Basel, Switzerland: Bank for International Settlements, BIS Papers No. 23 (May): 124–127 (http://www.bis.org/publ/bppdf/bispap23h.pdf).

People's Bank of China (2005b), "PBC Official on Further Developing RMB Business in Hong Kong," November 1 (http://www.pbc.gov.cn/english/detail.asp?col=6400&ID=606).

People's Bank of China (2006), "China Monetary Policy Report: Quarter Four, 2005," Beijing, March 16.

People's Bank of China (2007), "China Monetary Policy Report: Quarter One, 2007," Beijing, May 29.

People's Daily Online (2004), "China to Build Four Major Oil Reserve Bases," October 10 (http://english.people.com.cn/200410/10/eng20041010_159641.html).

People's Daily Online (2005a), "China to Wield Leverage of Exchange Rates on Macro Economy," July 25 (http://english.people.com.cn/200507/25/eng20050725_198011.html).

People's Daily Online (2005b), "Trade Surplus with the US Viewed from Another Angle," August 12 (http://english1.people.com.cn/200508/12/eng20050812_202051.html).

People's Daily Online (2005c), "RMB's Further Appreciation is Megatrend, Vice Central Banker," October 26 (http://english.peopledaily.com.cn/200510/26/print20051026_217008.html).

People's Daily Online (2006a), "Big State Bank Posts Profits Jump, Accelerates Listing," January 20 (http://english.peopledaily.com.cn/200601/20/eng20060120_236881.html).

People's Daily Online (2006b), "Mundell: Fast Growth in Economy, but not RMB Appreciation," February 14 (http://english1.people.com.cn/200602/14/eng20060214_242688.html).

People's Daily Online (2006c), "Chinese Premier Addresses Media on Major Issues," March 15 (http://english.peopledaily.com.cn/200603/15/eng20060315_250735.html).

People's Daily Online (2007a), "Forming of Forex Investment Company Not to Impact U.S.-Dollar Denominated Assets: Premier," March 16 (http://english.people.com.cn/200703/16/eng20070316_358280.html).

People's Daily Online (2007b), "China Development Bank to Issue 5-bln yuan RMB Bond in Hong Kong," June 26 (http://english.people.com.cn/200706/26/eng20070626_387752.html).

People's Daily Online (2007c), "Bank Withdrawals Continue but Rate Falls," August 11 (http://english.people.com.cn/90001/90778/6237166.html).

Peyrefitte, Alain (1977), *The Chinese: Portrait of a People*, translated from the French by Graham Webb, Indianapolis/New York: Bobbs-Merrill.

Phillips, Kerk L., and Kunrong, Shen (2005), "What Effect Does the Size of the State-Owned Sector Have on Regional Growth in China?" *Journal of Asian Economics* 15 (January): 1079–1102.

Podpiera, Richard (2006), "Progress in China's Banking Sector Reform: Has Bank Behavior Changed?" Working Paper 06/71, International Monetary Fund, Washington, DC, March.

Poon, Winnie P. H., Firth, Michael, and Fung, Hung-Gay (1998), "The Spillover Effects of the Trading Suspension of the Treasury Bond Futures Market in China," *Journal of International Financial Markets, Institutions, and Money* 8 (June): 205–218.

Prasad, Eswar, and Wei, Shang-Jin (2007), "The Chinese Approach to Capital Inflows: Patterns and Possible Explanations," in Edwards, Sebastian (ed.), *Capital Controls and Capital Flows in Emerging Economies: Policies, Practices, and Consequences*, Chicago, IL: University of Chicago Press, pp. 421–480.

Qian, Ming (2006), "The Adjustment When Foreign Banks Enter the Chinese Banking System," *Economist Monthly*, No. 3, item number: 1009–3990 (2006) 03-0019-04 (in Chinese).

Qin, Duo (2003), "Determinants of Household Savings in China and Their Role in Quasi-Money Supply," *Economics of Transition* 11: 513–537.

Quddus, Munir, Liu, Jin-Tan, and Butler, John S. (1989), "Money, Prices, and Causality: The Chinese Hyperinflation, 1946–1949, Reexamined," *Journal of Macroeconomics* 11 (Summer): 447–453.

Rajan, Ramkishen S., and Kiran, Jose (2006), "Will the Greenback Remain the World's Reserve Currency?" *Intereconomics* 41 (May/June): 124–129.

Rawski, Thomas G. (1989), *Economic Growth in Prewar China*, Berkeley: University of California Press.

Rawski, Thomas G. (1993), "Milton Friedman, Silver, and China," *Journal of Political Economy* 101 (August): 755–758.

Ren, Daniel (2007), "Rally Puts ICBC on Top of the World," *South China Morning Post*, July 24, p. B1.

Research Group of Price Reform, Chinese Academy of Social Sciences (1987), "Ponder of Price Reform for 7 Years," in Gao Shang quan. et al. (eds.), *China: Development and Reform*, Chengdu: Sichuan ren min chu ban she, pp. 132–147 (in Chinese).

Rodrik, Dani (2006), "What's So Special about China's Exports?" *China & World Economy* 14 (September–October): 1–19.

Rosenthal, Leonard, and Young, Colin (1990), "The Seemingly Anomalous Price Behavior of Royal Dutch/Shell and Unilever N.V./PLC," *Journal of Financial Economics* 26 (July): 123–141.

Roubini, Nouriel (2007), "Why China Should Abandon Its Dollar Peg," *International Finance* 10 (Spring): 71–89.

Salter, Sir Arthur (1934), *China and Silver*, New York: Economic Forum Inc.

Sargent, Thomas J., and Wallace, Neil (1973), "Rational Expectations and the Dynamics of Hyperinflation," *International Economic Review* 14 (June): 328–350.

Schellekens, Philip (2005), "Deflation in Hong Kong SAR," *Pacific Economic Review* 10 (June): 243–260.

Schenk, Catherine R. (2000), "Another Asian Financial Crisis: Monetary Links between Hong Kong and China 1945–50," *Modern Asian Studies* 34 (July): 739–764.

Schenk, Catherine R. (2002), "Sterling, Hong Kong, and China in the 1930s and 1950s." Paper presented at the XIII Economic History Congress, Buenos Aires, Argentina, July 22–26 (http://eh.net/XIIICongress/cd/papers/8Schenk373.pdf).

Schindler, John W., and Beckett, Dustin H. (2005), "Adjusting Chinese Bilateral Trade Data: How Big is China's Trade Surplus?" *International Journal of Applied Economics* 2 (September): 27–55.

Setser, Brad (2006), "The Chinese Conundrum: External Financial Strength, Domestic Financial Weakness," *CESifo Economic Studies* 52 (June): 364–395.

Shen, Chung-Hua (2002), "The Choice of Intermediate Targets–Money or Interest Rate: The Case of Taiwan," in Dwyer, Gerald P., Jr., Lin, Jin-Lung, Shea, Jia-Dong, and Wu, Chung-Shu (eds.), *Monetary Policy and Taiwan's Economy*, Northampton, MA: Edward Elgar, pp. 147–166.

Shen, L. Y. (1941), *China's Currency Reform: A Historical Survey*, Shanghai: Mercury Press.

Shenzhen Daily (2005), "Foreign Investors to be Allowed to Buy A Shares," November 7 (http://english.mofcom.gov.cn/aarticle/newsrelease/significantnews/200511/20051100730600.html).

Shi, Jianhuai (2006), "Are Currency Appreciations Contractionary in China?" Working Paper No. 12551, National Bureau of Economic Research, Cambridge, MA, September (http://www.nber.org/papers/w12551).

Shi, Jianhuai, and Yu, Haifeng (2005), "Renminbi Equilibrium Exchange Rate and China's Exchange Rate Misalignment: 1991–2004," *Jing ji yan jiu*, no. 4: 34–45 (in Chinese).

Shih, Victor (2004), "Factions Matter: Personal Networks and the Distribution of Bank Loans in China," *Journal of Contemporary China* 13 (February): 3–19.

Shih, Victor, Zhang, Qi, and Liu, Mingxing (2007), "Comparing the Performance of Chinese Banks: A Principal Component Approach," *China Economic Review* 18: 15–34.

Shijie ribao [World Daily] (1996), "Chongqing Controls Price Increases Effectively," February 22 (in Chinese).

Siddique, Abu (2006), "Globalization and Economic Development," in Wu, Yanrui (ed.), *Economic Growth, Transition and Globalization in China,* Northampton, MA: Edward Elgar, pp. 214–238.

Siebert, Horst (2007), "China: Coming to Grips with the New Global Player," *World Economy* 30 (June): 893–922.

Siklos, Pierre L. (1993), "Income Velocity and Institutional Change: Some New Time Series Evidence," *Journal of Money, Credit, and Banking* 25 (August): 377–392.

Silver and Prices in China: Report of the Committee for the Study of Silver Values and Commodity Prices, Ministry of Industries (1935), Shanghai: Commercial Press.

Siregar, Reza, and Rajan, Ramkishen S. (2006), "Models of Equilibrium Real Exchange Rates Revisited: A Selective Review of the Literature," mimeo, University of Adelaide, Australia, August.

Sito, Peggy (2007), "Ban on Pre-Sale of Flats Proposed," *South China Morning Post,* July 26, p. B1.

Song, Guoqing (1995), "Interest Rate, Inflation Expectations, and Savings Propensity," *Jing ji yan jiu,* no. 7: 3–10 (in Chinese).

Stiglitz, Joseph (2005), "US Has Little to Teach China about Steady Economy," *Financial Times,* July 26 (http://www.ft.com).

Sun, Huayu, and Ma, Yue (2004), "Money and Price Relationship in China," *Journal of Chinese Economic and Business Studies* 2 (September): 225–247.

Sutter, Karen M. (2002), "Business Dynamism across the Taiwan Strait: The Implications for Cross-Strait Relations," *Asian Survey* 42 (May–June): 522–540.

Taipei Times (2003), "Locals Invest US$66.8bn in China Last Year," January 17, p. 11 (http://www.taipeitimes.com).

Tallman, Ellis W., Tang, De-Piao, and Wang, Ping (2003), "Nominal and Real Disturbances and Money Demand in Chinese Hyperinflation," *Economic Inquiry* 41 (April): 234–249.

Tamagna, Frank M. (1942), *Banking and Finance in China,* New York: Institute of Pacific Relations.

T'ang, Leang-Li (1936), *China's New Currency System,* Shanghai: China United Press.

Tang, De-Piao, and Hu, Teh-Wei (1983), "Money, Prices, and Causality: The Chinese Hyperinflation, 1946–1949," *Journal of Macroeconomics* 5 (Fall): 503–510.

Taylor, John B. (1993), "Discretion versus Policy Rules in Practice," *Carnegie-Rochester Conference Series on Public Policy* 39 (November): 195–214.

Thomas, Stephen, and Ji, Chen (2006), "Banking on Reform," *China Business Review,* May–June (http://www.chinabusinessreview.com).

Tsai, Kellee S. (2002), *Back-Alley Banking: Private Entrepreneurs in China,* Ithaca, NY: Cornell University Press.

Tucker, Sundeep, and Anderlini, Jamil (2007), "BoCom Reclassification Ends Bank's Hopes of Full Control," *Financial Times,* April 12, p. 18.

Tung, Chen-Yuan (2004), "Economic Relations between Taiwan and China," UNISCI Discussion Papers (Madrid, Spain: Research Unit on International Security and Cooperation), No. 4, January (http://www.ucm.es/info/unisci/TUNG4M.pdf).

United Nations Conference on Trade and Development (2006), *World Investment Report 2006 – FDI from Developing and Transition Economies: Implications for Development,* New York and Geneva: United Nations (http://www.unctad. org/en/docs/wir2006_en.pdf).

US Department of State (1949), *United States Relations with China, With Special Reference to the Period 1944–1949,* Washington, DC: Department of State Publication 3573, Far Eastern Series 30, August.

US Department of the Treasury, Federal Reserve Bank of New York, and Board of Governors of the Federal Reserve System (2007), *Report on Foreign Portfolio Holdings of U.S. Securities as of June 30, 2006,* Washington, DC, May (http://www.treas. gov/tic/shl2006r.pdf).

von Furstenberg, George M., and Wei, Jianjun (2004), "Overcoming Chinese Monetary Division and External Anchoring in East Asia," *Asian Economic Papers* 3: 27–54.

Wang, J., Burton, B. M., and Power, D. M. (2004), "Analysis of the Overreaction Effect in the Chinese Stock Market," *Applied Economics Letters* 11 (June): 437–442.

Wang, Steven Shuye, and Firth, Michael (2004), "Do Bears and Bulls Swim Across Oceans? Market Information Transmission between Greater China and the Rest of the World," *Journal of International Financial Markets, Institutions, and Money* 14 (July): 235–254.

Wang, Steven Shuye, and Jiang, Li (2004), "Location of Trade, Ownership Restrictions, and Market Illiquidity: Examining Chinese A- and H-shares," *Journal of Banking & Finance* 28 (June): 1273–1297.

Warnock, Francis E., and Warnock, Veronica Cacdac (2006), "International Capital Flows and U.S. Interest Rates," Working Paper No. 12560, National Bureau of Economic Research, Cambridge, MA, October (http://www.nber.org/papers/w12560).

Wasserstrom, Jeffrey N. (2003), "The Second Coming of Global Shanghai," *World Policy Journal* 20 (Summer): 51–60.

Wei, Shang-Jin (2000), "Noise Trading in the Chinese Stock Market," in Chen, Baizhu, Dietrich, J. Kimball, and Feng, Yi, (eds.), *Financial Market Reform in China: Progress, Problems, and Prospects,* Boulder, CO: Westview Press, pp. 221–241.

Wei, Shang-Jin, Liu, Ligang, Wang, Zhi, and Woo, Wing T. (2000), "The China Money Puzzle: Will Devaluation of the Yuan Help or Hurt the Hong Kong Dollar?" *China Economic Review* 11: 171–188.

Westerfield, Ray B. (1936), *Our Silver Debacle,* New York: Ronald Press.

Whalley, John, and Xin, Xian (2006), "China's FDI and Non-FDI Economies and the Sustainability of Future High Chinese Growth," Working Paper No. 12249, National Bureau of Economic Research, Cambridge, MA, May (http://www.nber. org/papers/w12249).

Williamson, John (2005), "A Currency Basket for East Asia, Not Just China," Policy Brief No. PB05-1, Institute for International Economics, Washington, DC, August (http://www.iie.com/publications/pb/pb05-1.pdf).

Wong, Christine P. W., Heady, Christopher, and Woo, Wing T. (1995), *Fiscal Management and Economic Reform in the People's Republic of China,* New York: Oxford University Press.

Wong, John (1998), "Will China Be the Next Financial Domino?" *China's Economy and the Asian Financial Crisis,* Singapore: East Asian Institute Occasional Paper No. 4.

Wong, Sonia M. L. (2006), "China's Stock Market: A Marriage of Capitalism and Socialism," *Cato Journal* 26 (Fall): 389–424.

World Bank (1994), *China: Foreign Trade Reform*, Washington, DC.

World Bank (1995), *China: Macroeconomic Stability in a Decentralized Economy*, Washington, DC.

World Bank (1996), *The Chinese Economy: Fighting Inflation, Deepening Reforms*, Washington, DC.

World Bank (1999), *China: Weathering the Storm and Learning the Lessons*, Washington, DC.

Wu, Deming (2004), "Was There Deflation in China between 1997 and 2002? An Empirical Study of Price Movement in China," Unpublished Ph.D. Dissertation, Stanford University. Stanford, CA, June.

Wu, Gang (1958), *Historical Material Relating to the Inflation in Old China*. Shanghai: Shanghai ren min chu ban she (in Chinese).

Wu, Jinglian (2005), *Understanding and Interpreting Chinese Economic Reform*, Mason, OH: Thomson.

Wu, Tsong-Min (1997), "The Nationalist Government's Economic Policies Regarding Taiwan: 1945–1949," *Taiwan Economic Review* 25 (December): 521–554 (in Chinese).

Wu, Zhiwen (2003), "The China Paradox: A Critical Review and a New Hypothesis," *Jing ji xue ji kan* 3 (October): 39–70 (in Chinese).

Xafa, Miranda (2007), "Global Imbalances: Do They Matter?" *Cato Journal* 27 (Winter): 59–68.

Xie, Ping (2004), "China's Monetary Policy: 1998–2002," Working Paper No. 217, Stanford Center for International Development, Stanford, CA, June.

Xu, Changsheng (2002), "Real and Monetary Factors Contributing to China's Present Deflation since the Asian Financial Crisis," in Hooley, Richard, and Yoo, Jang-Hee (eds.), *The Post-Financial Crisis Challenges for Asian Industrialization*, Amsterdam: Elsevier Scientific, pp. 509–520.

Xu, Xinpeng (2006), "A Currency Union for Hong Kong and Mainland China," *Journal of International Money and Finance* 25 (October): 894–911.

Xu, Yingfeng (2008), "Lessons from Taiwan's Experience of Currency Appreciation," *China Economic Review* 19: 53–65.

Yang, Jiawen (2004), "Nontradables and the Valuation of RMB – An Evaluation of the Big Mac Index," *China Economic Review* 15: 353–359.

Yang, Ting, and Lau, Sie Ting (2006), "Choice of Listing Location: Experience of Chinese Firms," *Pacific-Basin Finance Journal* 14 (June): 311–326.

Yang, Ya-Hwei, and Shea, Jia-Dong (2005), "Deflation and Monetary Policy in Taiwan," Working Paper No. 11244, National Bureau of Economic Research, Cambridge, MA, March (http://www.nber.org/papers/w11244).

Yardeni, Edward (2004), "Use SPR to Cap Oil at $40 Now!" *Investment Strategy Weekly*, Prudential Equity Group, New York, August 16.

Yeh, Andrew (2006), "China Sells First Pools of NPLs," *Financial Times*, November 24, p. 30.

Yeh, K. C. (1979), "China's National Income, 1931–36," in Hou, Chi-ming and Yu, Tzong-shian (eds.), *Modern Chinese Economic History*, Taipei, Taiwan: Institute of Economics, Academia Sinica, pp. 95–128.

Yi, Gang (1994), *Money, Banking, and Financial Markets in China*, Boulder, CO: Westview Press.

Young, Arthur N. (1971), *China's Nation-Building Effort, 1927–1937: The Financial and Economic Record,* Stanford, CA: Hoover Institution Press.

Yuan, Minggang (2002), "Analysis of the Co-Existence of an Increasing Growth Rate and Aggravating Deflation," September 19 (http://www.forumcn.com) (in Chinese).

Zhang, Gaiyan, and Fung, Hung-Gay (2006), "On the Imbalance between the Real Estate Market and the Stock Markets in China," *The Chinese Economy* 39 (March–April): 26–39.

Zhang, Kevin Honglin (2005), "Why Does So Much FDI from Hong Kong and Taiwan Go to Mainland China?" *China Economic Review* 16 (2005): 293–307.

Zhang, Jian, Fung, Hung-Gay, and Kummer, Donald (2006), "Can Renminbi Appreciation Reduce the US Trade Deficit?" *China & World Economy* 14 (February): 44–56.

Zhang, Jikang, and Liang, Yuanyuan (2006), "The Institutional and Structural Problems of China's Foreign Exchange Market and Implications for the New Exchange Rate Regime," *China: An International Journal* 4 (March): 60–85.

Zhang, Peter G. (2004), *Chinese Yuan (Renminbi) Derivative Products,* Hackensack, NJ: World Scientific.

Zhang, Xiaojing, and Sun, Tao (2006), "China's Current Real Estate Cycle and Potential Financial Risks," *China & World Economy* 14 (August): 57–74.

Zhang, Yin, and Wan, Guanghua (2004), "Output and Price Fluctuations in China's Reform Years," Research Paper No. 2004/56, United Nations University-World Institute for Development Economics Research, Helsinki, Finland.

Zhang, Zhaoyang (1999), "China's Exchange Rate Reform and Its Impact on the Balance of Trade and Domestic Inflation," *Asia Pacific Journal of Economics and Business* 3 (December): 4–22.

Zhang, Zhichao (2001), "Real Exchange Rate Misalignment in China: An Empirical Investigation," *Journal of Comparative Economics* 29 (March): 80–94.

Zhang, Zhichao (2003), "China's Foreign Exchange Policy in a Time of Change," in Preston, P. W., and Haacke, Preston (eds.), *Contemporary China: The Dynamics of Change at the Start of the New Millennium,* New York: RoutledgeCurzon, pp. 45–63.

Zhang, Zhichao (2006), "Capital Controls in China: Recent Developments and Reform Prospects," mimeo, Durham Business School, University of Durham, England, February.

Zheng, Jian (2002), "Deflation: A Representation of the Economy's Adjustment," September 21 (http://www.forumcn.com) (in Chinese).

Zheng, Yongnian, and Yi, Jingtao (2007), "China's Rapid Accumulation of Foreign Exchange Reserves and Its Policy Implications," *China & World Economy* 15 (January–February): 14–25.

Zhou, Xiaochuan (2006a), "China's Corporate Bond Market Development: Lessons Learned," *BIS Papers* (Bank for International Settlements), no. 26, part 2 (February): 7–10.

Zhou, Xiaochuan (2006b), "Statement on Behalf of China," Fourteenth Meeting of the International Monetary and Financial Committee, Singapore, September 17 (http://www.imf.org/external/am/2006/imfc/statement/eng/chn.pdf).

Zhou, Zhongfei, and Li, Jingwei (2007), "Independence and Accountability of the People's Bank of China: A Legal Perspective," in Barth, James R., Zhou, Zhongfei, Arner, Douglas W., Hsu, Barry F. C., and Wang, Wei (eds.), *Financial Restructuring* and *Reform in Post-WTO China*, Alphen aan den Rijn, Netherlands: Kluwer Law International.

Zhu, Youping (2002), "Irrational Expectations Lead to Failure of the Transmission Mechanism – A Structural Explanation for Sustained Low Price Levels," October 9 (http://www.forumcn.com) (in Chinese).

Author Index

Subject Index

255

DATE DUE